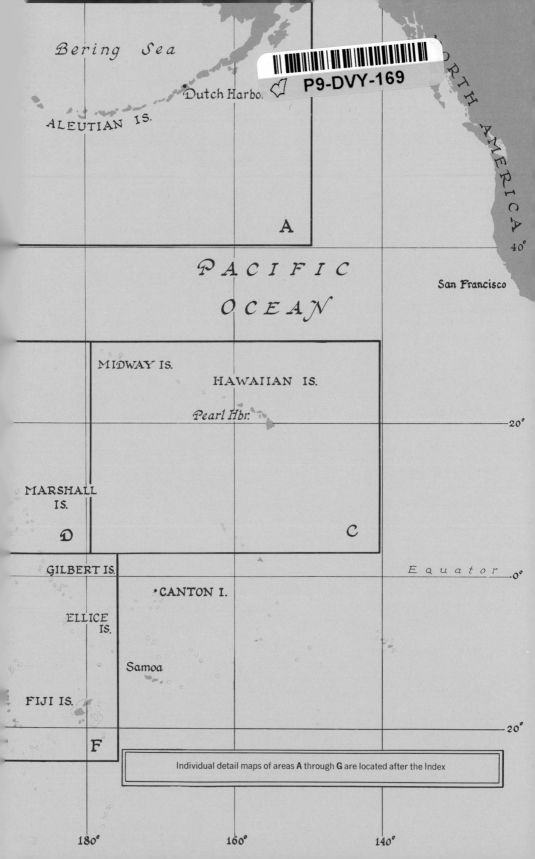

Bering Sea

Dutch Harbo. P9-DVY-169

ALEUTIAN IS.

NORTH AMERICA

A

40°

PACIFIC

OCEAN

San Francisco

MIDWAY IS.

HAWAIIAN IS.

Pearl Hbr.

20°

MARSHALL
IS.

D

C

GILBERT IS.

Equator 0°

CANTON I.

ELLICE
IS.

Samoa

FIJI IS.

20°

F

Individual detail maps of areas **A** through **G** are located after the Index

180°   160°   140°

DOUBLE-EDGED
SECRETS

Joseph J. Rochefort
Courtesy: Mrs. Janet Rochefort Elerding

W. J. HOLMES

DOUBLE-EDGED SECRETS

U. S. Naval Intelligence Operations in the Pacific during World War II

NAVAL INSTITUTE PRESS
Annapolis, Maryland

Copyright © 1979
by the United States Naval Institute
Annapolis, Maryland

Charts by Dorothy deFontaine

Library of Congress Catalog Card Number: 78-70779
ISBN 0-87021-162-5

Printed in the United States of America

9 8 7 6 5 4 3

To
the memory of
JOSEPH JOHN ROCHEFORT
1899–1976
Captain, U.S. Navy

FOREWORD

WHEN I was a student at the University of Hawaii following World War II, I knew Dean W. J. Holmes as a topflight professor of engineering. But to those who were involved in naval intelligence operations against Japan during World War II, he will always be remembered as Commander (and later Captain) Holmes of the Combat Intelligence Unit, one of the select few who handled the supersecret "Ultra" messages which the U.S. Navy produced from having broken Japanese codes. This work of Holmes was so secret that even after the war, when I was his student, I could only guess at what his role had been in the Pacific victory.

Double-Edged Secrets is the eyewitness story of the remarkable organization that collected, analyzed, and disseminated naval intelligence throughout World War II. Making use of the unique insights intercepted Japanese messages afforded U.S. Navy planning, Holmes now brings illuminating new dimensions to the story of the war in the Pacific, especially concerning such events as the attack on Pearl Harbor, the breaking of the incredibly complex Japanese ciphers, the use of Ultra intelligence, the Battle of Midway, the targeting of U.S. submarines against Japanese aircraft carriers, American anti-submarine warfare, and the decision to shoot down Admiral Yamamoto's plane. Holmes's story is the raw material of adventure fiction—but it is all true, and it is told in a manner that is at the same time fascinating and professional.

Although *Double-Edged Secrets* is about intelligence during World War II, it has lessons for us today. In my capacity as the first chairman of the U.S. Senate's Select Committee on Intelligence, and now as a continuing member of that committee, I have come to learn more and more about the crucial service that U.S. intelligence has performed for the American people. An important part of my work on this committee concerns the dilemma which is the heart—and the title—of this book: the contradiction that secrecy can sometimes harm national security as well as the enemy. Many instructive incidents illustrating this dilemma are provided throughout the book.

Holmes describes the predicament faced in deciding whether or not to use Ultra information to intercept and shoot down the plane carrying Admiral Yamamoto, Japan's most outstanding naval officer. Fortunately, the dramatic death of Yamamoto did not tip off the Japanese that their communications were insecure.

A more tragic outcome resulted from the decision not to disseminate Ultra information concerning the positions of Japanese submarines late in the war. This information was given extremely limited distribution lest the Japanese should discover that their most sophisticated code had been broken. As a result, the USS *Indianapolis* never learned that there was a Japanese submarine in her path. The *Indianapolis* went down in fifteen minutes, and the total loss came to 883 men.

In relating these examples, Holmes skillfully acquaints the reader with the deeply perplexing operational and moral questions that faced U.S. commanders as a result of the extraordinary insight provided them through cryptanalysis. The source was so exceedingly valuable that it had to be protected at all costs, yet should such costs include, for example, the many lives aboard the *Indianapolis*? It is in studying these decisions—and their consequences—that we may better learn to resolve the continuing problem of secrecy.

All in all, *Double-Edged Secrets* is much more than just a thrilling story and a lesson concerning the dilemmas of sensitive intelligence. Based on Holmes's unique personal experience, it is a tribute to the courageous and brilliant men whose work was so secret that they could not be recognized, and whose contribution was so vital that it is no exaggeration to say that without it the Pacific conflict might have been waged on the coast of California. In addition to "intelligence," these men had imagination, enthusiasm, a very-much-needed sense of humor, and an unflagging capacity for good, hard work. One of the most enterprising and important of these unsung heroes is the author of this enjoyable and rewarding book.

DANIEL K. INOUYE
U.S. Senator from Hawaii

PREFACE

No RECORDS were kept of some of the incidents related in this book and the records of others have been too highly classified to be consulted. The thirty-nine-volume *Hearings Before the Joint Committee on the Investigation of the Pearl Harbor Attack*, seventy-ninth Congress, is the source of most of the information on communications intelligence before that attack, and Samuel Eliot Morison's fifteen-volume *History of United States Naval Operations in World War II* is the reference for the general history of that war; but the principal source of information is personal recollection. The book is a first-person account of experience in a highly successful intelligence organization that conducted its business without the cloak-and-dagger actions, assassinations, murders, sedition, and seduction featured in many books about intelligence. Yet, it elucidates principles of intelligence which, had they been applied during the past thirty years, might have saved the United States from much trauma.

Experience proved that intelligence functions best when limited to its proper tasks: the collection, collation, evaluation, and distribution of information concerning the enemy. Although, for best efficiency, those who work in intelligence must cooperate closely with those who use it, they must never attempt to usurp the functions of either those who make plans or those who direct operations.

As this book demonstrates, secrecy is often essential to the security and continuing production of intelligence, but it is a double-edged weapon that must be wielded carefully lest it wound the wielder more deeply than the enemy. Restricting intelligence to "those who need to know" sometimes requires both omniscience and omnipotence.

Without the help of Drew W. Kohler, this work could not have been completed. He was my translator, typist, consultant, and critic. David A. Ward contributed many valuable corrections and criticisms. John A. Harrison is a mine of information on the Translation Section. I am grateful to Donald M. Showers for steering the manuscript through the maze of Washington's intelligence community, in order to obtain security clearance. Jack S. Holtwick and Paul T. Yardley read and corrected parts of the manuscript. I have contributed all the errors. I am grateful to Richard W. Emory and Elizabeth B. Holmes for support and encouragement. I am deeply indebted to Mary Veronica Amoss, whose patient and skillful editing has removed my many inconsistencies, redundancies, and errors and greatly improved the organization of the text to make this a more readable book.

About my colleagues who served in the Fleet Radio Unit, Pacific, and the Joint Intelligence Center, Pacific Ocean Area, I feel:

> And they were stronger hands than mine
> That digged the Ruby from the earth—
> More cunning brains that made it worth
> The large desire of a king,
> And stouter hearts that through the brine
> Went down the perfect Pearl to bring.

> Rudyard Kipling
> Dedication to *Soldiers Three*

DOUBLE-EDGED
SECRETS

CHAPTER 1

WHEN THE FIRST BOMBS FELL on Pearl Harbor I was fourteen miles away at home in bed, the best place for a naval intelligence officer to be that Sunday morning. In December 1941 it was obvious that the remaining days of peace were few. I had been on duty all the previous weekend and lazy Sunday mornings were too precious to waste. The only person awake at our house was our eleven-year-old son, Eric.

We had assigned to Eric the regular task of preparing Sunday morning breakfast, to educate him for a future when it would be wise for any young man to have basic competence in the kitchen. He had become so adept that we knew it was an emergency that brought him, breathless and round-eyed with excitement, into our bedroom.

"The *Advertiser* didn't come," he exclaimed. "Mr. Herndon says to get up, the Japs are taking the island and you have no coffee."

His mother opened her sleepy eyes and replied, "Call up the *Advertiser*. There is a fresh can of coffee in the lower closet."

"The Japs aren't taking this island," I reassured him. "They are thousands of miles away, taking an island in the Dutch East Indies."

With that, the telephone rang. Denzel Carr, in a hurried and excited voice, announced, "This is the District Intelligence duty officer. General Quarters!" and hung up before I could ask a question.

In the few minutes required to get into my uniform, I had time to reflect that the sadistic high brass would probably pick this as the ideal time for a practice alert. A Sunday morning alert would cause a minimum of interference with Honolulu's business. This Sunday both of the aircraft carriers that were stationed in the Hawaiian Islands were busy delivering planes to Wake and Midway. Since no carrier planes were available for antisubmarine patrol of operating areas, all the battleships, rather than the usual one-third of the fleet, were in port at Pearl Harbor to be safe from submarine attack.

On this Sunday morning, therefore, the fleet staff had an irresistible opportunity to disrupt the maximum amount of rare Sunday relaxation with a practice alert. On the other hand, war was expected any moment. It might already have exploded in the South China Sea or the East Indies, as we expected. This might be the first real all-hands alert, in which case information I had carefully collected during the past few months would immediately be needed to provide protection for ships at sea in the eastern Pacific.

Like all sound strategists, my wife, Isabelle, believed that it was bad tactics to go to war on an empty stomach. She quickly relieved Eric in the kitchen. As I backed my little Studebaker Champion out of the garage, she came hurrying out of the back door and recommended, "Wait just a minute and the coffee will be ready. You will be gone all morning and you need some breakfast." But it was too late. I paused only to tell her, "Call up the Lanquists. If the beach areas are evacuated you should be sure you have a place to go."

Families living in the beach areas had been instructed to make arrangements to retreat inland in an emergency. My wife kept a box of canned food and a jug of drinking water stored in the back of her Ford to be always ready to go. The Lanquists, who lived up Nuuanu Valley, had agreed to receive refugees from our home on Black Point. I waved good-bye and backed into the street. That was the last peaceful Sunday morning at our house for a long time.

The coast artillery company that manned the Diamond Head batteries was assembling for muster at Fort Ruger as I drove through. When I topped the rise and looked down on Waikiki I saw a string of black bursts of antiaircraft fire out over the reef. I took it as an indication that this was all part of a realistic practice alert, for the bursts appeared to be placed only over the water, where there would be no danger of anyone being hit by shell fragments. The streets of Honolulu were even quieter than usual for a Sunday morning. I was near the center of town before cars started streaming in from the side streets. Then the traffic clotted rapidly, all headed in the direction of Pearl Harbor.

By the time we reached Kalihi, the traffic bound for Pearl Harbor preempted the right of way, ignoring all traffic lights, and we all speeded together in the same direction until suddenly everything came to a halt just as I was passing Oahu Prison. As far ahead as I could see, the road was jammed with cars. In the distance, above the cane fields, a great pillar of ominous black smoke arose, advertising disaster at our destination. A car pulled out into the left lane, followed immediately by a string of others until quickly all four lanes were packed into a solid and unmoving mass headed toward

Pearl Harbor. A fire engine, trapped in the frozen traffic, screamed in frustration for the right of way. Someone shouted to me that the Japs were strafing the road ahead. On the rough left shoulder of the road a covey of cars came bumping along from the Pearl Harbor direction. In some of them we could see obviously injured people. For the first time I knew for sure that this was not a drill.

The traffic started moving again as suddenly as it had stopped. After the next intersection, the road was clear and I sped on with the others to the main gate of the Navy Yard. The Marine sentry recognized the identifying sticker on my car and waved me on in. This must have been the brief lull in the battle, about nine o'clock. I drove directly to the Administration Building and around back to the half-empty parking lot. In the harbor close by, but screened from my view by the shop buildings, thousands of men had died and thousands of others were then manning guns or desperately trying to save their burning and sinking ships; but the parking lot was as quiet and peaceful as on any other Sunday morning. I parked my car and walked down to the basement where I belonged.

I reported to my boss, Joseph J. Rochefort, a tall, lean commander with a conciliatory smile that nullified his habit of caustic speech, and at last had an opportunity to ask someone for information.

"Japanese air attack on battleship row," Rochefort informed me. "It looks bad."

Durwood G. "Tex" Rorie, the chief petty officer who acted as administrative assistant, appeared. "As I came down from Aiea, planes with Japanese markings were making low-level torpedo attacks," he reported. "I saw *Oklahoma* hit by torpedoes and roll completely over."

"*Arizona* blew up about the same time," someone else added. The lull in the battle that had coincided with my arrival ended with the sound of heavy gunfire which rapidly increased to a crescendo. Several heavy explosions rocked the solid earth, and our basement trembled. Of course, none of us could see what went on above ground. The lights went out, plunging us into total darkness for a few minutes, then flickered briefly and came back on again. It was past ten o'clock before relative calm returned above us.

My job at Pearl Harbor was to keep track of the positions of all noncombatant ships at sea in the eastern Pacific. Their predicted noon positions were plotted on charts each day. William Dunbar, the yeoman who assisted me, helped me spread out these charts across the chart desk and bring them up to date. We had anticipated that, on the outbreak of war, knowledge of the location of these ships would be helpful to provide escort and protection for our ships or to help search planes avoid mistakes in identification. We knew also that Japanese tankers were being routed across the South Pacific, and despite their evasive routings, we were able to keep track of them. We hoped that cruisers might intercept some of these tankers if war came suddenly.

A few minutes after the first Japanese planes appeared over Pearl Harbor, the Commander in Chief, Pacific Fleet, (CinCPac) reported the attack to Washington and Manila, and radio station KGMB at Honolulu repeatedly broadcast that Pearl Harbor was under attack, "this is not a drill." About eleven-thirty CinCPac broadcast instructions to all merchant ships at sea to proceed immediately to the closest friendly port. After that, the value of our information on ships' positions decreased rapidly. All ships were maintaining radio silence and running for cover by evasive routes. As for the Japanese tankers: any cruiser that could get to sea had more important tasks closer to home than a wild-goose chase after high-speed tankers thousands of miles away. It was not surprising that there were no calls that morning for the information we had so painstakingly compiled.

About noon I got permission to come up out of the basement and see what was going on at the waterfront. As I came into the bright sunlight, the first thing I noticed was a shell hole clear through the powerhouse stack; a direct hit by one of our own antiaircraft guns. No other damage to the Navy Yard shops was visible. From the dock, I could see battleship row along Ford Island, across the harbor. It was dense with smoke, obscuring details, but the extent of disaster was apparent. The *Oklahoma*'s bottom bulged obscenely above the oily water. The *Arizona*'s masts were cocked at a crazy angle above a pall of smoke. The *West Virginia* was burning furiously. The *Nevada* was aground at Hospital Point. For the moment no guns were firing.

Many men were wandering about as aimlessly as I was. I encountered Commander Edmond P. Speight, captain of the minelayer *Ogalala*, and asked him where his ship was. Wordlessly he pointed down. There she was, a few yards away, lying alongside the dock, but with her bottom up and her keel just below dock level. Everyone was frustrated and unable to find anything constructive to do. When I reported this to Rochefort I was vaguely aware that the burden of frustration must have lain most heavily upon him.

Reports of enemy sightings and activity began coming in to the Hawaiian Sea Frontier's operations office above us. These were routed by voice tube and message drop to the Combat Intelligence Unit, where we kept a log of reports and plotted positions to try to establish some kind of pattern. No better experience could have been devised to instill into a combat intelligence officer the cynical skepticism to doubt even eyewitness accounts reported by sincere and normally reliable observers. Stress and surprise, hysteria and self-delusion, colored everything, and rumors snowballed as they were passed down the line. No one who has not experienced it can realize how difficult it is to track the shadow of truth through the fog of war.

Subsequent information has proved beyond reasonable doubt that no Japanese surface ships approached any Hawaiian island closer than 180 miles that morning. After eleven o'clock there were no Japanese planes over Oahu. Japanese submarines within sight of land remained submerged during daylight. Yet, landing operations were reported on Oahu's northern shore. Paratroopers were seen dropping on Ewa Plain; their uniforms were carefully described. Two Japanese carriers with eight escorts and three troopships were reported forty miles off Barber's Point, only a few miles from the entrance to Pearl Harbor. A formation of twelve Japanese battleships was reported south of Kauai. Mysterious vessels were observed entering Lahaina Roads, the fleet anchorage seventy miles southeast of Pearl Harbor. These and many other instances of hostile activity and sabotage that just did not happen were faithfully reported.

About eleven o'clock, CinCPac telephoned that they had picked up a radio message from the Navy's strategic direction finder at Lualualei reporting an enemy aircraft carrier transmitting on bearing 357? This direction finder normally reported to Combat Intelligence by telephone but, early that morning, telephone communication was cut off, so the direction-finder operators resorted to radio broadcast to get out their important information. The cut telephone connection was believed to have been the work of saboteurs until it was later discovered that service on this line had been interrupted by Army communications personnel setting up new circuits.

The bearing reported was correct—the Japanese carrier was nearly due north—but all other information at CinCPac headquarters, much of it based on false contacts, indicated that Japanese surface activity was concentrated to the south. The Marshall Islands, where the Japanese had their nearest naval bases and from which it seemed most probable an attack would come, were to the southwest. As many direction finders in those days were unable to distinguish between the real and the reciprocal bearing of a transmission,

CinCPac directed Admiral William F. Halsey in the aircraft carrier *Enterprise* to search for the enemy to the southward. The most important contribution of communications intelligence that day, therefore, sent Halsey at high speed directly away from the Japanese task force. It was a most fortunate error, for had Halsey steamed north and encountered six Japanese aircraft carriers, probably neither the *Enterprise* nor Halsey would have survived the first day of the war.

Japanese submarines were reported everywhere. More than an hour before the air attack started, the destroyer *Ward*, patrolling the defensive sea area off Pearl Harbor's entrance buoys, reported attacking a submerged submarine. A few minutes after the air attack started, the seaplane tender *Curtiss*, moored inside Pearl Harbor, opened fire on the periscope of a submerged submarine, which the destroyer *Monaghan*, having gone to the *Curtiss's* assistance, fired on, depth-charged, and rammed.

Many times I had piloted a surfaced submarine through Pearl Harbor Channel. I knew that, even on the surface, a submarine had to navigate that long channel with caution, so I evaluated as ridiculous the report that a submerged Japanese submarine was inside Pearl Harbor. It was, in fact, one of the few accurate sighting reports to reach us that day, as was proved a few days later when the crushed and broken hull of the midget submarine that the *Monaghan* and *Curtiss* had sunk was recovered. The submarine that the *Ward* sank also turned out to be a midget.

Late that afternoon I was discussing these submarine activities with Commander Charles B. Momsen, of the Hawaiian Sea Frontier, an old colleague of my submarine service, when I discovered that the telephone service into Honolulu was functioning normally. I picked up Momsen's telephone and dialed my home number. My wife, Izzy, answered promptly and calmly reported that everything was quiet around the Diamond Head area. Momsen and I had just agreed that it was quite possible that the Japanese, having knocked out the naval and air defenses of Oahu, would return that night to bombard the coastal defenses. Diamond Head would make a good target for them. Cruisers could safely lie outside the range of its old coast-defense guns and bombard Diamond Head at leisure. There were two 8-inch guns practically in our back yard on Black Point. I couldn't very well explain all this on the telephone, but I told Izzy to go on up to Nuuanu Valley with Eric to spend the night with the Lanquists, as we had planned. She protested that Civil Defense had warned everyone to stay off the roads. The family of John Detar, captain of the submarine *Tuna*, had taken refuge with her

6

and she thought they would all be better off at home, but when I insisted she promised to go.

———————

Though no one seemed inclined to leave the basement for long, we had only a couple of cots for the thirty men working there, and we could not exist forever on coffee and sandwiches brought in from the Navy Yard cafeteria. We established a system of watches, and by evening I had a few hours with no specific duties to perform. I backed my car out of the parking area and drove to Honolulu to check up on the safety of my wife and son. It was still light and traffic was practically nonexistent. I found them and the Detar family safe but crowded in with the Lanquists. By morning the greatest danger of bombardment would be over and they would be able to go back to Black Point.

It was late and very dark when I started back to Pearl Harbor. Not a light showed in all of Honolulu as I cautiously felt my way without lights down Nuuanu Avenue. If I put my foot on the brake, the tail lights blazed like red beacons, so I had to control the car with the hand parking brake. I followed the curb line of the road, most of the time in low gear, and worked my way slowly to the center of town. A masked flashlight signaled me to stop and a Honolulu policeman stepped off the curb to ask me where I was going. When I told him my destination was Pearl Harbor, he said he had a shipfitter trying to get to the naval base, where he was badly needed. Silently, my passenger climbed in beside me. I was grateful for his company and assistance in watching the road ahead.

It was so dark we had difficulty staying on the road where there was no curb to guide us. Every once in a while, we encountered a roadblock manned by nervous sentries who stopped us but let us proceed as soon as we were recognized. On one occasion, when the car was slow to stop with only the hand brake, a jittery sentry ordered both of us out of the car to face the leveled rifles of several of his comrades while he reluctantly concluded we were not saboteurs cleverly disguised and bent on some nefarious mission. We both sighed with relief when we safely passed the Navy Yard gate. In the darkness I never had a good look at my passenger's face and our conversation was limited to the problem of staying in the road so I never learned his name, but I am sure that he felt as I did, that on the night of 7 December we were in much greater danger from Oahu's defenders than from its enemies.

On the completely blacked-out island, familiar things assumed strange threatening shapes. Almost anything that moved in the cane fields was shot at by nervous sentries, and the chatter of one machine gun would wake its neighbor into action like barking dogs along a country lane. Phantom aircraft drew frantic fire from every tense gunner.

That night, among many other wild reports, we received one that a dirigible had been sighted over Honolulu, two degrees to the right of the moon and four degrees below it. There was, at that time, no dirigible in existence. Unfortunately not all planes sighted were phantom. Four of six planes from the *Enterprise*, attempting to make an announced landing at Ford Island, were shot down with lamentable efficiency.

The next morning, groups of us went in turn over to the officers' mess for breakfast. The route led past the Navy Yard flagstaff, and my group reached it just in time for eight o'clock colors. The guard and band had been paraded. We stood at stiff attention and saluted as the flag was smartly two-blocked. The music of the national anthem rolled out over the oil-dark water of Pearl Harbor and over the bodies of three thousand sailors who had died there in the previous dawn's early light.

CHAPTER 2

AN UNUSUAL COMBINATION of circumstances had steered me, at the beginning of the war, into the Combat Intelligence office of the Fourteenth Naval District at Pearl Harbor. I had neither training and experience nor any of the skills expected of an intelligence officer. Six years before, I was a lieutenant, a graduate of the Naval Academy with thirteen years of commissioned service, and in command of the submarine *S-30*, at Pearl Harbor. I had arthritis of the spine, which had progressed so far that it could no longer be concealed on annual physical examination. This ended my career as a submarine officer. I fought it to the end, but the sad day finally came in 1936, when I walked down the steps of the Submarine Base Administration Building, en route to be retired for physical disability, then drove home to put away my uniform; probably forever. No one could foresee that almost exactly ten years later I would again walk down those same steps, again to be retired, but the second time as a captain, U.S. Navy.

Fortunately, I had a master's degree in engineering from Columbia University, so I was able to find a job, which was not easy in 1936. I was glad to start all over again at the bottom of the ladder in a new profession. I became an instructor in engineering at the University of Hawaii. During my summer vacations from the university I wrote short stories under the pen name of Alec Hudson for *The Saturday Evening Post*, and this combination promised to be a new and challenging career for me.

In June 1941 Admiral Claude C. Bloch, commandant of the Fourteenth Naval District, sent for me and asked me if I would like to return to active duty in the Navy. As the international situation grew ominous, the Navy began recalling many of its retired officers to active duty. During 1940 I had twice been asked to return to active duty. There was no possibility of a permanent future for me in the Navy, and a short tour would disrupt my new civilian

Claude C. Bloch
Courtesy: U.S. Naval Academy Alumni Association

career, so I was not too disappointed when the doctors refused to certify me physically. However, I assured Admiral Bloch that I certainly wanted to be back in uniform if the United States went to war, and he told me that the doctors would pass me this time. The medics had recently been authorized to consider the kind of duty an officer would be required to perform as well as his physical condition. Admiral Bloch said he wanted me to be a combat intelligence officer and that he would inform the hospital that this would be light duty. So I passed my physicals for "limited shore duty only." I am sure Admiral Bloch intended that my duty would be light, but there were many times before it was over when my reach for the limits of my duties exceeded my grasp, both physically and mentally.

The nature of the duties of a combat intelligence officer of a naval district was completely unknown to me. "Combat intelligence officer" was a new billet just being allocated to units of the fleet and to some naval districts. In some battleships, I knew, the most important duty assigned to new combat intelligence officers was keeping track of ship's laundry when the ship was in port. When I confessed my ignorance to Admiral Bloch he said he didn't know what a combat intelligence officer did either; I could write my own ticket. In this, I believe, he was not altogether frank. I learned much later that he had talked to Commander Rochefort about the possibilities of my joining the Communications Intelligence Unit. Rochefort was not enthusiastic. He had enough trouble without being burdened with an untrained officer physically qualified for limited shore duty only.

A retired officer recalled to active duty could expect to be assigned dull routine jobs from which he would release an officer qualified for more strenuous duty. At first, this seemed to be my fate. District Intelligence, primarily concerned with counterintelligence, had offices in Honolulu. Although I was nominally attached to District Intelligence, my duties were different and I was assigned to work under the Fourteenth Naval District's operations officer at Pearl Harbor, several miles from Honolulu. Thus, I was in a semidetached status. The operations officer regarded me as a temporary encumbrance and provided me with neither assistance nor facilities in his crowded office. I didn't have a desk to work at or even a chair to sit on (a real handicap for anyone with arthritis of the spine) until I brought my own chair from home. I had no connection with Communications Intelligence and very little contact with Fleet Intelligence or CinCPac, whose headquarters were at the Submarine Base, Pearl Harbor. From the beginning there was confusion as to how my activity fitted into the standard organizational chart, and this confusion grew and was compounded in higher and higher echelons as time went on. Sometimes this was a handicap, but generally it was an asset, because I could often call on several different sources for assistance and could innocently remain ignorant of much inhibiting red tape.

There was then no center of information in the Fourteenth Naval District for the current location of ships at sea. CinCPac's Operations Division kept track of fleet vessels operating in the Hawaiian area, but many of the details were left to subordinate commanders, and all of them together knew next to nothing about the operations of merchant ships. After a short course of study of Rainbow Five, the current war plan, and of the orders and organization to divide the responsibility of defense between the Army, the fleet, and the naval district, I decided that a good way to start would be to collect and plot all available information on merchant shipping in the area. Fortunately the newspapers provided good information on many ship movements. Also the people in the offices of the shipping companies in Honolulu proved to be most cooperative. On my way to the Navy Yard each morning, I stopped in to chat with them and collect all the local shipping gossip. By collating several sources of information, I soon had charts that furnished a picture of ship movements, which was of service to several different offices in and around Pearl Harbor. This is when District Intelligence assigned to me Yeoman William Dunbar, to help broaden my activities.

My broader activity soon brought me into a minor conflict of interest, the significance of which I did not recognize at the time. Many merchant vessels at sea originated a radio message each day, reporting weather data at their position. For this they used a standard international weather cipher. In Honolulu these messages were received by a commercial radio and cable company and forwarded to San Francisco, where they were used in forecasting West Coast weather. The first two cipher groups of these standard form messages gave the position of the originating ship. This radio company was thus a source of the daily positions of many ships at sea. I went to them to investigate the possibility of picking up a list of ship positions each morning.

The office manager told me that he would be glad to comply with my request, but he was forbidden by the Federal Communications Act of 1934 to disclose to anyone, other than the addressees, any information contained in messages filed with his company. He admitted he might be induced to stick his neck out in a national emergency, but he wanted a more authoritative request than a casual one from an unknown lieutenant. I understood his position. I thanked him sincerely, satisfied that I had laid the groundwork for a source of information that would be quickly available if it were needed.

The next day the district's operations officer told me that he had been informed that I was soliciting illegal information from a radio company. He explained that Captain Irving H. Mayfield, the district intelligence officer, reserved to himself the authority to make any such requests. He also informed me that the Communications Act of 1934 provided penalties of a ten-thousand-dollar fine and a year in jail for anyone who violated the security of messages filed with a U.S. communications agency. Under these circumstances, he suggested that I had better expend my energies in some other direction.

This incident is interesting because of a coincidence that I did not learn about until later. In the regular commercial radio offices of Honolulu, the Japanese consul general, Nagao Kita, frequently filed coded messages to Tokyo. These included many messages from a special vice consul, Takeo Yoshikawa, a former ensign in the Imperial Japanese Navy, whose duty it was to observe and report all activities at Pearl Harbor. The Japanese placed no reliance on the Federal Communications Act to safeguard their coded communications. They were confident that their codes were secure against cryptanalytic attack. In this they were mistaken. Their diplomatic codes had been compromised and the consul general in Hawaii was indebted only to the Communications Act of 1934 for protection of his communications with Tokyo.

At about this same time Ambassador Joseph C. Grew, in Japan, was filing his diplomatic coded messages with Japanese communications agencies. He remarks in his book *Ten Years in Japan* that many of the reports his embassy sent to Washington became promptly known to the Japanese authorities because the Japanese had broken all but one of the American diplomatic codes. Copies of coded messages filed in Tokyo were sent to the Japanese Foreign Office before the messages were released for transmittal to Washington. Grew was sure, however, that one code was perfectly safe—a dangerous assumption because the first step toward a code being compromised is for the user to feel perfectly safe.

Before World War II, most of the world's diplomatic codes were compromised. Nations with competent cryptanalysts were reading each other's encrypted diplomatic messages, each country usually remaining confident that its own codes were safe. Japanese diplomatic messages, transmitted by Japanese radio systems, were being efficiently intercepted by the U.S. Army and the U.S. Navy and were being read in Washington. Although nobody was willing to question it, there was a comforting theory that the Communications Act of 1934 did not make illegal the interception of a foreign radio message on a foreign radio channel. Japanese consular messages in possession of a U.S. communications company in Hawaii, however, were safe. Nowhere other than the United States did such a situation exist.

In the summer of 1941 information on naval ships' locations was classified. Only the captain of the yard (and Japanese Vice Consul Yoshikawa) had up-to-the-minute information on every ship's berthing assignment at the many docks and anchorages of Pearl Harbor. Sometimes, when an officer reporting for duty asked where his ship was, the captain of the yard's clerks would reply that they were not authorized to give out that classified information. Of course, an officer thus thwarted had only to drive up to the heights above Pearl Harbor, survey all the harbor spread out before him, and pick out his ship. Anyone who did this might well encounter Yoshikawa, who regularly made such observations and then promptly reported the information to Tokyo by public communication facilities under the protection of American laws.

The positions of ships at sea were not so easily available. Yoshikawa tried hard without success to discover where naval vessels went when they left Pearl Harbor and disappeared over the horizon. The Japanese could easily monitor the radio traffic of U.S. merchant shipping and compile information denied to me by the Communications Act, but communications security gradually tightened. In the fall, weather reports from ships were sent only in a secret cipher and that may have given the Japanese cryptanalysts a little difficulty. In October all U.S. merchant vessels were withdrawn from the northern and central Pacific routes. Ships bound for the Philippines were routed south through Torres Strait, between New Guinea and the tip of Cape York Peninsula, Australia. Some of them were organized in escorted convoys, and all of them maintained radio silence. The port director at Pearl Harbor was responsible for their routing and at first depended upon Combat Intelligence's plot for information on ships' positions. The operations office was too open and accessible to permit the display of such classified information. When the new wing of the Administration Building was completed, it was decided to move me in with Commander Rochefort's Communications Intelligence Unit and to restrict severely the number of people who had access to my plotting charts.

Rochefort was then in charge of a group that conducted a mysterious operation in a room behind the supply office. Whatever they were doing required the use of keypunchers, sorters, collators, and machine printers, all standard IBM equipment today, but at that time quite exotic. Their machinery and the lack of any forthright explanation of their activity aroused speculation and prying by the overly curious. There were even amused suggestions that "Rochefort was trying to break the Japanese code."

The basement of the new wing of the Administration Building had been designed to provide security for Rochefort's work. There was then no name in general use for this group. The code name "Hypo," then the standard name for the "H" flag in the International Signal Code, was used within the organization and was sometimes loosely used for the whole activity, although strictly it applied only to the Hawaiian intercept station.

When we all moved into the basement together, Rochefort took advantage of the secrecy associated with ship movements to hide what his group was doing behind my charts. He adopted Combat Intelligence Unit as a cover name for the whole outfit. It was a case of the tip of the tail wagging the dog, but it worked. It met the need for an overt name that gave no clue to the real activity, and it satisfied the snoopers, for they then thought they knew what went on behind the security curtain. For me, personally, it removed all danger that my wartime service would be in a dull routine job. My situation was clear. I continued to perform the combat intelligence functions that I had developed. I worked for Rochefort and under his direction, but I remained on the rolls of the Fourteenth Naval District's intelligence office, and sometimes this tenuous relationship proved useful.

Later, radio intelligence was placed directly under the U.S. Pacific Fleet and renamed Fleet Radio Unit, Pacific, known more commonly by the acronym FRUPac. Although use of the term "FRUPac" is anachronistic when referring to activity prior to September 1943, it is the most convenient way to designate the radio intelligence group at Pearl Harbor.

Dunbar and I moved into the basement with a chart desk and plotting equipment, a good portfolio of Pacific Ocean charts, copies of Sailing Directions and Coast Pilots of Pacific areas, and a few books of my own, of which Bryan's *Coral Islands* was one of the most useful. We also acquired a large wall chart which at first we glued to the basement wall, but later put on a steel backing so we could indicate daily ship movements with small magnets.

It was distinctly understood that we were with, but not of, FRUPac. We were not told anything about FRUPac and were cautioned not to be curious about its operation. Space was allotted to us near the back door, which communicated with the port director's office on the floor above, and through which we could approach our area without passing through FRUPac. So far as possible, we were expected to remain in our own space. Thus, it was literally through the back door that I entered FRUPac, for although the restrictions were carefully observed at first, circumstances slowly eroded them.

Shortly after we were relocated, I learned that the U.S. Coast Guard monitored and routinely deciphered the weather reports of all ships within radio range. These intercepts were forwarded to FRUPac daily, which greatly simplified my data collection and gave me better and more timely information on the positions of many ships. It also confirmed my supposition that FRUPac was in the radio-interception business and had the support of at least one organization capable of intercepting on a useful scale.

The Japanese were also interested in weather over the Pacific Ocean. Their tankers, desperately trying to outflank the American, British, and Dutch oil embargo, were hauling oil from South America by unusual routes across the South Pacific. From the broad blank spaces on the map which they traversed, no weather information was otherwise available. The tankers faithfully reported their weather observations to Japan, and FRUPac intercepted these messages. After a while the positions of the Japanese tankers were given to me so that I could trace their secret tracks across the vast and lonely South Pacific.

It required no great deductive power to realize that interception of the tankers' weather reports was an accomplishment of a higher order of magnitude than the simple interception of our own weather messages. Radio messages sent by European countries were in the international telegraphic code of the standard alphabet, although of course they could be encoded or enciphered, or both, to make them more secure. Japanese is written mostly in Chinese characters (*kanji*) but it may also be written in a phonetic syllabary (*kana*). The *romaji* form of *kana* employs roman letters, but *kana* has its own telegraphic code to represent the fifty-one symbols in the system. Most of the Japanese radio traffic was in *kana* code, but the numerals were in international telegraphic code: it was necessary for an operator to be adept in both *kana* telegraphic code and in international telegraphic code in order to copy it. Fortunately our radio monitors did not also have to know the Japanese language, but they obviously required special skills, a special organization, and special equipment to monitor the Japanese radio frequencies.

The Japanese were very sensitive to communications security. Many months before the war they began transmitting their weather messages in secret ciphers. To get any information from Japanese weather reports it was necessary to break their ciphers. Through plotting the tanker tracks, I became aware that this was the special task of a young radioman, Anthony Ethier, who occupied a desk in a quiet corner of the basement. Sometime in October 1941 he was joined by a chief petty officer, William Livingston. Together, they worked on Japanese weather messages, occasionally receiving some help from Rochefort and others in his organization.

Combat Intelligence, under Rochefort, was a unique military organization. Not much attention was paid to uniforms or to military punctilio of any kind. Although there was never any doubt as to who was boss, a man's status depended upon factors other than rank. Outside the basement, Livingston was just one chief petty officer among many, and Ethier was only another sailor in a white hat, but once safely behind the steel doors their status was higher than that of many junior officers. They had a job to do. They were given wide latitude on how to do it. They could call on anybody in the basement to help them and everybody tacitly understood that their success demonstrated rare talent.

Japanese weather ciphers were quite sophisticated, and they were changed frequently to hinder cryptanalysis. I knew very little about cryptography, but I knew that I could not do what Livingston and Ethier were doing in a routine fashion, and I was anxious to give them any help I could. The system of Japanese shore-based weather stations was being rapidly expanded. Frequently, after the name of a new weather station was determined, it was difficult to find it on the map. Livingston sometimes came to us with questions, "Where is Roi?" "Where is Kosol?"*

At first it appeared to be a simple job of tracking down a place-name on charts, sailing-direction indices, or gazetteers; but it was often more difficult than that. Places in the Pacific islands often had three or more names, derived from the original native names or left over from English, French, Spanish, German, or Japanese explorations and occupations. Names often had radical variations in spelling.

The rendering of a foreign place-name in Japanese *kana* generally resulted in weird spelling and pronunciation, incomprehensible to anyone as ignorant as I was of the Japanese language. Dunbar and I started a card file of Pacific island place-names, cross-referenced for the many variations we encountered. As it grew, the file became valuable to others, because Japanese activity had a habit of following the trail blazed by the establishment of weather stations.

*The endpapers of this book consist of a map of the Pacific Ocean, and the areas outlined thereon are shown, on a larger scale, on the pages following the index.

CHAPTER 3

EARLY IN NOVEMBER 1941 the situation in the Pacific became alarming. We realized that war was imminent, and the Combat Intelligence Unit began to maintain a continuous watch. Few officers were available for Sunday or holiday watches or for night duty after their regular day's work. My name was included in FRUPac's watch list, despite my ignorance of much that went on in the basement. Actually when the watch officer was the only person on duty at night, there was little he could do other than recognize an emergency and call for help. Even this required broader knowledge than I then had, so Rochefort directed that I should be given traffic intelligence summaries to acquaint me with the current strategic situation in the Pacific.

Traffic intelligence summaries were produced each day by two traffic analysts, Lieutenant Commander Thomas A. Huckins, a tall, fair-haired, well-built man who spoke with a careful drawl, and John A. Williams, a short, tense, very nervous lieutenant with a sallow complexion. No one ever volunteered any information to me about their methods, or, until I was admitted to the privileged fold, about their conclusions. Huckins had been in the same company with me, two classes my junior, at the Naval Academy, but until the way was cleared by Rochefort we never discussed the subject of traffic analysis. I did know that, theoretically, it was possible to gain valuable information merely from the quantity, origins, addressees, priorities, and other characteristics of radio traffic, and I could not help but observe that Huckins and Williams were eternally shuffling a large volume of messages. Each evening, their distilled observations of the day's traffic were typed out as a summary, which had to be delivered to Lieutenant Commander Edwin T. Layton, the fleet intelligence officer, before eight o'clock in the morning. Because I delivered a chart overlay of ships' positions every morning to Layton at CinCPac headquarters, I frequently acted as

officer messenger for other secret material also. I soon learned of the importance Layton placed on the traffic intelligence summary for his intelligence briefings of the Commander in Chief, Pacific Fleet, Admiral Husband E. Kimmel, each morning at eight-thirty.

My first reaction to reading these daily reports was one of disappointment. They appeared to be a mixture of gobbledegook and vague innuendoes, with very little solid information. The task of intercepting a large number of Japanese naval messages and rapidly transmitting them to the traffic analysis desk required an efficient and competent organization, much of which was in an intercept station far from my range of observation. The labor and talent expended seemed to me to deserve greater rewards.

For some time the U.S. Navy had been frequently changing ciphers for its secret radio calls in order to confuse enemy traffic analysts. The Japanese used similar security measures. At midnight, Tokyo time, 1 November 1941, they changed all their naval call signs identifying the originators and addressees of radio messages. This caused considerable difficulty to our traffic analysts, but in a few days some of the calls had been identified and, by the middle of the month, the new Japanese call sign cipher had been effectively broken. I never understood the methods the analysts used.

"An unidentified call in the Palau area originated several messages addressed to Commander, Second Fleet," meant very little to me. "Several new calls believed to be submarines were associated today with Saipan" was an observation that gave me little useful information when I first encountered it.

Gradually, however, some of the "unidentified calls" assumed a kind of identity, simply because they were repeated from day to day. One originator of messages, with an unidentified radio call sign, which radio direction finders fixed as being in the area of the Palau Islands, was engaged in heavy communications with Japanese air organizations and with Commander, Second Fleet, which made it probable that a Japanese task force, including an aircraft carrier, was being assembled at Palau. We knew from sightings and other sources that a much larger force was moving south toward Takao, Formosa. Commander, Second Fleet, was busy communicating with both task forces, probably indicating coordination of their effort in some forthcoming operation. The center of Japanese naval power was evidently shifting southward toward Malaya and the Dutch East Indies.

Direction finders, as well as traffic patterns, indicated that submarines were assembling around Saipan. Direction-finding on high frequencies was not as accurate as on the lower frequency used to assist navigators and, in addition, the Japanese Navy was understandably not at all cooperative with our efforts to locate their transmitting naval units. Obtaining a fix required instant coordination of widely separated direction finders. Generally, the best that could be expected was identification of the area of the transmission within three or four hundred miles. But this was good enough, over a period of a few days, to tell us that the submarine concentration around Saipan was moving out of the Marianas eastward toward the Marshalls and Hawaii.

Logical deductions concerning the activities of the Japanese Navy could be based on traffic analysis alone. Often, after he had identified the addressees in the message heading, the analyst permitted his imagination to suggest the subject matter of the encoded body of the message and to project Japanese naval operations into the future. Unfortunately, even if all the call signs had been correctly identified, several different, equally logical deductions could usually be drawn from the pattern and volume of radio traffic. It was necessary to read at least parts of some of the messages to reach firm conclusions from the many possibilities. As all radio traffic was encoded, this required the ability to read some of the Japanese naval codes.

Every navy, and the Japanese Navy in particular, used not one but many codes and ciphers. The most secure ones were the most complicated, requiring considerable time and special equipment to encode and decode, and generally these were reserved for the most sensitive and important messages. Simpler codes, easier to use and more widely distributed, were used for less important traffic. Some, like the weather ciphers, were designed to be used for vulnerable reports whose compromise might give useful, but not vital, information to the enemy. Some had to be used in special situations, as in single-seater airplanes, where codes must require minimum equipment and be easy to use. Such codes might be cracked by determined cryptographic attack, but they served their purpose if the enemy was so delayed in decoding them that he could no longer profit by the ephemeral secrets that they protected. It was possible to obtain some useful information from minor codes, the nickel and dime stuff, as Rochefort called them, but breaking a major naval code was another matter.

Years before, when I was a communications officer in a small submarine, I became interested in cryptography. I solved some of the exercise cryptograms in the monthly communications bulletins and I read a few books on the subject, including an Army pamphlet, *Elements of Cryptanalysis*, and Herbert O. Yardley's *American*

Black Chamber. A book by Fletcher Pratt, *Secret and Urgent*, recounted several incidents when Union forces obtained important information from the decryption of Confederate secret messages. There were also stories of the achievements of British cryptanalysts in World War I. But the simple ciphers used by the Confederates were as obsolete as their muzzle-loading cannon, and the British achievements all seemed to revolve around some kind of a break that gave the cryptanalysts a "crib." The American Black Chamber had its outstanding success with diplomatic codes, which were generally more vulnerable than naval codes. The prospects of breaking a major Japanese naval code seemed impossibly remote.

Wesley A. Wright, better known as "Ham," a heavy-set man with craggy features, a large nose, and a thin moustache, worked in the cipher section. He must have been unduly impressed with my civilian status as an assistant professor of engineering and mathematics. He came to me one day for help in devising a mathematical formula for manipulating groups of five-digit numbers. I quickly discovered that a mathematical solution to his problem was beyond my capability, but his questions indicated that the cipher section was working on a very complicated enciphered numerical code. What little I knew of cryptographic history indicated that breaks in codes of such complexity had been very few indeed. Probably, they had never occurred except by a combination of lucky accidents relentlessly followed up by men of rare genius.

In cold appraisal, the men in the basement did not appear to fit into the category of geniuses. They worked hard, long hours. Some of them were very clever and resourceful with unusual techniques. They had more detailed knowledge of Japanese naval communications systems than I had acquired of U.S. naval communications systems in twenty years of naval experience. They had an efficient and smooth-working organization, but the results they obtained did not appear proportionate to their efforts. Most officers working in the Navy Yard, busy with nuts and bolts and fuel and ammunition, were inclined to view code-breaking with amused tolerance. I was better informed. I knew that the communications intelligence organization was much more competent than anyone had any right to expect, but I was not able to recognize any large outcropping of genius. In the longer view, the Navy's selection boards were not able to recognize exceptional ability there, either.

Commander Rochefort, the leader and the ablest of the group, had not been selected as "best fitted" for promotion. He had achieved his rank as commander after being selected as "fitted and retained" —a kind of limbo that classified him as too valuable to lose but not

Thomas H. Dyer

good enough for further promotion. Thomas H. Dyer, a short, dark-haired man with a black moustache and large glasses, whose informal manner and careless dress were more characteristic of a mathematics professor than of a naval officer, was head of the cipher section. He had had trouble with selection from lieutenant to lieutenant commander. The first time he was considered by a selection board he had insufficient sea service in rank to make the grade. His work in cryptography had kept him in shore jobs. By some kind of manipulation in the office of the Secretary of the Navy, he was designated for "Engineering Duty Only" before the board met the following year. This excused him from the sea-service requirements and he thus achieved the rank of lieutenant commander.

Thomas B. Birtley, whose talents as a Japanese-language officer and a cryptanalyst were desperately needed in communications intelligence, had been ordered away from the unit to a sea job the previous summer because he did not have sufficient sea duty to qualify for promotion to commander. Ransom Fullinwider, another language officer, was also in a shaky position for lack of sea service. Huckins, who was a classmate of Dyer, had been passed over the first time he was up for selection, but had then made lieutenant commander the following year.

Evidently service in communications intelligence did not impress naval selection boards, and young officers anxious to make a service reputation at sea in preparation for command were not attracted to that kind of work. Long experience, hard work, and dedicated service were needed to acquire the necessary skills in cryptography, traffic analysis, and the Japanese language, and to develop the organization even to limited usefulness. Only extraordinary ability and rare genius could carry it any further. I was unable to see where it was coming from.

Japan had ships, building and built, with characteristics of displacement, gun caliber, and speed that the authoritative *Jane's Fighting Ships* had never heard of. There were few opportunities to observe Japanese modern major combat vessels and little was published about their operations. Japan's long war with China had made it possible for her to maintain extraordinary security measures. Foreigners in Japan were closely watched and effectively denied access to much background information corresponding to that which was readily available about the U.S. Navy in the press, in publications, and from political debate.

The Japanese language is inscrutable. Few Americans could read it, and only about forty naval officers had any knowledge of the special idiom and ideographs peculiar to naval operations. Even after a Japanese naval message had been decoded, it often remained a "riddle wrapped in a mystery." The Japanese naval communications system was close-knit, self-contained, and protected by the vast distances of the Pacific. It was difficult to find a flaw in the armor of its security.

The chief of naval operations and the chief of staff of the U.S. Army had issued orders that only those who were specifically cleared and "whose responsibilities required them to know" could receive communications intelligence. Each individual cleared was required to sign an agreement that he would not disclose the information to anyone not "cleared for Ultra," that is, for intelligence obtained by decryption. As I was not cleared, I was told nothing and picked up only little by little some of the knowledge needed to understand what was going on under my nose, but I soon learned that most of what we knew about Japanese fleet operations came from intercepted communications.

A good knowledge of the organization of the Japanese fleet was essential to an understanding of its operation. Like the U.S. Navy, the Japanese Navy was divided into fleets, squadrons, and divisions for administrative purposes. For specific operations, units and divisions were temporarily assigned to task forces under a commander designated for the duration of an operation. Knowledge of which units were actively communicating with each other and with which commander offered a clue to the composition of task forces. The strength and composition of a task force offered clues to the magnitude and nature of the task. The geographical position of shore stations handling messages to and from ships or to and from task-force commanders gave some idea of where the forces were.

If this concatenation of deductions could be corroborated by other information, the conclusions were generally reliable. Otherwise, deduction piled on deduction could result in a construction that leaned far out from the truth. In November 1941, little information was available to verify traffic analysis. The Japanese-Chinese war had dried up sources of information from ports on the coast of China and from Japan. All American ships had been withdrawn from the North Pacific, and that great area, bounded by Hawaii on the south, the Aleutians on the north, Japan on the west, and the west coast of the United States and Canada on the east, was a deserted ocean.

It was obvious that if I was to learn anything from the traffic intelligence summaries, I would have to become familiar with the organization of the Japanese Navy. CinCPac's intelligence officer, Layton, had recently published, in an issue of the *Pacific Fleet Intelligence Bulletin*, an estimated organization chart of the Japanese fleet. With this chart, and with the illustrations in *Jane's Fighting Ships* to lend some reality to the many strange-sounding names, my education as an intelligence officer really began. Anyone who wishes to understand the development of combat intelligence should have a similar tabulation for reference.

COMBINED FLEET
Admiral Isoroku Yamamoto—Commander in Chief

FIRST FLEET—Battle Force

Battleship Division 1   *Nagato, Mutsu, Yamashiro*
Battleship Division 2   *Fuso, Ise, Hyuga*
Battleship Division 3   *Hiei, Kirishima, Kongo, Haruna*
Cruiser Division 6   *Kako, Furutaka, Aoba, Kinugasa*
Cruiser Division 9   *Kitagami, Oi*
Destroyer Squadron 1   *Abukuma* (light cruiser) and 12 destroyers
Destroyer Squadron 3   *Sendai* (light cruiser) and 16 destroyers

SECOND FLEET—Scouting Fleet

Cruiser Division 4   *Atago, Takao, Chokai, Maya*
Cruiser Division 5   *Myoko, Haguro*
Cruiser Division 7   *Mogami, Mikuma, Suzuya, Kumano*

Cruiser Division 8   *Tone, Chikuma*
Destroyer Squadron 2   *Jintsu* (light cruiser) and 12 destroyers
Destroyer Squadron 4   *Naka* (light cruiser) and 16 destroyers

THIRD FLEET—Blockade and Transport Force
Cruiser Division 16   *Ashigara, Kuma, Kinu, Nagara*
Destroyer Squadron 5   *Natori* (light cruiser) and 12 destroyers

FOURTH FLEET—South Sea Fleet
Flagship   *Kashima* (light cruiser)
Cruiser Division 18   *Tenryu, Tatsuta*
Destroyer Squadron 6   *Yubari* (light cruiser) and 8 destroyers

FIFTH FLEET—Northern Force
Cruiser Division 21   *Nachi, Tama, Kiso*, and 2 destroyers

SIXTH FLEET—Submarine Force
Katori, Yura, Isuzu (light cruisers) and 42 submarines

FIRST AIR FLEET—Carrier Force
Carrier Division 1   *Kaga, Akagi*
Carrier Division 2   *Hiryu, Soryu*
Carrier Division 4   *Ryujo, Zuiho, Hosho*
Carrier Division 5   *Shokaku, Zuikaku*

COMBINED AIR FORCE—Shore-based Naval Air Forces
Eleventh Air Fleet—based on Formosa
Air Squadron 21—based in Indochina
Air Squadron 23—based in Indochina
Air Squadrons—training in Japan
Other shore-based naval air force units

During the last week in November tensions increased. One morning Admiral Kimmel and Admiral Bloch together appeared in the basement. It was something like two mountains coming to Mohammed, but the basement was the most secure place for a secret conference. I learned later that Kimmel had sent instructions to Rochefort to prepare an estimate of the current disposition and intentions of the Japanese fleet, and to submit it by dispatch to communications intelligence units in Washington and Corregidor for comment. These two units and the one in Hawaii constantly exchanged technical information but left the individual commanders under whom they served to reach their own conclusions. Kimmel had therefore set in motion an unusual exchange of messages.

Rochefort responded with his estimate on 26 November. For the past month, he said, the commander of the Japanese Second Fleet had been organizing a task force which comprised most of the Second and Third fleets, plus Destroyer Squadron 3 and units of

Battleship Division 3 from the First Fleet. The greater part of the Combined Air Force, which consisted of shore-based naval air squadrons, was also under his orders. This force was assembling in Formosa and Indochina. Cruiser Division 7 and Destroyer Squadron 3 had advanced into the South China Sea. Commander, Second Fleet, had also exchanged many messages with units at Palau. Rochefort estimated that at least one-third of the Japanese submarine force, together with Air Squadron 24 and one or two units of the First Air Fleet, was in the Marshall Islands. From this, Rochefort concluded that a strong naval force based in Hainan and Formosa, with components in Palau and the Marshalls, was poised to attack Southeast Asia and the Netherlands East Indies.

Corregidor agreed on the composition and intention of the forces converging on Indochina, but could not agree on the strong submarine concentration or the presence of carrier units in the Marshalls. They believed that Japanese aircraft carriers were still in the Sasebo-Kure area of Japan and the First Fleet was in the Inland Sea.

Possibly triggered by these exchanges, the chief of naval operations, Admiral Harold R. Stark, on 27 November sent Admiral Kimmel and Admiral Thomas C. Hart, commander in chief, Asiatic Fleet, a message that began, "This dispatch is a war warning." He stated that negotiations between the United States and Japan had ceased and an aggressive move by Japan was expected within a few days. An amphibious expedition against either the Philippines, Thailand, the Kra Isthmus, or, possibly, Borneo was expected. Kimmel and Hart were ordered to execute appropriate defensive deployments in preparation for carrying out the Rainbow Five war plan.

Despite differences of opinion in regard to details, there was general agreement with regard to Japan's most probable move. Two coordinated forces were expected to execute a typical Japanese pincers movement against Malaya and the East Indies. The stronger leg of the pincers would come down through the South China Sea, and the other leg would advance from Palau against the Borneo area. A large part of the Japanese submarine force and a detachment of aircraft carriers would probably take up defensive positions in the Mandate, or Caroline and Marshall, Islands to guard the eastern flank of the operation from any opposition by the U.S. fleet in Hawaii.

The battleships of the First Fleet and the carriers of the First Air Fleet were expected to follow traditional Japanese strategy and wait in home waters. Only after the sea, the weather, the logistics of long supply lines, and constant harassing attacks by aggressive Japanese light forces had reduced their opponent's strength to manageable proportions would the Japanese offer decisive battle. This was the strategy ordained by the venerated Admiral Heihachiro Togo and by which he had destroyed the Imperial Russian Fleet at the Battle of Tsushima in 1905.

The Anglo-Dutch-American oil embargo had impaled Japan on the horns of a cruel dilemma. If she remained on the defensive, the depletion of her oil reserves would cripple her military operations in China and shortly render her completely impotent. This energy crisis forced her either to knuckle under to Allied demands or to move against the Netherlands East Indies and seize the essential supply of oil. The Philippines would menace Japanese supply lines in an East Indies operation. They were weakly defended, but were being rapidly strengthened. Japan might logically decide to take them at the start of a campaign, although this would bring America into the war immediately. Many strategists reasoned that Japan would be more subtle and bypass the Philippines. An attack on British or Dutch possessions would probably bring America into the war eventually, but if there were no direct attacks on U.S. possessions, Congress would debate so long that Japan would become too strongly entrenched to be dislodged before Germany won the war in Europe.

When November passed without open hostilities, tension eased a little. On 30 November the *Honolulu Advertiser* headlined "Japan May Strike Over the Weekend," but the next day headlines in the *Honolulu Star-Bulletin* read "Japan Envoys Resume Talks Amid Tension." On 2 December the *Advertiser* reported "Japan Called Still Hopeful of Making Peace with U.S." and "Japan Gives Two Weeks More to Negotiations." The newspapers had securely hedged their positions and could truthfully claim "We told you so," no matter what happened.

At zero hour, Tokyo time, on 1 December all Japanese naval radio calls were changed again. This shift, only one month after the previous change, was ominous. It handicapped the traffic analysts temporarily but, within two days, two hundred of the most frequently used calls were identified. However, these identifications did not include a single aircraft carrier call. Since 25 November no identified Japanese aircraft carrier had originated a message or been addressed for action or for information. This most unusual situation occasioned several comments in the traffic intelligence summaries.

Corregidor reported that nine Japanese submarines and a convoy of twenty-one transports had been sighted southbound through the South China Sea. From Singapore the British reported that Japanese battleships and cruisers had been sighted off the southern tip of Indochina. Reconnaissance planes reported a large convoy anchored in Camranh Bay. These sightings were consistent with Allied estimates of Japanese intentions.

The actual strength, disposition, and movements of the forces under Commander, Second Fleet, corresponded closely with Rochefort's estimates of 26 November. One unit of the First Air Fleet, the aircraft carrier *Ryujo*, was at Palau rather than in the Marshalls. Most of the battleships of the First Fleet were in the Sasebo-Kure area. Air Squadron 24 was in the Marshalls, and one-half rather than the estimated one-third of the submarines of the Sixth Fleet were in the Marshalls or en route to Hawaii directly from Japanese bases. The mystery of where the aircraft carriers of the First Air Fleet were, the key to the entire situation, remained unresolved.

Japanese planners recognized that the southward thrust of a big amphibious force supported by a major part of the Japanese Navy could not be completely hidden. No extraordinary security measures were taken to conceal it. In strictest secrecy, another task force, the Kido Butai, or Striking Force, under Admiral Chuichi Nagumo, Commander, First Air Fleet, was being assembled at Etorofu, in the Kuril Islands. Japanese strategists correctly calculated that the attention directed to the main southern movement would help to conceal the audacious operations of Nagumo's force in the north.

On 26 November the Kido Butai sortied from its secret anchorage, eastbound across the empty North Pacific Ocean. In the Kido Butai were the six most powerful carriers of the First Air Fleet (the *Akagi*, *Kaga*, *Hiryu*, *Soryu*, *Shokaku*, and *Zuikaku*), two fast battleships (the *Hiei* and *Kirishima*), two heavy cruisers (the *Tone* and *Chikuma*), the light cruiser *Abukuma* and nine destroyers of Destroyer Squadron 1, an advance patrol of three submarines, and a train of eight tankers. No one, Japanese or American, in the United States or in Hawaii, was aware of this sortie, and very few Japanese officials in Japan knew anything about it. The Kido Butai proceeded to a position 42°N 170°W, there to await orders that depended upon the outcome of the diplomatic negotiations with the United States. On 30 November Japan made the final decision for war. The next day the Kido Butai was ordered to execute the carefully planned attack on Pearl Harbor.

From that moment there was nothing anyone in Hawaii could have done to materially change the outcome. Numerous critiques have correctly enumerated those things that were done and should not have been done and those things that were left undone and should have been done, but generally they have ignored the one dominant fact. There were no Allied forces, or possible combination of forces, between the east coast of Africa and the west coast of the United States that could have hoped successfully to challenge the Kido Butai. Surprise made the Japanese task much easier, but they also had six aircraft carriers against only two that could possibly have been brought to oppose them. With its fleet speed of 27 knots, the Kido Butai could easily have stayed outside the gun range of old U.S. battleships, which would have had difficulty maintaining a fleet speed of 19 knots. Neither Army nor Navy shore-based air constituted any serious threat to the Japanese carriers. The Kido Butai was master of the Pacific Ocean.

CHAPTER 4

DECEMBER 7TH 1941 was a watershed in the lives of nearly everyone in Hawaii. Suddenly even the bright sky and the smiling sea concealed menacing enemies. Monday dawned on a different world with different problems, different objectives, and different schedules differently oriented than before Sunday's sunrise. The Combat Intelligence Unit was no exception to changes in a changing world.

After one experience, no one wanted to make the drive on the dark roads between Honolulu and Pearl Harbor. Automobile headlights were altered to show only a permissible little spot of blue light, but it took a real emergency or urgent duty to entice sensible men out on the road after sunset. At first we tried twenty-four-hour watches, relieving at noon, but this was inefficient and, for many, being absent from their jobs for twenty-four hours was intolerable. Short December days could not be divided into equitable watches that obviated night driving. Every system tried slowly eroded until nearly everyone worked seven days a week during daylight and divided up additional night watches so that the organization was fully functional at all times.

Information on the location of merchant vessels dried up, as ships at sea clamped down a tight radio silence. Convoys were routed and controlled by the port director, who maintained a chart of their positions in his office directly above us. There was no need to duplicate his work, so our efforts were more and more directed to keeping track of Japanese submarines. However, we continued to plot the courses of ships we had been tracking until we were sure they had reached port. This proved to be well worth the effort.

A week before the attack on Pearl Harbor the SS *Steel Voyager* set out from Panama for the long haul to Honolulu. When news of the attack shattered the peace of the Pacific, she was closer to Honolulu than to any other port of refuge. We guessed that she would keep quiet and keep plugging along to her destination.

One night, radio direction finders fixed the position of a Japanese submarine on the great-circle track of the lone freighter and dead ahead of her estimated position. The port director sent out a blind broadcast message to the *Voyager*, directing her around the danger. Our estimate of her position proved to be correct. Her captain made a radical change of course to avoid the submarine. A few days later he safely made port. He claimed that he had been saved by the warning message.

Another instance involved the *William Ward Burrows*, a naval transport under the command of Captain Ross A. Dierdorff, which had departed from Pearl Harbor before 7 December on a supply mission to Johnston Island, a small atoll seven hundred miles southwest of Oahu. On the night of 15 December, Johnston was shelled by a Japanese force thought to be a cruiser and a destroyer, but which was actually the two submarines *I-16* and *I-22*. The *Burrows* had completed her mission and left Johnston a few hours before the bombardment. Dierdorff proposed to return to the island to render assistance, but the Commandant, Fourteenth Naval District, having received information that there were no casualties on the island, directed the ship to return to Pearl Harbor.

I remember that night very well. There was a voice tube between my plotting table and the district operations office two floors above, but down it had come few requests for information. Suddenly I received a peremptory demand for the position of the *William Ward Burrows*. It required only a minute to prick it off on the chart, and I answered "17-10 N, 168-40 W."

A moment later the voice tube rumbled with the demand, "Check that position."

I recognized the irate voice of a captain who was noted for his antagonism to the whole Combat Intelligence Unit, so I carefully checked my data before confirming my first answer, and explained that my estimate was based on the assumption that the *Burrows* was carrying out her assigned schedule on time. In answer, the voice tube roared orders for me to report immediately in the operations office with my charts.

While collecting my charts and notes I realized that if a mistake had been made my hide would be nailed to the wall, but as I started for the door I encountered a grim-faced Rochefort, adjusting his tie and straightening his hat, preparatory to leaving the basement.

"I will answer that call," he told me, and relieving me of the charts he marched up the stairs to face the challenge.

Ten minutes later he returned, barely suppressing a grin. A green and flustered watch officer in the operations office had forgotten that the 180th meridian ran down between Johnston and Wake, dividing west longitude from east. He had plotted the position I gave in east longitude, putting the *Burrows* in a precarious spot between Wake and the Marshalls. Rochefort immediately spotted the error and delivered a cynical lecture on elementary geography to a red-faced operations watch.

Rochefort was amused, but I was not. I was impressed with his instant assumption of complete responsibility for his organization, and his readiness to stand between one of his junior officers and wrath from without. It was one example of the leadership that inspired into that outfit an ironclad morale that knit us forever into a unit.

On the night of 6 December, five two-man midget submarines were released from large submarines just south of the entrance to Pearl Harbor, with the mission to penetrate the harbor and torpedo ships there. Three seaplane-carrying submarines that had scouted ahead of the Kido Butai, and two others that had reconnoitered Samoa and the Aleutians, joined the blockade of twenty fleet submarines that surrounded Oahu as soon as their tasks were finished. Three rear admirals commanding submarine squadrons were embarked in the blockading submarines. The light cruiser *Katori*, flagship of the Japanese Sixth Fleet, was anchored at Kwajalein to coordinate by radio the submarines' part in the attack. This situation generated a large volume of radio communications between the individual submarines and their squadron commanders, and with the commander of the Sixth Fleet.

From traffic intelligence we were able to determine the positions of Japanese submarines quickly and accurately but there were few U.S. antisubmarine vessels available for inshore patrol. A Japanese submarine could bob up to the surface, send a quick radio message, and submerge again to safety before an antisubmarine patrol could be directed to the spot. Many depth charges were dropped on phantom targets, and there were many frustrations.

One night an Army observation post on Kahala Beach, to the east of Diamond Head, reported that a submarine was lying just outside the reef, charging her batteries. They could see her silhouette and hear the throb of her engines. The report was relayed to Combat Intelligence for checking against the known location of friendly forces. There were no friendly forces in the vicinity. A Japanese submarine had recently been fixed in that locality by direction finders. Less than a block from where I lived on Black Point, a battery of two coast-defense guns looked down on Kahala Reef. Maybe the submarine was close inshore to communicate with spies, but whatever her mission, the Black Point battery then had the opportunity to be the first coast-defense battery to fire at a real enemy target since the Civil War.

My wife and son were much too close to the action to suit me. I hoped that when the battery opened up, the submarine would be too busy getting the hell out of there to return the fire, but anything could happen. I waited anxiously for a report of the action. An hour later the Army observers reported that the submarine had moved a mile down the beach, still under the guns, and that was the last report we had.

It was two or three days before I got home. All that I had heard about the submarine off Kahala was very secret, so I cautiously asked Izzy if there had been any unusual excitement the previous Monday night. Excitement! Army trucks had charged up and down the normally quiet street all night. Izzy was air-raid warden for Black Point and on Tuesday morning all the neighbors came rushing to her for information. To quiet the panic, she telephoned to the adjutant at Fort Ruger for explanations. He sent the chaplain down to reassure the local inhabitants. With what he told Izzy and what I already knew, Izzy and I were able to reconstruct the sequence of events.

The coast-defense battery on the end of Black Point had been there for many years. Its two 8-inch guns were ancient and short-ranged, but they were well placed to defend the beaches at Diamond Head and Kahala. During the years the guns had been there, Black Point had developed as a beach colony, occupied mainly by artists and submarine officers' families. When word came down the line that night to "open fire on a surfaced submarine in grid position Helen seven five," the battery was ready. The two big guns were swung around to the proper bearing and the gunpointers found they were looking right into the windows of the house we knew as "George Hunter's old house," not fifty yards away. Moreover, ranged down the slope to the water's edge, under the muzzles of the guns, were twenty other houses where families were sleeping in blissful ignorance of what was happening on the other side of the chain-link fence that divided the Army from the civilian area.

Quite properly, Fort Ruger's commanding officer decided that, submarine or no submarine, he had to evacuate the area before he could open fire. By the time that was done, the submarine had completed its business off Kahala Beach and was long gone from there. The next morning the Army tore down "George Hunter's old house," but the other inhabitants slowly filtered back to their abandoned homes.

Considering the trauma of the sudden transition from peace and security to war and disaster, Hawaii's civilians and the equally green military and naval personnel cooperated very well. An antiaircraft battery was placed behind the guns at Black Point and a new coast-defense battery was added on the slopes of Diamond Head. Before these or the 12-inch guns of Fort DeRussy on Waikiki Beach were fired in practice, the Army went from door to door warning people to move their dishes from shelves to the floor and to open windows to prevent their being shattered by concussion. The beaches were protected by machine guns behind barbed-wire barricades. On many nights, a sentry mistaking a cloud shadow on a wave for a landing boat would open up with his machine gun, and nervous sentries on his flanks would take up the fire. You could hear the alarm spread up the coast from post to post far into the distance.

Two or three times a week there would be air-raid alerts. When the siren sounded, Izzy would put on her steel helmet, snatch up her gas mask and her air-raid warden's flashlight, and dash off to "man" the Kahala civil-defense center. Most of the alerts were false alarms. Prompt air reinforcements from the mainland right after the attack made it possible for daily air searches to be conducted as far as 600 miles out in the more vulnerable sectors. The only Japanese forces in the vicinity were submarines, but no one was willing to take any chances. Unknown to us then, some of the largest Japanese submarines carried light observation seaplanes, so there really was more substance than imagination to at least some of the alerts.

Early one morning, the most probable hour for an air raid, while I was on my way to Pearl Harbor, the air-raid warning sounded. At the siren's scream, all cars except those heading for action stations were required to pull over to the side of the road and stop until the all-clear signal. Since I was en route to Combat Intelligence, I stepped on the accelerator, speeded into the Navy Yard, and dashed down into the basement to arrive at the crux of the crisis.

Admiral Bloch, with steel helmet, gas mask, and pistol, was there, conferring with Rochefort over the charts of Oahu. Combat reports were pouring in from the operations office above. A formation of three enemy cruisers was reported on the horizon of Oahu's northern shore. Shore defenses reported coming under fire, with heavy shells falling on the beaches. Shore batteries reported taking landing craft under fire. Fighter planes were locked in desperate battle over Ewa Plain, just west of Pearl Harbor. Then suddenly it all died down.

34

The enemy cruisers turned out to be three small converted seaplane tenders en route from California to the Naval Air Station at Pearl Harbor. Their attempts to identify themselves by signal searchlight had been mistaken for gun flashes from enemy ships. The defending shore batteries had opened up on phantom landing craft in the surf. Splashes from the shore batteries' short salvos explained the reports of heavy shells falling on the beach. Pilots of fighter planes, scrambling from both Army and Navy airfields, tested their guns by firing a few bursts as soon as they reached altitude, and the chatter of their machine guns had been reported as an air battle over Ewa Plain. Everybody felt silly after it was all over, but nobody had been hurt and everybody profited to some extent by the realistic battle practice.

The Naval Air Station had enjoyed a great deal of independence in scheduling its operations and it had failed to report to either the fleet operations office or to the Fourteenth Naval District's Combat Intelligence Unit, the anticipated arrival of its seaplane tenders. The ships, approaching from the eastward, had inadvertently circumvented the short-legged air search in that sector and had rashly made landfall on Oahu at the most sensitive hour of dawn. After this experience, the Naval Air Station cooperated enthusiastically with Combat Intelligence. An officer from the Naval Air Station came to Combat Intelligence each night at midnight to exchange information. We would give him a plot of the predicted positions of all ships in the area, except for fleet formations, and he would give us a plot of the next day's air searches.

This arrangement was instrumental in saving a gallant little ship some time later. More than a month after the Pearl Harbor attack, a search plane out nearly six hundred miles west of Honolulu reported sighting "a mother ship towing three small submarines." One of the midget submarines that had taken part in the attack on Pearl Harbor had been captured intact and it was obvious that it had not reached Pearl Harbor under its own power. The search plane's report was therefore like a "tally-ho" to an overeager foxhunt until Combat Intelligence's plot revealed more probable identification.

The *Albert Foss*, a seagoing tug, had departed Wake Island on 6 December with three empty barges, and settled down at her maximum towing speed of 2½ knots for the 2,200-mile haul to Honolulu. The next day, while she was just over the horizon from Wake, that island was bombed by Japanese planes. The captain saw some of the attacking planes and heard the news on the radio. A lesser man would have cut the tow and run, but he kept towing straight ahead, convinced that his best contribution to the war effort would be to complete the job he had set out to do. For a month, he kept plodding along through seas traversed by submarines and task forces, unsighted and undaunted, only to be identified as an enemy on the last leg of his wearisome voyage. Fortunately, against all reason, we had kept him on our plot and we hurriedly passed along the information that the *Albert Foss* and her tow would be in the vicinity of the reported sighting; if she were still afloat. Probably the Naval Air Station had already reached that same conclusion and warned the search plane, for the *Albert Foss* was not bombed. She safely made port about a week later. I have never met that skipper but I have always admired his guts.

That was about the last real service rendered by the ships' plot in the basement. When the joint Army-Navy Defense Center of the Hawaiian Sea Frontier was established in the tunnels under Red Hill, the plot moved up there where it could be better coordinated with the air searches and with the port director's plot of convoy routes. Dunbar and I stayed behind in the basement. The Communications Intelligence Unit had suddenly developed an insatiable need for manpower. We were already working on its fringes and were irresistibly drawn into deeper and deeper involvement.

The reason for all this activity I did not know or need to know in order to be useful. There was a great deal of ordinary administrative work to be accomplished. No one, other than the regulars, was allowed behind the steel doors, so the organization had to be self-supporting. Chief Rorie, an old-timer in communications intelligence, supervised the work assignments, security, janitorial service, and supplies. No one questioned his authority inside the basement, but we had to have a commissioned officer to work with the Navy Yard, the Submarine Force, CinCPac's staff, and other outside agencies. Lieutenant Jack S. Holtwick, who already had charge of the mysterious machine room into which I never intruded, had handled this additional duty. As the volume of work increased, however, the entire attention of this wiry, quick, and energetic young officer was required to program and supervise the business machines and the very secret coding machine. The more routine chores fell on me. Also, as the organization grew, so grew the demands of the cryptanalysts for odd bits of information—place-names; charts and maps; positions of our own forces, especially submarines; news reports; and other information whose relevance I could only conjecture.

When the language school in Japan closed down in the fall of 1941, Gilven M. Slonim, Forrest R. Biard, John G. Roenigk, Arthur L. Benedict, and John R. Bromley, who had all been officer students there, arrived to join FRUPac late in November, as did Allyn Cole,

36

Jack S. Holtwick

who had been a language officer with the Corregidor unit. Shortly after 7 December, Joseph Finnegan, a language officer on duty with one of the fleet staffs, was ordered to FRUPac. He was a burly, black-haired Irishman. He and Major Alva B. Lasswell, a tall, sandy-haired, cigar-smoking Marine, familiarly known as "Red," became the most productive of the cryptographer-translators. Barney Calhoun joined the cipher section and Philip Leigh reinforced the traffic analysts. Late in December, Lieutenant Thomas Steele, a Naval Reservist, brought a group of cipher experts out from the mainland.

The new language officers had hardly reported when, to comply with instructions from Washington, four of them had to be assigned to the intercept station to maintain a continuous watch on Japanese voice circuits. This was a futile assignment that kept them fully occupied until after the attack and left too few language officers available for more important tasks.

All of these people had special skills and experiences. When they joined a functioning organization they became immediately productive, but the demand for trained people greatly exceeded the supply. Admiral Bloch offered the band of the battleship *California* as trainees, and Rochefort promptly accepted. The *California* was resting on the bottom of Pearl Harbor, her main deck under water. Her band had survived but their instruments had not, so they were among the technologically unemployed. Many of these musicians turned out to be such competent cryptanalysts after a short period of instruction that a theory was advanced that there must be a psychological connection between music and cryptanalysis.

Very early in December a messenger from the District Intelligence Office delivered to Rochefort a package of encrypted messages. Of course, I did not know about this until later, and I doubt that Rochefort then knew how the messages had been obtained. Captain Mayfield had long been quietly trying to circumvent the Communications Act of 1934 to get at the protected communications between the Japanese consul general in Hawaii and the Foreign Office in Tokyo. The previous summer, by trying to pick up ships' weather reports at a commercial cable office, I had bulled into his delicate negotiations. Mayfield had tapped the Japanese consul's telephone line, but that yielded no useful information. The encrypted messages filed with the local communications company remained sacred until some time in November when David Sarnoff, president of Radio Corporation of America, visited Honolulu. Admiral Bloch persuaded Sarnoff to authorize the delivery of RCA file copies of Japanese messages to Captain Mayfield. The first batch came in less than a week before the attack on Pearl Harbor.

These messages were in diplomatic cipher. FRUPac was assigned to work on naval codes and was not prepared to work on the consular messages. However, Farnsley C. Woodward, a chief radioman in the cipher section, had had experience with diplomatic messages. He recognized that the messages were in two different ciphers. One of them was too complicated for him to tackle alone, but the other one he would be able to break, given time and a sufficient number of messages. Woodward and Lasswell worked night and day deciphering and translating the consular messages, but before the morning of 7 December they found only dull and useless ones about routine consular business.

After the Japanese attack, the Naval District Intelligence Office and the Honolulu police raided the Japanese consulate before all its files had been burned, and managed to seize some messages that yielded interesting information. Among them were those of Takeo Yoshikawa, who had made frequent reports on torpedo nets and the arrival, departure, and berthing assignments of ships at Pearl Harbor. One message reported on the harbor's air defense and remarked on the absence of barrage balloons.

About 10 December the cryptanalysts discovered another interesting message. It had been sent by Consul General Kita on 6 December, but of course there was no way for the cryptanalysts to read it or even identify it as important until the code had been at least partially broken. This message revealed that Otto Kuehn, a German national who had been residing in Honolulu for several years, was a Japanese intelligence agent. Anticipating the loss of radio and cable communications between the consul general and Tokyo, Kuehn had devised a bizarre system of communication. He proposed to inform Japanese submarines off Hawaii of U.S. ship movements in and out of Pearl Harbor by arrangements of lights in windows at night, and of drying sheets on a clothes line near his house in Kailua by day. He planned to transmit other information to Japan or to Japanese ships at sea by coded paid advertisements in radio broadcasts. Kita had to transmit the proposed schedule to Tokyo in a vulnerable cipher because the more secure diplomatic code had already been burned.

I do not remember how or why I learned about this message, but I had met Kuehn, and his wife and daughter, on several occasions. Unfortunately for Kuehn, his avid interest in things naval and military and his unconcealed Nazi connections had attracted the FBI and both Navy and Army intelligence to him. He was picked up within hours of the attack. I doubt that his proposed means of communicating got through to the Japanese, although the submarine loitering off the beach at Kahala might have been at the wrong beach and looking for signal lights in windows.

Admiral Bloch showed the message to Secretary of the Navy Frank Knox, who was then at Pearl Harbor. The secretary directed that it should be shown only to Mayfield and Kimmel. Communications Intelligence would far rather have a spy go free than reveal that we could read Japanese coded messages. Several times provost marshal agents came down to our basement to confer with Rochefort, but I have no idea how much he revealed to them. Kuehn was tried by a military court and sentenced to death, although no cryptographer testified at his trial.

This incident had an interesting sequel. Kuehn's death sentence was commuted to life imprisonment and he was shipped off to the U.S. mainland for confinement. When the war ended, he was returned to Germany and released there. After he died, his widow came to the United States and petitioned to recover the value of the house they had bought in Kailua and which had been confiscated. Some twenty years after the war, I visited Japan and made the acquaintance of several Japanese ex-naval officers who had been engaged in planning and intelligence. Captain Toshikazu Ohmae remarked to me one day that he was on the last voyage of a Japanese merchant ship to Honolulu just before the war broke out. His mission was the delivery of twenty-five thousand dollars to Kuehn to pay for the Kailua house. I asked him if Japan had ever received anything for the money and he ruefully admitted that she had not. If Mrs. Kuehn ever received compensation for the Kailua house, she should reimburse the Japanese government. It was their money.

In the meantime, Hawaii and the Pacific Fleet were settling down for a long war. Despite our confusion, frustration, and shortage of antisubmarine vessels, the Japanese submarines swarming around Hawaii accomplished relatively little. The Japanese awarded high posthumous honors to the crews of the five two-man submarines, all of which were sunk or captured on the first day of the war without having inflicted any significant damage. The twenty-five large submarines involved in the Hawaii operation did little better. They sank the *Cynthia Olsen* and the *Lahaina*, both small freighters, about midway between Honolulu and the mainland and, in the first month of the war, sank two other freighters closer to Honolulu. An observation plane from the *I-7* successfully reconnoitered Pearl Harbor on 17 December and furnished Tokyo with accurate information on the results of the Japanese air attack. The *I-70* was sunk north of Oahu by planes from the *Enterprise*, and the other blockading submarines were so frequently bombed and harassed that they were unable to torpedo any combat ships. For this happy immunity Communications Intelligence deserved some of the credit.

The Pacific Fleet staff had difficulty pulling itself together. In prewar planning Admiral Kimmel had anticipated that a Japanese attack on Wake Island might present an opportunity for naval action. On 16 December, after many delays, a complicated operation involving three separate carrier task forces got under way to relieve Wake. The next day, President Franklin D. Roosevelt removed Kimmel from all duty, more than a week before Admiral Chester W. Nimitz arrived to take over. Thus, the expedition to relieve Wake, already handicapped by inadequate logistic support and poor leadership afloat, was further burdened by lack of decisive direction from the interim commander of the Pacific Fleet and his staff at Pearl Harbor. The opportunity to attack the Japanese invasion forces was lost. Wake Island surrendered to the Japanese on 23 December. That date, rather than 7 December, was the nadir of morale for the Pacific Fleet. It was a high price to pay to provide a scapegoat for the Pearl Harbor disaster.

There were many inconsequential omissions in the defenses of Pearl Harbor, but in more than thirty years of postmortems no one has proposed a course of action Kimmel could have taken that would have greatly changed the situation for the better. At the beginning of a war, all leaders are untested and, if one is knocked out of the box in the first inning, it may be good policy to try another. A disastrous defeat generates psychological scars in even the best of leaders. General Douglas A. MacArthur was so scarred by the loss of the Philippines that the only line of action he was able to consider was returning there; and Allied defeats in Southeast Asia made General Joseph W. Stilwell more determined to win the war in Burma than to defeat Japan.

A decision to relieve a defeated commander is not a question of justice. There is no justice in a war that sends one man to safe duty in a basement while thousands of his comrades are dying in desperate battle within a mile of where he sits. Kimmel should have been relieved but not in disgrace, and the decision to relieve him at that particularly critical moment was an error in judgment greater than any Kimmel ever committed. That Nimitz was the one chosen to replace him was the great good fortune of the United States.

It was a miserable Christmas. Luckier than most of my fellows, I had a few hours to spend with my family before I had to be back on duty at sunset. I spent most of my time blacking out my tiny "study" by sealing its windows with heavy building paper so there would be one place in the house where we could have a light at night. Nervous patrols were apt to shoot at any light that showed after dark. Many of our friends were at sea, in submarines and in the task forces, and their families momentarily expected to be evacuated to the mainland. For some of the latter, our house on Black Point was a comfortable refuge. Izzy and Eric were permanent residents of Hawaii and not on the evacuation list. I dreaded making the decision if an opportunity should come for them to leave. Izzy would have refused to go if she had an option, but it would be selfish of me to let her stay.

There were many indications that life in Hawaii would be harsh for everybody. Japanese submarines had begun shelling the beaches in surprise night attacks. So far they had not shelled Oahu. None of their bombardments had caused much damage. Japanese submarine commanders apparently liked to expend their deck-gun ammunition before leaving their area at the end of a patrol, and this habit helped us anticipate when an area would be clear of submarines. But a hit from a wild shell fired at random was just as deadly as any other, and Black Point was backed up against a myriad legitimate military targets. On the other hand, evacuation to the mainland meant a long, slow voyage in a convoy through seas infested with hostile submarines. There was little peace on earth or good will to men that Christmas.

Light was just around the corner. Nimitz arrived on Christmas Day to take over command of the Pacific Fleet. I met him one morning in the corridor at CinCPac headquarters, which was then on the second floor of the submarine base's supply building. He greeted me by name, and evidently knew that I had been retired for physical disability and recalled to active duty. He had little reason to remember me. I had been engineering officer of the *Barracuda* when he was commander of Submarine Division 20. The only other occasion I could remember talking to him was when Izzy and I made our white-gloved social call on the division commander and Mrs. Nimitz in Coronado eleven years before. Just seeing him at Pearl Harbor gave me the feeling that we had turned the corner.

The aura of calm confidence that radiated from Admiral Nimitz renewed everyone's morale, but it must have been a heavy burden for him to maintain. Many years after the war when Izzy and I visited Admiral and Mrs. Nimitz at Berkeley, California, he told me what his arrival at Pearl Harbor was like. Two years before that he had commanded a division of battleships in traditional spit, polish, and punctilio. That Christmas morning the motor whaleboat that transported him across the harbor afforded him a depressing view of five battered, capsized, and sunken battleships, still unable to move from where they had been blasted. As he passed an inlet crowded with ships' boats, a staff officer explained that those boats were loaded with dead sailors. When Admiral William S. Pye, who had commanded the Battle Force, succeeded to interim command of the fleet, he brought with him many of his Battle Force staff, without relieving Kimmel's old CinCPac staff. The result was confusion superimposed upon disaster. Admiral Nimitz told me that the fleet surgeon was dosing many of the staff with whatever they used for tranquilizers in those days. Kimmel was still in Honolulu, appearing before the Roberts Commission, which was there to investigate the defeat at Pearl Harbor. Who could have foreseen that, within six months, the black despair of disaster and defeat would be dispelled by a brilliant victory?

One afternoon in the last few days of 1941, three members of the Roberts Commission, Admiral William H. Standley, Admiral Joseph M. Reeves, and Justice Owen J. Roberts, came down into the basement. The two admirals engaged Rochefort in a close conference, but Justice Roberts asked to see the charts and logs we had kept during the attack. The Roberts Commission had been instructed to avoid talking to people about communications intelligence, and Roberts probably disassociated himself from the two admirals in meticulous observance of the limits of his jurisdiction. I was unaware of all this, so while I was showing him the charts I mentioned some of the relevant information we had gained since the attack by decrypting Japanese consular messages.

Had we intercepted the Japanese consul general's communications earlier we might have deduced that Pearl Harbor would be one of the first Japanese air targets and been forewarned. Like nearly everyone else, including the Roberts Commission, I then believed that only two Japanese aircraft carriers had taken part in the Pearl Harbor strike and, had we not been surprised, we might have defeated the attack. This hypothesis was disproved by information we acquired later, but I believed it then, and lamented our timidity in respecting the sanctions of the Communications Act of 1934 that protected the Japanese consul general's communications.

Justice Roberts remarked that if naval officers in their zeal to defend the United States could disregard its laws, we would already have lost much of the liberty we were trying to defend. I was deeply impressed by the magnanimity of his arguments, which I interpreted to mean that those who made the laws that had handicapped Pearl Harbor's defenders shared with them the responsibility for the disaster. Years later, when I read the complete Roberts Report, I realized that I had misconstrued his meaning.

In Justice Roberts's authoritative opinion nearly all communications intelligence activity was illegal, and presumably should have been stopped when the Communications Act became law. Had that happened, surely Midway would have been a Japanese victory and probably Hawaii would have been invaded by the Japanese in the fall of 1942. The maintenance of a balance between privacy and freedom on one hand and safety and survival on the other has been a difficult problem throughout all our history.

When the Roberts Commission departed we could put the past behind us and face a difficult future. The new year began with Nimitz firmly in the saddle. Rochefort summed it up when he exclaimed:

"Forget Pearl Harbor and get on with the war!"

CHAPTER 5

FOUR YEARS OF WAR DISCLOSED, in passing, much more about the attack on Pearl Harbor, but it was not until twenty years after the war ended that I could try to piece everything together. Then I had time to read the 39-volume report of the seventy-ninth Congress's *Hearings Before the Joint Committee on the Investigation of the Pearl Harbor Attack*, which includes the Roberts Report and the proceedings of several other courts, commissions, and investigations. From this monumental record I learned much that I had not previously known about communications intelligence. It was a business in which one hand frequently did not know what the other one was doing, and the reason for that lay in its peculiar history.

In 1925 the Code and Signal Section of the Navy's Communications Division in Washington, under Lieutenant Laurence F. Safford, began to develop a system of cryptanalytic and traffic-analysis centers, intercept stations, and radio direction finders, of which FRUPac was to become a part. At that time, the principal cryptanalytic agency of the United States was the Black Chamber, a clandestine, semiofficial organization located in New York and jointly supported by the State Department and the War Department. Herbert O. Yardley, who had served with the State Department and with the U.S. Army in France in World War I, directed its operations. In 1929, Herbert Hoover's new Secretary of State, Henry L. Stimson, abruptly withdrew his department's support from the Black Chamber on ethical grounds: "Gentlemen do not read each other's mail." Ripples from the proclamation of that punctilious principle extended down to Pearl Harbor and beyond.

Yardley responded by publishing *The American Black Chamber*, which revealed, among other secrets, that American cryptanalysts had broken the diplomatic codes used by the Japanese during the disarmament conference of 1922. Not only did Yardley's revelations cause the Japanese immediately to tighten up all their communica-

44

tions security, but they probably also inspired the stringent provisions in the Communications Act of 1934 protecting the privacy of electronic communications.

Stimson's action surely closed down the Black Chamber for good and took the State Department out of the cryptanalysis business. The Army consolidated all its cryptographic work, both code-making and code-breaking, under its Signal Intelligence Service, or SIS. In 1940 William F. Friedman, the Army's chief cryptographer, led SIS in the cryptanalytical feat of breaking the new "unbreakable" Japanese cipher. SIS built four so-called purple machines to decipher Japanese secret diplomatic messages. By 7 December 1941, the Army had 220 people in cryptanalysis in Washington and 150 more out in the field, who were intercepting and forwarding messages to the Washington center. Almost all of the Army's effort was being expended on diplomatic traffic. No Japanese military codes were being read.

In the meantime, the Navy's Code and Signal Section had evolved into Op-20-G, and was engaged in both code-making and code-breaking. The Navy was also involved in working on Japanese diplomatic traffic. A machine built by Lieutenant Jack Holtwick to decrypt the Japanese naval attaché's cipher was in use until 1939. In 1940, in a noteworthy example of cooperation, the Army and the Navy pooled their interception facilities and their cryptanalytical resources working in Washington on Japanese diplomatic communications.

The Japanese were then using the "purple" machine cipher for the highest level of diplomatic messages, a second code for the next highest level, and another for the third level of secrecy. With the purple machine, it was sometimes possible to deliver decrypted Japanese dispatches to Secretary of State Cordell Hull and the president of the United States before Japanese code clerks could deliver them to their own ambassador. During 1941 all but four of the Japanese diplomatic dispatches between Tokyo and Washington in purple cipher were intercepted by the U.S. Army or the U.S. Navy, decoded, and distributed to a small and select list of American officials.

In December 1941, Op-20-G was again directed by Laurence Safford. The Navy was less centralized than the Army. It had two major communications intelligence centers in the Pacific. On the island of Corregidor, in Manila Bay, it had an organization which, with its outlying intercept and direction-finder stations, employed about fifty officers and men under Lieutenant Rudolph J. Fabian. This unit kept liaison with the U.S. Army in the Philippines. Op-20-G assigned to it the tasks of interception of Japanese naval and diplomatic radio traffic, traffic analysis, and cryptanalysis of a five-digit Japanese naval code. The unit was equipped with one of the four purple machines and read and translated Japanese purple and other diplomatic codes. The five-digit code was in the initial stages of recovery. Corregidor and Washington exchanged recoveries, but neither could yet read any messages in this code. Through Lieutenant Commander Redfield Mason, the Asiatic Fleet's intelligence officer, who was a Japanese-language student and a gifted cryptanalyst, Admiral Hart was kept informed of communications intelligence. Admiral Kimmel was kept informed through Lieutenant Commander Layton, the Pacific Fleet's intelligence officer. Between Combat Intelligence and the fleet intelligence officers there was a constant flow of information.

FRUPac at Pearl Harbor had the most skillful and experienced communications intelligence team. It was assigned by Op-20-G to attack all Japanese naval codes except the five-digit one, work on that code being divided between Washington and Corregidor. Earlier versions of the Japanese flag-officer code had yielded the best intelligence but, although FRUPac was working hard on it, the latest version resisted all their efforts. At Pearl Harbor only the weather codes and a few minor codes could be read. Nearly all current information on movements of the Japanese Navy came from the traffic-analysis people. FRUPac's intercept station was on Oahu, and the mid-Pacific direction-finder net had several stations throughout the Pacific area.

In 1941 FRUPac had ten officers and twenty men in the Combat Intelligence Unit at Pearl Harbor and from fifty to sixty more in outlying stations. It did not have enough people or enough equipment to monitor all the Japanese naval circuits, and no attempt was made to intercept army or diplomatic traffic. Op-20-G in Washington had a greater number of people than Hawaii and Corregidor. A few were old-timers with more than ten years' experience, but there was a great national shortage of competent translators, cryptanalysts, and radio operators who could copy *kana*. Ninety per cent of Op-20-G's personnel were in training and had less than one year's experience. Recruitment and training were, therefore, among the most important functions of the Washington unit.

All naval communications intelligence was under the supervision and coordination of Op-20-G, which maintained a widespread network of intercept stations on the mainland of the United States. "Raw material" from these stations, from FRUPac, and from Corregidor flowed into Op-20-G. With this material they conducted basic research and assisted in code breaks. They kept the Office of

Naval Operations informed of communications intelligence through the Office of Naval Intelligence and shared equally with Army SIS the task of informing the State Department and the president of the United States.

It was a well-designed organization but, as American-Japanese relations slid slowly down the slippery path to war, both Op-20-G and SIS became overwhelmed by the swelling volume of diplomatic traffic. By the fall of 1941 they were processing fifty to seventy-five, and sometimes more than one hundred, messages a day. For this task, Op-20-G had six translators, most of them civilians, working under the direction of Lieutenant Commander Alwin D. Kramer. SIS had equal capability. Diplomatic messages relating to the delicate and explosive Japanese-American negotiations then going on in Washington were in the purple-machine cipher. These had to be given the highest priority. Other encrypted messages were more time-consuming to decode and generally less important. They could not be worked until the high-priority ones had been cleared.

About the middle of November, the Japanese Foreign Office sent out what was later to become known as the "winds message." This message set up a "hidden phrase code" that was to be concealed in the weather report of the Japanese voice news broadcast, when and if diplomatic relations reached a crisis and normal international communications from Japan were cut off. Certain precise phrases included in the weather report in a specific manner would alert Japanese diplomatic and consular offices all over the world to a diplomatic crisis with America, or Russia, or Britain: for example, the phrase *Higashi no kaze ame* ("East wind rain") was to designate a crisis in relations with the United States. Those offices were then to burn their codes and secret files to prevent them from falling into enemy hands.

The message of instructions was translated by Op-20-G about the 28th of November. By then it was evident that Japan was headed for open hostilities in Southeast Asia. If we could pick up the "winds-execute" message, we would know when the Japanese were about to strike. Numerous intercept stations tuned in to catch the word. Op-20-G began to receive transcripts of Japanese news broadcasts in a teletyped torrent, piled on top of its other burdens.

By 3 December it was known from several sources that Japanese agencies overseas were burning their codes and destroying code machines. After that, the winds-execute message would add little to what was already known, but the efforts to catch it continued.

The conditions predicated for the use of the winds code did not actually occur before the Pearl Harbor attack. Right down to the time the bombs fell, diplomatic exchanges continued and communications channels remained open. It may be that the Japanese Foreign Office, which would have originated the winds-execute message, was as surprised as anyone else by the attack. Safford, however, was sure he had seen a winds-execute message that had been intercepted before 6 December. Sometime later he searched the files and was unable to find any trace of it.

The possibility of a deep-laid plot to conceal the failure to send out a timely warning to Pearl Harbor had political implications. That intrigued the Joint Congressional Committee into taking many pages of controversial testimony, but the major effect of the search for a winds-execute message was to tie up facilities that could have been better used.

During November and early December, Consul General Kita in Hawaii originated and received a number of messages concerning Vice Consul Yoshikawa's observations of Pearl Harbor. These messages, taken together and collated with traffic-analysis and other information, might well have revealed that Pearl Harbor would probably be an early target for Japanese air attack. Kimmel later said he felt sure he would have reached that conclusion if he had had all this information before the attack. He did not have it.

A few of Kita's messages were read in Washington, but were discounted as of no particular importance. Largely because of the demands of messages of higher priority, most of them were not translated until long after the attack was over. For this and other reasons, Kimmel received little benefit from the flood of purple-machine messages that were being translated in Washington.

Secrecy constipated the flow of information. Within the War and Navy departments, only a few high-ranking officials outside of SIS and Op-20-G were cleared to receive Ultra, sometimes known as "Magic," intelligence. Those who were cleared were severely restricted in how they could use the information and with whom they could discuss it. General Walter C. Short, commanding general of Army forces in Hawaii, was not cleared for Ultra, nor was any member of his staff: Army codes were not considered sufficiently secure to be entrusted with such material. Strict orders required SIS to have approval of General George C. Marshall, Army chief of staff, before sending information that might affect operations to any field command. Marshall tightly controlled the dissemination of all Ultra. It was practically impossible under the circumstances to furnish Short with the constant flow of information that he required, if he was to make intelligent strategic decisions.

In some ways, the Navy was in a little better situation. The intelligence officers of both the Pacific Fleet and the Asiatic Fleet were cleared for Ultra and experienced in its use. A system of radio communications using a special code existed, the code being held only by the commanders of the Pacific and Asiatic fleets and the three communications intelligence centers. Over this circuit, Ultra information, most of it technical, flowed daily. It would have required little effort and no additional security risk to keep Kimmel fully informed, but Naval Intelligence, like the Army's SIS, had to have approval for sending out intelligence that might affect operations. The Chief of Naval Operations had authority to release such information, as did Admiral Richmond K. Turner, the head of the War Plans Division in Naval Operations. Turner, like Marshall, throttled the flow of information to a very thin trickle. He was unaware of the task assignments set up by Op-20-G and thought that Kimmel was receiving diplomatic intercepts through FRUPac. In consequence, Kimmel was not much better served than was Short by the Washington intelligence organizations.

The reasons for extreme secrecy were sound. The Japanese had been known to change codes within twenty-four hours of suspecting that their communications security had been compromised. If that happened, an advantage that could have been decisive might be lost forever. The greater the number of people who knew about decryption and the more they knew, the greater was the chance of a disastrous leak. It was important that the secret should not be entrusted to anyone, regardless of rank, who had not been thoroughly indoctrinated. And a leak to the enemy was not the only hazard.

The history of the Black Chamber was an example of how the whole system of American cryptanalysis could be destroyed from within. Most of those involved, if they thought about it at all, were of the opinion that the Communications Act of 1934 did not apply to radio interception of foreign transmissions. A few better-informed individuals believed that the whole operation was illegal. Justice Roberts revealed in the report of his commission that he, himself, had written a Supreme Court decision to the effect that the Communications Act did apply to the interception of foreign radio transmissions.

All of us who intercepted, decrypted, disseminated, or used Japanese radio messages were in violation of the law. Justice Roberts's remark to me at Pearl Harbor in December 1941, about a naval officer's duty to obey the law, expressed a philosophy that placed a higher value on the fine points of a legal interpretation of a law than on the lives of more than two thousand sailors, whose bodies were still unburied. Undoubtedly there were many with the same philosophy, or with less worthy motives of politics or publicity, who would have sacrificed the whole cryptanalytical organization without regard to consequences.

There is sound military theory that a field commander should be given all pertinent information upon which to base his decisions or, if that is not possible, he should be given explicit orders. Kimmel and Short were given neither. The whole principle is academic, however. A warning of an hour, a day, or even a week, could not have obviated a disaster at Pearl Harbor. The Japanese had overwhelming force at the point of contact. Indeed, had there been a warning, the disaster might well have been aggravated. Had the slow old battleships, with or without two aircraft carriers, sortied in the face of the fast Japanese task force that included six aircraft carriers, the most probable outcome would have been the sinking of the battleships in deep water beyond hope of salvage, and much greater loss of life.

In 1929, Secretary of State Stimson had condemned cryptanalysis as unethical. In 1941, the State Department, with no cryptanalytical service of its own, relied on cryptanalysis for information on which to base critical negotiations with Japan. It was served with admirable efficiency by the Navy Department and the War Department, although the same Henry Stimson was then Secretary of War. The requirements of the State Department preempted the cryptanalytical resources of the military services. Diplomatically important messages in purple-machine cipher occupied most of the cryptographers' efforts. This was one cause of the abridged intelligence service to the fleet. Messages of great naval value in other codes were intercepted but not translated until too late. Yet these paradoxes and inconsistencies were understandable.

The cryptanalytical resources of the United States were never equal to all the demands placed upon them. Some close and hard decisions had to be made, then and afterward, in their employment. In the fall of 1941 the State Department had the ball. Only diplomacy had the potential to avoid or delay hostilities, for which the Army and the Navy were woefully unprepared.

General Marshall and Admiral Stark pleaded for negotiation of a modus vivendi with Japan, but Roosevelt and Hull decided that the Japanese price was too high. On 26 November 1941 Hull told Stimson that he had "washed his hands of it" and that it was now up to the Army and the Navy. On the same day he presented to the Japanese ambassador "An Outline of Proposed Basis for Agreement between the United States and Japan," which contained provisions he knew Japan would not accept. On 1 December Admiral Isoroku Yamamoto, commander in chief of the Combined Fleet, radioed to the Kido Butai, "Climb Mount Niitaka," meaning carry out the attack on Pearl Harbor as planned.

On the evening of 6 December and the morning of the seventh, Tokyo sent a long, fourteen-part message for the Japanese envoys in Washington to deliver to Hull, breaking diplomatic relations. Separate instructions directed them to deliver this message promptly at 1:00 p.m., Washington time, but the Japanese code clerks were delayed in decoding it. It was 2:00 p.m. and the attack on Pearl Harbor was in progress when the Japanese diplomats arrived at the State Department.

By 11:00 a.m. Op-20-G and SIS had read the message instructing the Japanese to deliver the fourteen-part message at 1:00 p.m., Washington time, and both immediately recognized its importance. Lieutenant Commander Kramer in Op-20-G noted that 1:00 p.m. in Washington was 7:30 a.m. at Pearl Harbor, shortly after the hour of dawn. It was noon, however, before Admiral Stark and General Marshall could confer and agree on what warning message should be sent to field and fleet commanders. The transmission of this message was also bungled and it did not reach Short and Kimmel in Honolulu, until the afternoon, Honolulu time, hours after the Japanese had completed their attack.

It was ironic that the United States profited so little from one of the greatest cryptanalytical feats of all history. Both the Army and the Navy knew they were unprepared for war in the Pacific and that time was needed to repair decades of neglect. Yet, even with the advantage of reading Japanese secret diplomatic messages, American diplomats were unable or unwilling to try to avoid or defer the opening of hostilities. And grace of even an hour's warning was lost through the ineptness of naval and military bureaucracy in Washington.

The disparity between American naval policy and foreign policy in the Pacific was of long standing. The naval disarmament conference of 1922 was a great step toward world peace, but reduction in naval armament should have been followed by adjustment of foreign policy to fit the new circumstances. With relative naval strengths fixed by international agreement, the United States could no longer underwrite the Open Door policy in China or ensure the safety of the Philippines. Yet we lingered on in the Philippines and supported China against Japan with aggressive economic and diplomatic measures. Over two thousand years ago, Demosthenes stated the thesis clearly: Courage and boldness of speech, unless they have material force at command, lead to peril in action.

In the years between the disarmament conference in 1922 and the attack on Pearl Harbor, the courage and boldness of our speech steadily increased while our relative naval strength declined. Our naval policy and our foreign policy in Asia were incompatible with each other. Both had the support of Congress and of the general public, but their incompatibility certainly led to peril in action.

CHAPTER 6

COMBAT INTELLIGENCE was ignorant of most of what had gone on in Washington and, even if we had known, it still would have come under the Rochefort dictum, "Forget Pearl Harbor and get on with the war."

In a year of work, enough progress had been made with the five-digit code to read a few snatches of it and to determine that it had become the major naval code. It had replaced the flag officers' code as the vehicle for most of the high-level Japanese naval traffic, but on 4 December it suddenly became unreadable. It had been changed. On 10 December Op-20-G directed FRUPac to join the attack on the new Japanese five-digit naval code.

The probability was high that the code would be changed again before it could be broken, but the density of traffic, the identity of originators and addressees, and what had been learned of its structure, all indicated to Washington that work on the five-digit code might be more profitable than work on any other code. Dyer and Wright at FRUPac, having noted the increased traffic in that code, had made preliminary examinations of it. They were happy to shift over from the flag officers' code and take a crack at the other one.

To a layman their mission seemed impossible. They had to unravel a five-digit, two-part code. The encode part consisted of columns of words or phrases opposite columns of five-digit code groups. To encode "battleship sighted," for example, the encoder looked up "battleship" and wrote down the number opposite it, say, 52173. He then looked up "sighted" and wrote down 38541, the number opposite it. The plain code message would be 52173-38541. The decoder used the decode part, which was arranged in numerical order, and reversed the process.

An uncomplicated two-part code presents no insurmountable difficulty to a good cryptanalyst. He needs only time, patience, an infinite capacity for work, a mind that can focus on one problem to the exclusion of everything else, a photographic memory, the inability to drop an unsolved problem, and a large volume of traffic. The IBM tabulating and sorting machines then in use could do some of the routine labor. And Dyer kept posted over his desk a sign which read, "You don't have to be crazy but it helps."

The Japanese were much too sophisticated to use a simple two-part code. The five-digit code was enciphered after it was encoded and before it was transmitted. To do this the Japanese constructed columns of one hundred thousand random mixed five-digit numbers to use as an enciphering table. After a message had been put in plain code, the encoder selected a starting point in the enciphering table and subtracted the numbers from that table in succession from successive code groups. When the addressee received the message he needed to know only the starting point in his identical deciphering table to reverse the process and add the deciphering numbers from the table to the message numbers to obtain the plain code.

One hundred thousand different groups of five-digit numbers are more than enough to make a good code. The Japanese used a vocabulary of only about one-third that number, with code groups only of numbers divisible by three. If a number is divisible by three the sum of its digits is divisible by three, and this gave the Japanese code clerks a simple test for garbles and mistakes. It also gave the cryptanalysts a handy tool to work with, but that was unintentional.

Corregidor made the difficult initial break, but in February Fabian and his crew had to be evacuated from that island by submarine. Japanese ruthlessness in the interrogation of prisoners of war was well known, and the importance of keeping live communications intelligence people out of their hands was fully appreciated. The Corregidor unit was reestablished in the southwest Pacific, but the move interrupted their work. Washington, with more personnel than that unit or FRUPac on Oahu, recovered the most enciphering additives, but cooperation among the three centers was so close that it would be impossible to assign relative credit. The whole organization was permeated with the spirit that it could accomplish anything if nobody cared who got the credit. For the next few months, however, between the attack on Pearl Harbor and the Battle of Midway, FRUPac was under the gun. It served CinCPac day and night, and CinCPac was then making important strategic decisions in the Pacific.

The manpower of FRUPac grew steadily, but during this critical period a team of eight experienced and dedicated communications intelligence veterans held in their hands the destiny of the war in the Pacific. The Navy's top cryptanalysts were Dyer, his chief assistant, Wright, and Holtwick who, like Dyer, was skilled in the use of business machines in this cryptic business. Huckins and Williams were among the best traffic analysts in the Navy. Finnegan and Lasswell were a phenomenal team of translator-cryptanalysts: as soon as plain text began to emerge from the welter of code numbers, the translators' work became of primary importance. Rochefort was probably the most skilled cryptanalyst in the Navy. His experience went back to 1925, when he, Safford, and Agnes Driscoll were the whole of the Navy's code-breaking crew. He had studied the Japanese language for three years in Tokyo. He was a first-rate traffic analyst. He also had the subtle ability to piece together scattered fragments of information and formulate them into useful intelligence. In estimating the probable intentions of the Japanese, Rochefort was equaled only by Layton.

Had I not witnessed it, I never would have believed that any group of men was capable of such sustained mental effort under such constant pressure for such a length of time. Rochefort, whose family had been evacuated to Pasadena, California, left the basement only to bathe, change clothes, or get an occasional meal to supplement a steady diet of coffee and sandwiches; like a destroyer skipper on the bridge during close-formation maneuvers. For weeks the only sleep he got was on a field cot pushed into a crowded corner; always nearly fully dressed, he was ready at a moment's notice to roll out and jump into carpet slippers and an old, red smoking jacket, which was his uniform of the day in the basement.

Dyer's wife was a Honolulu resident who, unlike most other Navy dependents, had escaped evacuation. She would pack a laborer's large lunch box full of sandwiches and send Dyer forth for a stint in the basement. When the sandwiches ran out, two or three days later, Rochefort would almost physically shove him up the stairs out of the basement to go home and get some decent rest away from the clack of the business machines. Rochefort knew that a top cryptanalyst with his teeth in a problem could never let it go. He might eat and converse or yield to exhaustion by taking short naps, but his mind would go right on shuffling combinations and permutations of code groups into a nervous breakdown. Rochefort conserved Dyer's genius in the way a cruiser commander might husband his fuel supply against the hours when it would have to be lavishly expended. Next to Rochefort, Dyer was senior officer, both in regard to rank and length of service in communications intelligence. Until after the Battle of Midway either he or Rochefort was always in the basement, and usually both of them were there.

Wesley A. Wright

The yeoman typists, punch-card operators, and clerks generally put in only a normal eighty-four-hour work week. Some of the rest of us lingered on after our regular hours, frustrated by a feeling of guilt that we were unable to do anything to lighten the load of the eight veterans who, more often than not, were there when we came to work and still there when we left.

Sealed off from the rest of the world like a submarine, the basement was completely dependent on air-conditioning, whose machinery was in a room that the maintenance men could reach without entering Combat Intelligence. They adjusted the machine so that it maintained a temperature of seventy-four degrees as steadily as though the thermometer were a painted dummy, but at two o'clock every morning, when Rorie mustered the yeomen to swab down the deck for the new day, the basement felt like the inside of a refrigerator. I brought in a wet-bulb thermometer which told me that the humidity was out of whack, but all attempts to control it failed until we discovered that the fresh-air intake was closed. It had been closed off the previous autumn when there was a dust problem from construction work nearby. For four months the only fresh air that had entered the basement was what we brought in in our pockets. We had two or three cases of pneumonia, and at one time I feared Rochefort would be laid low by it.

As the war in the Pacific went on, the Japanese were triumphant everywhere. The aircraft carrier *Saratoga* was torpedoed by a Japanese submarine on 11 January 1942, about four hundred miles south of Oahu, and had to return to the West Coast for repairs. Twelve days later, another Japanese submarine sank the oiler *Neches* a few hours after she departed from Pearl Harbor to rendezvous with a task force planning to bombard Wake. The *Neches* was the only tanker available in the central Pacific and the whole operation had to be called off. That same day, 23 January 1942, the Japanese Fourth Fleet, backed up by four carriers of the Kido Butai, covered a landing at Rabaul, New Britain. However, when Japanese submarines, en route home to Japan, attempted a night bombardment of Midway, they ran into trouble. Their radio communications had revealed to FRUPac that they were converging on those islands, and the Marines there were forewarned and prepared. The submarines' gunfire was returned so rapidly and accurately that they broke off the bombardment and dived.

At about that time, the *Gudgeon*, the first U.S. submarine to make a patrol off Japan, was returning to Pearl Harbor via Midway. Commander, Submarines, Pacific Fleet (ComSubPac), also warned by FRUPac of Japanese submarine activity in the vicinity of Midway, alerted her to the danger. The *Gudgeon* made a cautious submerged approach. She caught one of the Japanese submarines on the surface and sank it with a well-directed torpedo.

By the first of February, CinCPac was able to mount a series of carrier raids in the central Pacific, in an attempt to relieve the pressure in the Malay Peninsula and the Philippines. Submarines had left Pearl Harbor in late December to reconnoiter the Marshalls and the Carolines. Submarine captains going on patrol in those areas were sent to me for briefing on what enemy activity to expect. The Japanese mandated islands were terra incognita at the beginning of the war and I had little but misinformation on them to give the captains, but the briefings started a cooperation between the Submarine Force and Combat Intelligence that later paid big dividends.

Not until the submarine *Dolphin* returned from the Marshalls on 27 January 1942 did we learn that Kwajalein, rather than Jaluit, was the principal center of Japanese naval activity in the Marshalls. On the basis of that information, Kwajalein was added to the list of targets to be hit by the first U.S. carrier raid in the central Pacific. On 1 February, the *Enterprise* raided Kwajalein, Wotje, and Maloelap, and the carrier *Yorktown* hit Jaluit and the Gilberts. Bankson T. Holcomb, a Marine language officer from FRUPac, went out with Halsey on the Kwajalein raid. His account of the conduct of the raid and of Halsey's aggressive spirit brought a bright ray of hope into the basement. When the *Enterprise* departed from Pearl on 14 February to raid Wake and Marcus islands, Slonim was on board her as language officer, and he had with him a communications intelligence team of four radio operators who could copy Japanese radio messages. Fullinwider, with a similar team, went out in the carrier *Lexington*, and Biard was on board the *Yorktown*. There was considerable argument in FRUPac about whether these teams were more valuable on board carriers or back at FRUPac and the intercept station, where they were badly needed.

When the first radio intelligence teams proved valuable to the carrier task force commanders, the argument became academic. FRUPac had to provide the service, and the only way to do it was gracefully and efficiently. The radio operators could pick up the earliest signs of alarm at the target of the raid and the language officer could gauge the magnitude of the defending forces by the flow of radio traffic. Armed with a list of the major Japanese units' radio calls, the team also had the potential ability to detect the presence of major Japanese naval forces within strategic distance. Radio intelligence teams with the task forces could sometimes copy Japanese messages that escaped the shore-based intercept station but, since task forces operated in strict radio silence, FRUPac could not get these intercepts until a task force returned. Of course, we could broadcast to the forces, in special codes, information such as changes in call signs and any other radio intelligence we might acquire, particularly weather information. Ethier and Livingston were so efficient at breaking the Japanese weather cipher that it was possible to pick up the latest Japanese weather report from the target, decrypt it, re-encipher it in our own special cipher, and have it on a carrier before the first strike took off at dawn. The Japanese had an excellent weather service and we took full advantage of it.

Since, in the central Pacific, weather generally progresses from west to east, Japanese weather reports from the South Seas would be very valuable to our aerographers. I was surprised, therefore, to learn that they never got them from FRUPac. The reason for this omission was that Communications Intelligence would rather not use the information it collected at all than expand the circle of those who knew of our success in breaking even this minor Japanese code.

Although we were aware that the Japanese had instant statistics direct from our weather stations, we went right on keeping weather reports out of newspapers and radio broadcasts, and censors continued scissoring all references to weather from personal letters.

We and the Japanese could not have cooperated better if we had both broadcast the weather in the clear. But we thought we had the advantage because, while we knew that the Japanese could read our weather reports, the Japanese did not know that we knew. Weather played an important part in the second bombing of Pearl Harbor on 4 March 1942.

By that time a normal year's work had been compressed into three months, and FRUPac could read a few groups of the five-digit code, and, in addition to the weather cipher, they could read a minor code used in the Mandates. The Japanese used two-letter designators to replace frequently used place-names: traffic analysis and the course of events established that PP was Palau and PT was Truk. RR was Rabaul and several other two-letter designators with R as the initial letter also occurred. These always seemed to be for places in the vicinity of Rabaul. When the area designator AFG, which departed from the pattern of alliteration, began to appear, traffic analysis connected it with Jaluit and Kwajalein islands, in the Marshalls. It was also connected with both Air Squadron 24, known to be in the Marshall Islands, and with submarines of the Sixth Fleet. Several Japanese submarines were fixed by direction finder in the Hawaiian area, and on 2 March we estimated they were in the vicinity of French Frigate Shoal.

There had been very little Japanese submarine activity close to Hawaii since the *Neches* was sunk, and I was puzzled by the new buildup. I believe Rochefort had more information than he gave me, for on the afternoon of 3 March 1942 he warned CinCPac and Admiral Bloch that something was about to happen. I hung around, trying to be helpful, until Rochefort told me there was nothing I could do and it was time I went home to get some rest. He was right on both counts, so I picked up my lunch box, buckled on my gas mask and my .45 automatic pistol, both of which we all were required to carry, and drove home through the bright moonlight. It seemed that my head had no sooner hit the pillow than Izzy awoke me to report that District Intelligence had telephoned "all hands, general quarters" and that she had been ordered out as an air-raid warden in a full air alert.

A rainstorm over the Koolau Mountains blotted out the moonlight. As I drove down Dillingham Boulevard, on my way back to Pearl Harbor, a military policeman pulled me over to check my identification papers and my destination. Just then there were heavy explosions in the hills behind Honolulu.

Kauai radar had picked up enemy planes, or "bandits," coming in from the west shortly after midnight. They tracked right on course to Pearl Harbor. The Hawaiian Defense commander ordered "full alert." Patrol planes armed with torpedoes took off in search of a suspected seaplane carrier. Army fighters scrambled to meet the "bandits." Nimbus clouds over Pearl Harbor were thick and nobody saw anybody up there, but somebody dropped bombs on the slopes of Mount Tantalus.

The next morning I was on watch when Layton called up from CinCPac. Did I know what had happened last night? I did not, but I could guess that Japanese seaplanes had come in from the Marshall Islands, refueled from submarines at French Frigate Shoal, and then come in to bomb Oahu. "That's right," he replied, "and they copied the idea from Alec Hudson's story 'Rendezvous' in last August's *Saturday Evening Post*."

Layton's theory of the second bombing of Pearl Harbor prevailed over one, popular among naval aviators, that the "bandits" were in reality Army planes that had dropped bombs on Tantalus by mistake, and over another theory, popular among Army aviators, that Navy planes had jettisoned their bombs before landing and missed the Pacific Ocean, at which they aimed. As a result, the mine force was sent out to plant mine fields around French Frigate Shoal to discourage Japanese submarines from using that anchorage.

The May 1953 issue of the *Naval Institute Proceedings* published Layton's article on his exhaustive postwar research of what the Japanese called "K" operations. From a mass of captured documents, he tracked down the Japanese operation orders for the attack of 4 March and the reports of the Japanese aviators. Just as he had deduced, the Japanese sent two long-range seaplanes from the Marshalls to French Frigate Shoal, where they refueled from three submarines. Another submarine acted as a navigational beacon, and a fifth, the *I-23*, was stationed ten miles south of Pearl Harbor as a weather observer and as a lifeguard for the seaplanes. The Japanese depended on decryption of American weather reports for weather information, but the American weather cipher was changed on 1 March, leaving the *I-23* as the only observer of weather at the target. The *I-23* disappeared without a trace and without making a weather report.

So the planes were both figuratively and literally in the dark of a tropical rainstorm when they reached Pearl Harbor. Their target was the Ten Ten dock, a couple of hundred yards from the Combat Intelligence Unit. Had they been right on target, Combat Intelligence might well have been wiped out and the course of the war greatly changed. Bombing blind, they hit only some algaroba trees six miles away, and returned to the Marshall Islands.

At the time, of course, Layton was being facetious in alleging that the Japanese had borrowed their plans from *The Saturday Evening Post*, but "Rendezvous" did feature submarines refueling seaplanes in the lee of an uninhabited island. The Navy Department had, indeed, held up the publication of "Rendezvous" for over a year, and permitted it only after Alec Hudson had demonstrated that the idea was current in other navies.

As Layton points out in his article, "Intelligence officers [in reality Layton himself] recalling to mind the *Saturday Evening Post* story, had no difficulty in recognizing the raid as *Rendezvous in Reverse*." Had he not made the deduction he did and followed it up with vigorous action, French Frigate Shoal would probably not have been mined and kept under surveillance during the Midway operations three months later. The Japanese planned a second "K" operation before Midway in order to scout American surface forces. It failed because French Frigate Shoal was occupied by an American ship when the Japanese submarines arrived. The fact that the Japanese were not able to make any pre-battle seaplane searches from French Frigate, allowed Spruance to arrive north of Midway unsighted.

———

Rochefort was busy with work that only he could do, so I tried to take some of the administrative details off his hands. Secrecy was essential for FRUPac but it gummed up even the simplest of administrative work. One senior officer in the naval district resented that he was not permitted to enter Combat Intelligence. It was only natural that he would vent his feelings by being uncooperative, and he made things particularly difficult for me. Most people would have been only too glad to cooperate with us if we could have explained what we were doing, but the only justifications we were permitted to make were weak.

With more people in FRUPac, we needed more space. An area of the basement adjacent to Combat Intelligence had been left unfinished, and by knocking down partitions we could prepare to extend into it. The supply officer had overt and urgent need for the same space and it was not easy to take two-thirds of it away from him. When negotiations became really difficult we could always go direct to Admiral Bloch. He knew our situation and he would usually resolve a problem in our favor. It was the easiest way to influence people but not the best way to win friends.

The chief clerk could not see why we should be given priority on some office equipment in short supply. The hydrographic office

Edwin T. Layton

wanted justification for our request for complete portfolios of charts of the Aleutian Islands and the Dutch East Indies. It took a lot of wheeling and dealing. The Battle Force staff, then back in San Francisco, requested that the *California*'s band be returned to them. When Admiral Bloch turned down their request, some senior officer in the Battle Force questioned Bloch's jurisdiction. We had to carry the case to Admiral Nimitz to save our ex-bandsmen cryptanalysts from becoming bandsmen again, making music to improve the morale of the Market Street Commandos.

Most of my contemporaries were commanders and most of the younger officers of FRUPac had been promoted since joining the unit, but there was then no legal way to promote a retired officer recalled to active duty, so I remained a lieutenant. My low rank made no difference while I was in the basement, but sometimes it was a minor handicap in my negotiations with the Navy Yard. Fortunately, I had many personal friends in the yard and I knew all the ways and byways of its organization. Sometimes even this did not help. Frustration was a minor price to pay for the privilege of making a small contribution to what was cooking in the basement. I did not have the ability to stir the pot or taste the broth, but I could chop wood and carry water.

When work on the five-digit code reached the stage where language-officer cryptanalysts could read a few code groups, they frequently wanted background information. Finnegan, in particular, would sometimes demand information that was difficult to get and often seemed completely irrelevant. He was very inarticulate and sometimes unable to explain his requirements or his reasoning, but so many times he was right in his conclusions that I did my utmost to get whatever he wanted. He conducted cryptanalysis by hunches and intuition. He had the ability to take off in an illogical direction from a shaky premise and land squarely on a firm conclusion. En route, he might want Dunbar and me to produce charts of remote areas, find the eight-letter name of a place for which he had the middle four letters, and tell him what news had been broadcast from Honolulu three days back. Finnegan frequently wanted details of past and present submarine operations and they were easy for me to get. The Submarine Force was eager to cooperate.

The Japanese port director at Truk reported arrivals and departures of ships, using a minor code that we could often read. Generally, these messages were intercepted too late to be of tactical value, but early in February we picked up a report of a carrier leaving Truk, whose course would take her through a pass between Hall Island and Namonuito Atoll, Caroline Islands, the area of a patrolling submarine. I asked Rochefort to let me pass this information on to the Submarine Force.

If I had known more about communications intelligence than I did then, I would never have asked him. Rochefort knew all the risks. He knew that Op-20-G would have permitted him to use such information only if a major strategic objective were at stake. He also knew that the Japanese had eight or ten aircraft carriers in the Pacific to our four, and that the opportunity to ambush a Japanese aircraft carrier was worth considerable risk. Carefully, he instructed me to "sanitize" the information as much as possible: conceal its source, lie convincingly if questioned closely, and pass it orally to someone I had confidence would restrict it to as few people as possible.

Commander Charles W. Styer, an old friend of my submarine days, was chief of staff of ComSubPac. I told him I had some firm information that the *Grayling*, patrolling off Truk, could use, but I could not tell him where it came from because a leak probably would destroy the source. Could he use it? He could and did. A message was sent to the *Grayling*, telling her to guard the pass; an aircraft carrier was coming through. She got there in time to see the carrier come through but did not get a shot at her.

In early March we picked up important information from a partially decrypted message. The *Kaga*, one of the Kido Butai carriers that had led the attack on Pearl Harbor, had been damaged and was returning to Japan from the East Indies by way of Palau. We thought it had been damaged by a submarine torpedo but, in fact, it had been damaged in an encounter with a strictly neutral coral head. There were five U.S. submarines then off Japan and the Nansei Shoto, and we had the information early enough for Com-SubPac to spot four of them along the *Kaga*'s most likely route. The *Narwhal* got a long-range difficult shot at a carrier, probably not the *Kaga*, but missed. These two incidents convinced the Submarine Force that we could put their submarines on the track of important targets.

Lasswell and Finnegan made an ideal translator-cryptanalyst team. Lasswell approached cryptanalysis like a chess-player maneuvering relentlessly to untangle his problem. His desk was usually clear of everything but his current puzzle. He worked sitting upright at his desk, wearing a carefully pressed Marine Corps uniform of the day, his sole deviation being a green eyeshade for protection against the hours under fluorescent lights. Finnegan barricaded himself behind a desk with two flanking tables, all piled high with IBM printouts, newspapers, messages, crumpled cigarette packs, coffee cups, apple cores, and sundry material, through which he searched intently, usually with success, for some stray bit of corroboratory evidence he remembered having seen days or weeks before. He paid little attention to the hours of the day, or days of the week, and not infrequently he worked himself into such a state of exhaustion that his head dropped into the rat's nest on his desk and he reluctantly fell asleep. Rochefort was a master at matching the talents of these two translators. A Finnegan hunch checked out by Lasswell's siege tactics made a firm foundation on which to build.

Evidence accumulated day by day that the Japanese were about to open a new offensive in eastern New Guinea or the Solomon Islands. The Fourth Fleet flagship, the light cruiser *Kashima*, arrived at Truk and departed by way of South Pass, duly reported to Tokyo by Truk's port director. Shortly afterwards, traffic analysis discovered that the commander of the Fourth Fleet was at Rabaul. Place-names like Deboyne and Misima, in the Louisiade Archipelago, for which the Japanese apparently had no code groups or two-letter area designators, began to appear in messages, spelled out in *kana*. Laswell undertook to teach me the *kana* syllabary in both *katakana* and *romaji*. "First thing a Japanese kindergarten kid learns," Rochefort said, by way of encouragement.

One afternoon Finnegan gave me part of a place-name that he wanted completed. I tried various combinations of *kana* but none of them fit any names on the charts or in the gazetteers. I had pieced together WO-DO-RA-KU and sat surveying it in disgust when Rochefort happened to look over my shoulder.

"That's all right, Jasper," he remarked. "You've got it."

I was not only a slow learner, I was so retarded I could not recognize that "Wodoraku" was the *kana* spelling of Woodlark.

Woodlark Island was right in line with Misima and Deboyne, down off the tail of the New Guinea bird. The *Kamikawa Maru*, a converted Japanese seaplane carrier, was associated in traffic with messages concerning those islands. Were the Japanese establishing an advanced base from which seaplanes could scout for a task force that was to advance into the Coral Sea?

Four heavy cruisers, the *Aoba*, *Kako*, *Kinugasa*, and *Furutaka*, were reported by the port director as arriving at Truk. A new area designator, MO, made its appearance in coded messages. MO was Port Moresby, Finnegan insisted. Rochefort was skeptical, as he often pretended to be, to force Finnegan to dig up more evidence to support his hunches. When Lasswell backed up Finnegan, Rochefort was convinced. If Moresby had an area designator it must figure in Japanese long-range plans. The Japanese had occupied Lae, on New Guinea's northern shore, but between them and Moresby were the formidable Owen Stanley Range and one of the world's hairiest jungles. I went to the library of the University of Hawaii to consult books on New Guinea and was soon convinced that a land operation across the Owen Stanley Range would be impossible. The *Lexington* and *Yorktown* were in the Coral Sea. They had run up into the Gulf of Papua to fly planes across the Owen Stanley Mountains and raid Lae and Salamaua shortly after the Japanese occupation forces landed there. The Japanese knew there were two American carriers in the vicinity. They would need carriers to oppose them if they intended to round the tail of eastern New Guinea.

The Battle of the Java Sea, which took place on 27 February 1942, had cleared all Allied surface forces from north of the Malay Barrier. The Kido Butai had spread devastation from Darwin to Ceylon. By the middle of April, the British Eastern Fleet had been pushed back to the western side of the Indian Ocean. Except for the doomed remnants of American and Philippine forces still holding out on Corregidor, the Japanese Greater East Asia Co-Prosperity Sphere had spread its mantle over all Southeast Asia and the East Indies. The Kido Butai would soon be free for new enterprises in early May. Stragglers from the shattered U.S. Asiatic Fleet, coming back through Honolulu, recommended we dig in at the Rocky Mountains.

In March 1942, Washington asked Rochefort for his estimate of Japanese intentions. In a remarkable analysis he predicted that, with the East Indies secure and the Indian Ocean swept clear of threatening forces, the next Japanese campaign would be in the area of New Guinea. The Japanese Navy would follow that up with an all-out offensive in the central Pacific sometime in the summer.

Then, on 18 April 1942, Lieutenant Colonel James H. Doolittle led his sixteen U.S. Army B-25 bombers in the first air raid on Tokyo.

CHAPTER 7

LIEUTENANT SLONIM, with two radiomen, Cain and Rundle, from FRUPac, was with Halsey during the Doolittle raid. At three o'clock on the morning of 18 April 1942, and again at four-thirty, radar detected strange vessels ahead. The two carriers, the *Enterprise* and *Hornet*, with their screening cruisers in formation, maneuvered silently in the darkness to avoid them. Halsey had been briefed that submarines en route to patrol areas off Japan had encountered a ring of picket boats six hundred miles out from Tokyo, but to find them eight hundred miles out was an ominous surprise.

Huddled over their intercept receivers under the *Enterprise*'s flag bridge, Slonim and his crew listened tensely but heard no radio transmissions that would indicate alarm. Perhaps the night strangers were fishermen, or even radar phantoms. Then, the first search plane off the *Enterprise*'s deck at dawn reported a picket boat twenty miles ahead. Suddenly the cruiser *Nashville* veered from her course. Signal flags of varicolored bunting flew from her yardarm proclaiming, "Unidentified vessel sighted." A moment later she opened fire. There could be no doubt that the task force had run right into the picket line. With two picket boats within view, the possibility was remote that the task force could sink them both before one of them got off a warning message. Almost simultaneously with the *Nashville*'s first salvo, Slonim picked up frantic and garbled Japanese conversations on the radio, evidently originated in the vicinity of the task force.

Any doubts that the picket boats' alarm got through were soon dispelled. Within minutes, the Japanese civil defense circuits were on the air, and Slonim could hear excited Japanese conversation about carriers, planes, and gunfire. Immediate Japanese counterattack was certain. Search planes would take off, probably closely followed by every available bomber and torpedo plane of Air Squadron 26. Within a few hours a furious air battle over the task

William F. Halsey and Gilven M. Slonim

force could be expected. The *Hornet*, with sixteen Army bombers
on her flight deck, would be helpless in her own defense, and she
was still two hundred miles short of her planned launching point.

When Rundle copied an intercepted naval message, Slonim had
more to go on. The body of the message was in five-numeral code
beyond his ability to decrypt, but its heading carried important information. The message was from Radio Tokyo to a long list of
addressees. Some of the calls he could not identify from the call list
that had been given him by FRUPac at Pearl Harbor, but the Kido
Butai's call was prominent. If the Kido Butai was taking traffic
direct from Radio Tokyo, it was no longer in the Indian Ocean.
Halsey might be running into a hornets' nest not to the *Hornet*'s
liking. He had little choice but to launch the Army air strike immediately and retreat before he was trapped by greatly superior
forces.

FRUPac had little warning of the raid on Tokyo. On the evening before it was to take place, Rochefort came back from a conference at CinCPac headquarters with the electrifying news that
planes from Halsey's task force would bomb Tokyo during the
night of 18 April. FRUPac was usually given early information on
carrier raids, in order to pick up reports of the weather at the tar-

get, but this time the submarine *Thresher* was posted off Tokyo to make weather observations.

Information on Halsey's plans was closely guarded. Huckins was justly irked by the inadequate notice he received. There were not enough *kana* operators and intercept receivers to cover more than a few of the Japanese naval radio circuits. Planning for coverage of the most important traffic was always a matter of compromise. Given enough warning, he could have doubled the watch on the Tokyo circuit. He had no warning at all. Launched early, Doolittle's bombers flew off the *Hornet*'s deck before the intercept station and the direction-finder net could be fully alerted.

At that time Combat Intelligence had only one direct land line to the intercept station on Oahu. Most of the intercepted Japanese messages were brought down by jeep three or four times a day, a precarious trip at night over blacked-out roads. On the night of the Tokyo raid, it was hours before the traffic analysts had the pertinent traffic to work on, too late to be any help to Slonim. FRUPac could only confirm that the Kido Butai was back in the Pacific and taking an active part in the search for Halsey. The Second Fleet, which had sortied from the Inland Sea, and even some elements of the Fourth Fleet in the South Seas, were helping to search the entire North Pacific. In the basement we waited for a Japanese contact report and prayed it would never come. Halsey got clean away.

Everybody's morale got a big lift from the Doolittle raid, but in FRUPac we soon began to have second thoughts. It was magnificent, but was it war? Finnegan, industriously digging into his rat's nest of paper that nearly submerged him, was the first to voice doubts. It was becoming more and more apparent to him that the Japanese were about to try a power play around the southern end of the U.S. defense line while half of our available carrier forces were busy staging a grandstand play at the northern end. What military damage the raid had done was not known, and its psychological effect both in Japan and in the United States was difficult to assess. If it resulted in the loss of Port Moresby, it would be a first-class disaster.

Rochefort had predicted a Japanese offensive in the New Guinea area but the evidence was thin. Aerial reconnaissance confirmed the assembly of a large force of cruisers, destroyers, transports, and supply ships at Rabaul, but most information had to be pieced together from the fragments of whatever radio messages could be decrypted. The old Corregidor unit had been moved to the southwest Pacific. When the volume of Japanese radio traffic in the Rabaul area increased, that unit, being in the best position to exploit it, joined FRUPac and Op-20-G in the attack on the five-digit code. Every additive or code group recovered by any of the three units let more light into the dark language of this code, but only a few words of a few messages could yet be decrypted. From what little was learned, much could be inferred with the aid of traffic analysis. Day-by-day details of the Japanese order of battle unfolded.

Commander, Fourth Fleet, at Rabaul, sent several messages referring to a ship for which we found no single code group. It was, evidently, a new ship. Its name was encoded by two code groups identified only as "single characters used in a name." The traffic it generated was like that of an aircraft carrier, but it was not one of the known carriers. By some process of his own logic, Finnegan read the characters as "Ryukaku" and insisted that it was a new aircraft carrier. As "Ryukaku" it became known to the American Navy. Months later, captured documents revealed that it was a light carrier with about one-third the plane capacity of a big attack carrier and the Japanese had christened it *Shoho*. By any name, it was still a new carrier, and its association with the Fourth Fleet was ominous.

We knew nothing of the characteristics of the *Shoho* except that it was capable of supporting combat flight operations. Translated bits of messages, collated with traffic analysis, pieced together a reasonable estimate of its employment. The four heavy cruisers that had been reported arriving at Truk in early April, departed southbound. The port director at Truk very obligingly reported their departure in the minor code that FRUPac was then reading. Traffic analysis noted many messages associating these cruisers with the "Ryukaku." Finnegan discovered a reference to a new organization, the "MO Covering Force," whose commander was identified by traffic analysis as the commander of Cruiser Division Six in the *Aoba*. Finnegan also discovered references to the "MO Occupation Force" and to a second occupation force that seemed to be connected with an unidentified place in the Solomon Islands.

We already knew that the seaplane carrier *Kamikawa Maru*, in another task group, was busy among the small islands off the tail of New Guinea. The pieces of the intelligence puzzle fell together, with many gaps, to suggest a typically complex Japanese operational plan. The major thrust would be down around the eastern end of New Guinea and through the Coral Sea to occupy Port Moresby. Another force, of unknown strength, would seize an advanced base in the Solomon Islands. A powerful force of at least

70

four heavy cruisers and the "Ryukaku" would cover both these operations.

The answer to the big question "when" could only be estimated. The Japanese concealed references to important dates and times by further encipherment within their coded messages. Very few occurrences of this cipher were discovered, so it was impossible to break it. The date set for the operation had to be inferred from ships' movements and concentrations and from aerial reconnaissance. The best estimate was some time in the first week of May. Allied forces consisting of the *Lexington* and *Yorktown*, two Australian and six American cruisers, and eleven destroyers were due to rendezvous in the eastern end of the Coral Sea on 1 May. For a short time the prospect of an American and Australian preponderance of force at the point of contact appeared bright.

Then an intercepted Japanese message changed that prospect. Given the fact that only one in ten intercepted messages could be forced to yield information, a translator-cryptanalyst bucked a large element of chance. He might sweat for hours over a message only to be baffled by its stone-wall defense, or to discover in the end that it was of no current importance. Had he picked another message, it might have cracked wide open and spewed forth important secrets.

In early April traffic analysis linked Carrier Division Five, the *Shokaku* and *Zuikaku*, with the commander of the Fourth Fleet, and Rochefort was very curious about the association. Everyone was alerted. When the Kido Butai gave up the search for Halsey, a message was intercepted addressed to Carrier Division Five, with Commander, Fourth Fleet, as an information addressee. More than pure chance gave that message immediate attention. Enough of it could be decrypted to learn that Carrier Division Five and Cruiser Division Five, the *Myoko* and *Haguro*, were ordered detached from the Kido Butai and directed to proceed to Truk. It was quite clear that two big carriers and two more heavy cruisers had been assigned to the Moresby operation.

The prospective preponderance of strength swung heavily to the Japanese. Both sides had shore-based air forces, but the outcome would probably depend upon the opposing carrier forces. With Carrier Division Five added to the unknown strength of the "Ryukaku," the relative strengths were now 3:2 in favor of the Japanese.

There was opportunity as well as jeopardy in the intrusion of the *Shokaku* and *Zuikaku* into the arena. So long as the six big carriers of the Kido Butai stayed together, they would predominate over any opposing force in the Pacific. If a strong detachment from it could be isolated and trapped, the Kido Butai's strength might be reduced to manageable size. The *Hornet* and *Enterprise* were returning from the Doolittle raid; they were due to enter Pearl Harbor on 25 April. If they could join the *Lexington* and *Yorktown* in the Coral Sea in time, the whole course of the war might be changed. A chart study confirmed that it was possible. If Halsey bypassed Hawaii, fueled at sea, and cut down by French Frigate Shoal and Johnston Island in a high-speed run, he might arrive in time for the battle.

In the basement the chart desk was strewn with charts of New Britain, New Guinea, and the Solomon Islands. The air was thick with conversations about the *Kamikawa Maru*, the Moresby Occupation Force, and Rabaul. Each incoming message was quickly scanned for reference to the Fourth Fleet or Carrier Division Five. We lived and breathed and schemed in the atmosphere of the Coral Sea. Up above us, the Navy Yard was busy with salvage operations, black oil, and beans. Submarines stole silently out through the channel on patrol and returned. Each dawn, search planes labored to lift their heavy loads of fuel for the long day's grind out to six or seven hundred miles and home again. The newspapers were full of the Tokyo raid and the war in Europe and Burma. Names like Solomon Islands, Truk, and Coral Sea had not yet flashed above their horizon. Everyone was concerned with his own special problem, and no one outside the basement seemed aware of the gathering tornado.

I wanted Rochefort to go over to CinCPac headquarters and suggest to Admiral Nimitz that Halsey take that cutoff, bypassing Pearl Harbor, and make a high-speed run to join up with the *Lexington* and *Yorktown*. Together they would form a force that could clobber the Japanese carrier striking force, the MO Covering Force, and the MO Occupation Force, and win a victory that the United States greatly needed. He shrugged off my impertinent suggestion with a typically cynical remark. I had a lot to learn as an intelligence officer.

More than chart studies were required to prepare for such an operation. Lead time was necessary to work out the logistics and get tankers moving to rendezvous. In preparation for a war in the Pacific, patient peacetime exercises had perfected techniques for fueling and replenishing ships at sea, far from supporting bases. The *Yorktown* task force had patrolled a weary beat back and forth across the Coral Sea since early March, nursing from tankers at prearranged intervals. Black oil flowed through flexible fuel lines draped between ships propelled in unison through rolling seas, while mail and men and food and cigarettes and radar parts went back and forth over the highline. Tankers for such operations were almost as scarce as the carriers themselves. The hazard of running short of fuel was a task-force commander's nightmare. In the early months of the war many opportunities to do damage to the Japanese were missed because, like the dog that had to stop for a logistic emergency and so did not catch the rabbit, a task force often had to refuel at a critical moment.

Previous service on a big fleet staff had convinced Rochefort that many elements other than intelligence were involved in any action, and that the best results came from leaving operational matters to those who dealt with plans and operations. Rochefort was right, of course, as events were to prove. Like most naval and military intelligence officers, he subscribed to the principle that intelligence organizations should gather, collate, and disseminate information and not attempt to make operational decisions.

The *Hornet* and *Enterprise* arrived at Pearl Harbor on 25 April. They spent five days in port, refueling, replenishing, rearranging air groups, and rearming with a new type of bomb that had just reached Hawaii. On 30 April a task force built around the two carriers, under Halsey's command, departed for the Coral Sea, 3,500 miles away. The next day a Japanese task force, built around the *Shokaku* and *Zuikaku*, left Truk for the same destination with less than one-third of that distance to go. The Truk port director dutifully reported their departure, so we knew they would be in the Coral Sea long before Halsey could arrive.

The Battle of the Coral Sea started on 4 May 1942 with a U.S. carrier strike against Japanese invasion forces at Tulagi, in the Solomon Islands. It ended on 8 May with the first carrier–vs.–carrier battle ever fought. In the basement we watched all intercepted messages for news. The Japanese used the word *gekichin* to report the destruction of an enemy ship, and *chimbotsu* to described the sinking of one of their own ships. The traffic-analysis desk flagged every potentially important message and rushed it to Holtwick in the machine room. As each printout rolled off the machines, hungry eyes searched for the code group for *chimbotsu*. When they spotted it, we learned that the "Ryukaku" was *chimbotsu*. The *Shokaku* had been damaged and put out of action. The MO Occupation Force and the MO Covering Force were ordered back to Rabaul. Some days later, word filtered down to us in the basement that the *Lexington* had been lost and the *Yorktown* severely damaged. The trade-off of the *Lexington* for the *Shoho* ("Ryukaku") was greatly in Japan's favor, but Port Moresby had been saved from immediate danger.

73

The *Shokaku* and *Zuikaku* retired to Truk after the battle. The *Shokaku* had taken three dive-bomber hits and was badly damaged. We believed it had been hit by aerial torpedoes, as it should have been if American torpedoes had been nearly as good as the Japanese. If the *Shokaku* had underwater damage, it would be slowed down and make an easier target for submarines. In anticipation of heavy traffic, ComSubPac had stationed three submarines off Truk, but we had no information on which of five passes through the fringing reef the Japanese would use. They were using North Pass and South Pass; the other three were mined. The *Gar*, off Piaanu Pass, saw nothing. The *Greenling*, off Northeast Pass, saw a carrier steam safely across the big atoll and out through North Pass, hopelessly beyond the reach of the submarine's torpedoes. The *Tautog*, stationed south of Truk, saw no carriers, but she sank the submarine *I-28* and torpedoed the *Goyo Maru*, both of which had taken part in the Moresby operation.

Carrier Division Five and Cruiser Division Five were ordered to return to Japan from Truk. The *Shokaku*, with a destroyer escort, sailed alone a day or so ahead of the others by an evasive route. A message giving the route points through which it would pass was intercepted and decrypted, but the points' coordinates were in an unsolved secret grid, which the Japanese used in many of their encrypted messages further to conceal latitude and longitude coordinates. The Submarine Force therefore knew only the points of departure and arrival. There were several submarines within possible range of the direct route between Truk and Bungo Suido, the entrance to the Inland Sea. ComSubPac did his best to intercept the returning carriers, but the departure and arrival points of a long voyage are scant information for a submarine attempting to intercept a high-speed target on the high seas. Four submarines searched for the damaged carrier, and the *Triton* sighted it, making 16 knots, but just outside torpedo range.

It might have been a different story if we had had the solution to the Japanese grid. Submarines could have been stationed at the route points to ambush the homeward-bound carrier. Grid coordinates were given by four *kana* and a single digit. There had been several occurrences of such coordinates in Japanese messages. The approximate geographic position for some grid coordinates were known, and the distance between successive points for some others could be approximated. With a little imaginative chart work, the grid should be solvable. Chart work was in my line. Rochefort gave me the problem to work on. The U.S. Army used a rectangular grid for reporting positions in the Hawaiian area, probably more for convenience than for security. I was confident I could have solved the Army grid. The Japanese version had me completely frustrated.

Before Alec Hudson was permitted to publish "Rendezvous," the Navy Department required him to eliminate from the story all reference to rectangular grids. It was not a difficult change to make, but the requirement revealed a lack of background in naval history by the Navy Department censors. Rectangular grids were such a natural development that it would not be surprising if Themistocles used grid coordinates to make his rendezvous at Salamis. The Germans used a rectangular grid in the North Sea during World War I, and its compromise, by charts recovered from a dirigible shot down in France, is a well-known story. I wished that the Japanese had been as naive as the Navy Department censors thought they were. The Japanese grid was much more sophisticated than anything I had ever read about.

At the beginning of May an intercepted message revealed that the *Kasuga Maru* would arrive at Kwajalein on 4 May. Later renamed the *Taiyo*, it was one of five big Japanese merchant ships converted to auxiliary aircraft carriers, about which little was known to us at that time. The *Gato* was closely patrolling Kwajalein. With information I carried to the Submarine Force, she was alerted to the expected hour of the *Kasuga Maru*'s arrival. This time the submarine was at the right place at the right time. She fired five torpedoes and missed. Rochefort remarked that it did not do much good for me to carry information to my submarine friends if they could not make their torpedoes hit.

Some of the veterans in Communications Intelligence considered that passing information to the submarines was dangerous. They might have been mollified if the submarines had sunk an aircraft carrier. So far, I had passed on a considerable amount of sensitive intelligence to the submarines with no tangible results. Everyone was apprehensive of the Japanese becoming suspicious that their code was compromised. A change of code could throw us completely in the dark at just the time when information was of the greatest importance. I began to realize the weight of responsibility Rochefort had assumed by permitting me to converse with the Submarine Force.

The *Shokaku* arrived safely home on 17 May. The *Zuikaku* got in a few days later. On 16 May Nimitz ordered Halsey to return to Pearl Harbor. The *Lexington* was lost. It was estimated that it would require three months in the Navy Yard to repair the *Yorktown*'s battle damage. The *Saratoga* was still on the West Coast, repairing the torpedo damage she had taken in January. Nimitz had only Halsey's two carriers to rely on.

The *Shokaku* was damaged and out of action. The *Zuikaku* had lost most of its planes and pilots in battle. There were no planes or trained pilots for immediate replacement. The Japanese still had four first-line carriers in the Kido Butai and four additional light carriers that were battle-ready. Japanese planners were confident. They believed that their relative strength had been increased by the Battle of the Coral Sea.

CHAPTER 8

While Admiral Nimitz, at Pearl Harbor, was trying to estimate Japanese capabilities and intentions, Japanese naval planners were having troubles of their own. To the Allies, frustrated and defeated at every turn, it appeared that the Japanese war machine was proceeding at top speed along a well-prepared track under the sure hand of a master planner, with all the loyal sons of Nippon bending their utmost efforts in harmonious unison; but such was not the case. Before the war began, Japan's objectives for its first and second phases were agreed upon, but there were serious differences of opinion as to how these objectives were to be achieved.

I was curious about the preparation of Japanese plans during the first phase, when we were desperately trying to determine where the victorious Japanese Navy would strike next. My curiosity was only partially appeased by documents captured during the war and by the reports of the U.S. Strategic Bombing Survey after it. In 1959, however, I spent a couple of months in Japan. Captain Edward S. Pearce, U.S. Navy, an old friend, was then living in Tokyo. With his assistance and the good offices of the American embassy, I met many ex-officers of the Imperial Japanese Navy who had been involved in intelligence and planning.

Pearce was one of the fifty-odd U.S. naval officers who had completed a three-year course of study of the Japanese language in Tokyo during the twenty years before the war. As did many of the language officers, during his student days he developed an affinity for Japan and things Japanese, and perhaps more than most he made many friends in the Japanese Navy. He returned to Japan with the occupation forces after the war, and sometimes helped soften the hard lot of his old friends.

While he was a student in Japan, Pearce met a bachelor Japanese naval officer of his own age, and the two became firm friends and

77

drinking companions. A few years later, the Japanese officer was sent to Washington for duty with the Japanese embassy during a period when Pearce was also on duty in Washington. The friendship continued, although both men knew that they would probably one day be on opposite sides in a war. When the Japanese officer returned to Japan, he married and had a daughter.

Pearce became somewhat like a godfather to the little girl and sent her presents on birthdays and holidays. When he returned to Tokyo after the war, he learned that his friend had been killed at Rabaul. At the first opportunity, he set out to search for his friend's daughter, who would then be a young lady. When he found her, in Yamaguchi Prefecture, she was in the middle of a paddy, up to her knees in muck, planting rice. Standing on the dike of the paddy, Pearce called to her, and she came wading toward him through the mud.

"I am Captain Pearce," he told her.

"I know," she replied. "My father told me you would come for me if he did not come home from the war."

Whether or not this was typical, I soon discovered that a note or a telephone call from Eddie Pearce opened doors for me that would have otherwise remained closed. I learned much about the formulation of Japanese war plans in a comparatively short time.

In September 1940 Japan signed the Tripartite Pact with Germany and Italy. The Japanese Army was strongly in favor of this alliance, but the Navy was apprehensive. Participation in the pact meant that the old naval war plans were no longer adequate, and new ones had to be drawn up by the First Section of the Naval General Staff. Captain Sadatoshi Tomioka, with Commander Tatsukichi Miyo as his assistant for air, was assigned to the task. In 1959 I had long discussions with both of these officers, and learned to appreciate the dilemma in which they had been placed.

The key to the situation was oil. The Japanese Navy had accumulated a reserve of 6.5 million tons of oil, but this supply would be rapidly depleted by war operations. The Navy would not be able to sit tight and let the war come to it. In the first days of the war it would have to assume the offensive and go out to seize a source of oil. The First Section decided that the Dutch East Indies would have to be conquered at the outset to ensure a fuel supply. To protect their communications, they planned to occupy the Philippines and British Malaya. With these objectives for the first phase there was general agreement, but the Combined Fleet Staff did not agree with the Naval General Staff on how the job was to be done.

The Naval General Staff planned that the Main Body, under the direct command of Admiral Yamamoto, including most of the battleships of the First Fleet, would remain in home waters as a strategic reserve. The Southern Force, consisting of the Second and Third fleets reinforced by two battleships, one light aircraft carrier, and three air squadrons of the Eleventh Air Fleet, would annihilate enemy forces in the Philippines and the East Indies and support Army landing operations. The South Sea Force, consisting of the Fourth Fleet plus a division of heavy cruisers from the First Fleet, would defend the Marshalls and the Carolines and seize Guam, Wake, and Rabaul. The Advanced Expeditionary Force, consisting of most of the submarines of the Sixth Fleet, would invest Pearl Harbor and sink targets of opportunity.

On the principle of concentration of force, the Naval General Staff proposed to use the Kido Butai to cover the Southern Force in a quick capture of the vital East Indies oil fields, and to leave the initial attack on the American battle fleet at Pearl Harbor to the submarines. The similarity between the assignments that the Japanese Naval General Staff planned for its task forces and Rochefort's intelligence estimate of 26 November is striking, but both of them were reckoned without adequate consideration of Isoroku Yamamoto, commander in chief of the Combined Fleet.

Admiral Yamamoto was steadfastly opposed to the war but was resolved that if it came he would do his best to win it. He had had two tours of duty with the Japanese embassy in Washington and gone home with no love for Americans, but a healthy respect for the economic might of the United States. He knew he would have to take desperate chances. He decided to use Japan's great advantage in aircraft carrier strength to strike the American battle fleet at Pearl Harbor and prevent it from interfering with the Japanese occupation of the East Indies. To that end he set Captains Yasuji Watanabe and Kameto Kuroshima of the Combined Fleet Staff, Admiral Takejiro Ohnishi of the Eleventh Air Fleet, and Commander Minoru Genda of the First Air Fleet to drawing up plans for the Kido Butai's strike on Pearl Harbor.

Thus, the plan of the Naval General Staff and the plan of the Combined Fleet were in opposition, and powerful proponents lined up on both sides of the argument. Ordinarily the Naval General Staff would have won this argument, but Yamamoto was adamant. He threatened to resign as commander in chief of the Combined

Fleet if the war plans were not to his liking. This threat was decisive, and the plans for a surprise air attack on Pearl Harbor were approved.

Japanese war plans were based on the assumption that it would require a year and cost their Navy one-third of its strength to gain the objectives of the first phase. However, in four months most of those objectives were achieved at the cost of four destroyers, six submarines, and a few minor vessels. New ships joining the fleet, including the mighty battleship *Yamato* and the light carrier *Shoho*, more than made up the losses, and the Navy was stronger than ever. The insignificance of the losses and the magnitude of the victories caught the planners unprepared.

Japanese naval planners were, nevertheless, under no delusion that the war had been won. They estimated that by the middle of 1943 the American Navy would be strong enough to challenge both Japan and the long logistic lines of the Pacific Ocean together. The objectives of the second phase were to develop a strong defense line before that time, and to force the U.S. Navy to decisive action before it was ready. Again, there was complete agreement on the objectives, but again the Combined Fleet Staff disagreed with the Naval General Staff as to how they were to be achieved.

Miyo, who was air plans officer on the Naval General Staff, reasoned that a counterattack would be launched from Australia. That continent possessed the land mass for dispersed bases from which a massive air attack could be mounted. It was essential to impose some sort of barrier between Australia and the oil fields of Java and Borneo. Tomioka favored the direct method of invading Australia and seizing all of that continent's northern ports.

The Army vetoed any such ambitious plan. It would take ten divisions, the Army estimated, and these were not available without unacceptable weakening of the Kwantung Army, deployed in Manchuria. Tomioka believed five divisions could do the job, but a check on resources soon convinced him that there was insufficient shipping available to lift even that many divisions to Australia and support their operations. Invasion of Australia at that stage of the war was beyond the capabilities of Japan, swollen with victory and conscious of power though she was.

Tomioka and Miyo then decided that the next best plan was to occupy islands along the line of communications between the United States and Australia in order to prevent a rapid buildup of air and military strength in Australia. This the Navy could do, with only a minimum of assistance from the Army. Once entrenched along a defense line through the Solomon Islands to Fiji and Samoa, the Japanese Navy would have a stranglehold on Australia. Japan would be in such a strong strategic position that the United States would have to commit its full strength in an all-out effort to break the line. Nimitz would have to accept decisive battle under conditions imposed by Japan, in the South Seas, and at a time dictated by the emergency rather than when American naval strength was built up to the task. Miyo had based his prewar estimates and plans on just such a campaign.

In anticipation of the kind of island-hopping operation that this plan would entail, the Japanese Navy had organized its Naval Special Landing Forces, roughly the counterpart of the U.S. Marine Corps. Quite independent of the Army, these forces would be able to seize and hold an island base and, as soon as an airfield could be constructed, the air squadrons of the Eleventh Air Fleet would move in.

The naval air squadrons had no counterpart in any other navy. They were shore-based, but trained, equipped, organized, and integrated into the naval organization for cooperation with the fleet. Air squadrons operating from a chain of island bases within supporting distance of each other would be able to guard the Japanese defense line against anything but strong carrier attacks. The Kido Butai, behind a screen of island-based air squadrons, would be almost invincible, and Japan would be able to exploit and develop her newly won territory in security.

Independently of the Naval General Staff, the Combined Fleet Staff was working on plans for the second phase. Alarmed by American carrier raids in the central Pacific, it rejected Tomioka's plan. In a South Seas campaign, Pearl Harbor would have interior lines of communication: with the Japanese Navy fully committed at the southern end of the defense line, carrier task forces based at Pearl Harbor would be able to raid Tokyo; and if Japanese carrier forces were pulled back to cover the northern end, the southern end would be vulnerable. An attack on Midway, on the other hand, would put the entire Japanese fleet between Hawaii and Japan.

Admiral Matome Ugaki, chief of staff of the Combined Fleet, proposed a plan to invade Hawaii and destroy the American fleet. Detailed studies by Captains Kuroshima and Watanabe soon revealed that such an operation was beyond the logistic capability of Japan at that time. They settled on a plan to seize Midway in June, followed by Johnston Island later in the summer, and set up Hawaii for invasion in the fall of 1942.

About the middle of March, the Combined Fleet informed the Naval General Staff that it was studying a plan to attack Midway. On 30 March Captain Watanabe carried the preliminary plan from the flagship *Yamato* to Tokyo for presentation to the Naval General Staff. A violent argument ensued, but one of the results of the Pearl Harbor success was to put the planners of the Combined Fleet in the ascendancy, eclipsing the First Section of the Naval General Staff in its legitimate function. On 5 April the Naval General Staff agreed to the plan. However, arguments about its details continued.

On 18 April Lieutenant Colonel Doolittle led sixteen bombers off the flight deck of the *Hornet* to bomb Tokyo. That ended all opposition to an early Japanese attack on Midway.

Early June, when the moon would be right, was chosen for a landing on Midway. Much of the planning took place before the Second Fleet and the Kido Butai returned from their operations in the south. It was nearly May before staff officers who had major responsibility for the operations could discuss them with the Combined Fleet Staff, most of whom accepted the plans without objections. Admiral Nobutake Kondo, commander of the Second Fleet, favored the Naval General Staff's plan to invade Fiji and Samoa. Genda, who was operations officer of the First Air Fleet during the Battle of Midway, told me in 1959 that he had objected to the battle plans. The Combined Fleet Staff overrode all objections. In 1959, Kuroshima was still confident that there was nothing wrong with the Midway plans. He told me that if Nagumo, commanding the Kido Butai, had carried out his orders to seize every opportunity to attack the American aircraft carriers, it would have been a Japanese victory. He dismissed Genda's criticism with the remark, "Genda was a very junior officer."

The capture of Port Moresby had been planned for early March 1942, but the arrival of an American carrier task force in the Coral Sea delayed that operation until the Kido Butai had completed its campaign against Ceylon and returned to the Pacific from the Indian Ocean. Carrier Division Five was then ordered to support the Fourth Fleet in the Moresby operation. This delay gave U.S. naval communications intelligence time to recover enough of the five-digit Japanese naval code to disclose Japanese plans. The Battle of the Coral Sea took place on 8 May 1942. For the first time, the Japanese

Navy encountered effective resistance. The occupation of Port Moresby was thwarted.

Before the Doolittle raid Kuroshima had correctly estimated that there were two American carriers operating in the North Pacific and two in the Coral Sea. When the *Shokaku* and *Zuikaku* were detached from the Kido Butai to support the Port Moresby operation, he calculated that in any carrier battle the Japanese carriers would inflict at least as much damage as they received. Like a chess-player, he reckoned that an equal exchange favored the stronger side. He insisted that he had never included Carrier Division Five in his plans for Midway; with four carriers Nagumo should have had ample strength to accomplish all the Midway task assigned to him. At the end of the Coral Sea action Kuroshima's calculations were correct. From then on, however, an unknown element entered into the equation and distorted his projections.

On 5 May, Imperial General Headquarters Navy Order Number 18 was issued, directing the commander in chief of the Combined Fleet to occupy Midway and islands in the western Aleutians. It was a very complex operation that would widely disperse major Japanese forces over the North Pacific, outside the range of mutual support and subject to defeat in detail by an alert, aggressive enemy, even though that enemy were greatly inferior in strength to the Combined Fleet. There was barely time to get ready. Much of the information that the scattered forces required had to be sent to them by radio. Even before Navy Order Number 18 was issued, Rochefort had predicted the general trend of coming events.

Before leaving Japan, I had a memorable visit to Eta Jima, the Japanese Naval Academy. The U.S. naval attaché arranged it for me, and thereby set up a coincidence stranger than fiction. Admiral Suguru Suzuki, superintendent of the academy, invited me to lunch with his staff. During the course of the lunch, he asked me if I knew that Pearl Harbor was bombed twice. Indeed I did. I was there on both occasions. Admiral Suzuki then told me that he had planned the second bombing. So I asked him if he had ever heard of Alec Hudson or read *The Saturday Evening Post*. He said no, and the conversation somehow changed to another subject, so I could not explain that he had just shattered Alec Hudson's only claim to fame as a Japanese naval planner.

I had to leave the luncheon hurriedly to catch the boat to Kure. Unexpectedly, I encountered Mrs. Suzuki at the exit to the admiral's home. She was on her knees, bowed low in the traditional obeisance of a Japanese hostess to a departing guest. I did not know whether I should bow, or kneel, or curtsy, or offer to shake hands. As I hesitated, she looked up at me with a frank and friendly smile.

"Do you know Captain Pearce?" she inquired.

I did, I did indeed, and I would be glad to convey her greetings to him when I returned to Tokyo. Moreover, I would ask Eddie Pearce to instruct me in what I was supposed to do with my hands and my feet in such a situation.

CHAPTER 9

Rochefort had predicted that the Port Moresby operation would be followed by a bigger operation in the central Pacific. Japanese preparations for such an offensive were perceptible before the Battle of the Coral Sea. On 10 March 1942 a seaplane of the type used in the second bombing of Pearl Harbor attempted to reconnoiter Midway. The Marines there had been tipped off by Communications Intelligence and were ready. The big seaplane was shot down before it could complete its mission.

In May radio traffic typical of air operations indicated increased Japanese air activity in the Marshalls. The *Kasuga Maru*, having escaped the *Gato*'s torpedoes, had completed its mission of ferrying air reinforcements to Kwajalein. The considerable radio traffic between Air Squadron 24, with headquarters at Kwajalein, and submarines of the Japanese Sixth Fleet was reminiscent of that which had preceded the "K" operation at French Frigate Shoal and the second bombing of Pearl Harbor.

The whole traffic pattern suggested the formation of new task forces, geographic redistribution of naval units, and a buildup of forces around Saipan. The Fourth Fleet in the Mandates, the Second Fleet, and the Kido Butai were all involved. Their commanders were action or information addressees of many messages from the commander in chief of the Combined Fleet. A new two-letter area designator, AF, was discovered in some of these messages.

It was reasonable to deduce that AF was associated with AFG, identified as French Frigate Shoal by the "K" operation. A similar occurrence of a three-letter designator, built up from a two-letter designator, had been worked out in the Solomon Islands. Parallelism suggested that AF and AFG were close to each other and that therefore AF was somewhere in the Hawaiian Island chain. When an AF Occupation Force was mentioned in a partially decrypted message, the situation became alarming.

The Port Moresby operation demonstrated the ability of FRU-Pac to predict Japanese operations by this line of reasoning. The constant flow of information from Combat Intelligence to CinCPac Intelligence pulled these two organizations closely together. CinCPac's operations officers became familiar with the sometimes imperfect but always important communications intelligence material, and gained confidence in its use.

Nimitz recalled Halsey on 16 May. The round trip of Halsey's carrier task force to the Solomon Islands was not entirely wasted. The day before its recall, Halsey's task force was sighted by a Japanese search plane. Japanese planners believed that two American carriers had been sunk during the Battle of the Coral Sea and that only two remained in the Pacific. When both of them were spotted, 3,500 miles from Hawaii, the Japanese were reassured that they could occupy Midway before American carriers could interfere with the operation.

———————

The large volume of radio traffic during the Battle of the Coral Sea resulted in the "recovery" of many code values in the five-digit code. By early May one-third of the groups of that code could be read. Since the most frequently used groups were the first to be recovered, the larger part of the body of messages in the five-digit code could be decrypted, if time and manpower were available. There were often gaps in the readable text of messages but, even if no more than a word or two of a message could be decrypted, it was sometimes significant.

Only a fraction of the vast volume of Japanese radio traffic could be intercepted. Traffic analysts scanned the volume of traffic across the radio spectrum, and Huckins usually assigned the Japanese circuits to be guarded by the intercept station. More messages were intercepted than the cryptanalysts could profitably work on. Selection of those that were to receive primary attention was more of an art than a science. The identities of the originator and the addressees, the block of additives used in the encipherment, the priority given to the message, its length, the time of transmission, and Finnegan's hunches, were all important elements to be considered.

Keeping track of the readable fragments and correlating them with each other became a problem. Perhaps it could have best been done by IBM machinery, but Dyer, who used a punch-card sorter like a surgeon's scalpel to dissect both code and enciphering tables, needed unlimited access to the machinery. Holtwick had all the available machinery programmed twenty-four hours each day, and the translators could not wait for machine time. Rochefort scribbled out the translated scraps of messages in his illegible scrawl and threw them across the desk for Dunbar and me to catalogue and record. Our effort to file them chronologically and produce them again whenever they were called for failed almost immediately. A translator would often need to compare all the messages relating to a specific unit, place, or subject. If he wanted everything referring to the *Shokaku*, he would certainly need not only to have all the messages in which that carrier's name or radio call sign appeared, but also to check up on Carrier Division Five and the First Air Fleet as well. The traffic analysts might want to examine other associations, and Dyer or Wright might want some different arrangement. We were constantly arranging, rearranging, and disarranging the whole mess.

I went to a friend of mine who was the chief clerk of the Navy Yard, and cajoled him into giving me a couple of visual file cabinets of the type used by supply officers for ready reference to inventory cards. We then transcribed pertinent portions of translated messages, traffic-analysis reports, and other data on five-by-eight-inch index cards, making a separate card for each ship, organization, and place-name. The coordinated information would then be available at the flip of a finger. This worked for a little while but, under the pressure of the sheer volume of material, it, too, failed.

Eventually we progressed to making multiple copies of each translation, together with its message heading, on five-by-eight-inch slips of paper. We filed these copies under as many headings as we thought might be useful, behind index cards in long, open, wooden boxes. Excerpts from traffic-intelligence reports and any other bits of information we acquired were "carded" and filed along with the messages. It would have been much simpler if xerography had been invented, but we had to use the hectograph process of duplication. Dunbar soon needed a couple of yeomen to help him type and duplicate the slips. The purple ink used in the hectographing became our trademark, emblazoned impartially on product and producers.

The original purpose of our system was to feed information back to the translators, the traffic analysts, and the cryptanalysts, but it soon had other uses. We arranged the index cards of Japanese naval units according to the organization of the Japanese fleet, by type, division, and fleet, because this was the most convenient arrangement for the translators who used the material. Traffic analysts were constantly discovering changes in, or revising their estimates of, Japanese fleet organization. Each week we drew up and duplicated, for everyone's use, a corrected estimate of that organization, noting as we did so any recent information on where the ships or units were. Thus, we became involved in the Japanese "naval order of battle" before we ever heard the phrase or knew what it meant. Each morning we clipped together copies of the previous day's acquisitions to make up the day's "book," copies of which went to the translators and to the traffic analysts. When Layton heard of these compilations, he asked for copies to help him make his own estimates.

Japanese Imperial General Headquarters neglected to send FRUPac a copy of its Navy Order Number 18, directing Yamamoto to occupy Midway and key points in the western Aleutians, but shortly after its issuance on 5 May references to Attu, Kiska, and Dutch Harbor began to appear in messages. A number of Japanese submarines had been sighted off British Columbia and the coast of Oregon. From the beginning, Combat Intelligence and CinCPac Intelligence concurred in the premise that AF was Midway. Op-20-G in Washington now pointed out that the A in AF was similar to the P in PP, designating Palau, and the initial R common to the designators for places in the vicinity of Rabaul, so the A might refer to the Aleutians. On 21 May CinCPac formed the Northern Force, with five cruisers and ten destroyers, under command of Admiral Robert A. Theobald, to defend the Aleutians.

Nimitz continued to assemble all other available forces to defend Midway, but the identification of AF was an item on which he could not afford to be wrong. All the evidence that had been adduced was consistent with Midway as AF. The original identification had been one of Finnegan's hunches, and the challenge spurred him to frantic research, burrowing through the stacks of paper he had accumulated on his desk.

Soon after the Japanese captured Wake they set up a radio intelligence station there. Nearly every day that station originated a message to Tokyo summarizing the information Japanese radio intelligence had gained from monitoring U.S. naval radio traffic and news broadcasts from radio stations in Hawaii and on the West Coast. Finnegan learned to spot these messages as soon as they came in. One such message reported that intercepted naval radio traffic indicated that long-range air searches were being conducted from AF daily, and that AF was an active submarine base frequently communicating with submarines. This message tended to confirm Midway as AF but it was not altogether inconsistent with Dutch Harbor, nor did it rule out Oahu.

On 20 May Yamamoto issued an operation order detailing the complete Japanese order of battle for the assault on AF and the Aleutians. This long message was intercepted in its entirety and was immediately identified as what it was. Five days later, Rochefort personally delivered Yamamoto's operation order, nearly 90 per cent decrypted, to Admiral Nimitz. The Kido Butai, with four carriers supported by two fast battleships, two heavy cruisers, and three destroyer divisions, was directed to obliterate the air defenses of AF and bomb the shore installations. After that, the AF Occupation Force would reduce the beach defenses and land the assault forces. Two light carriers, escorted by several cruisers and destroyers, were directed to raid Dutch Harbor by air and then support the occupation of Attu and Kiska. The air attack on Dutch Harbor was scheduled to take place before the first attack on AF, and thus divert American defenders from AF.

This ruled out the Aleutians as AF. Both Rochefort and Layton drew other inferences from this message to confirm their conclusion that Midway was AF. Admiral Ernest J. King, Commander in Chief, U.S. Fleet (CominCh), however, with the same information passed on to him by Op-20-G, was apprehensive that AF might be Oahu or even some objective on the west coast of the United States.

Rarely has a fleet commander been confronted with a dilemma such as then faced Admiral Nimitz. His intelligence organization convinced him that the Japanese intended to capture Midway. According to sacrosanct Naval War College doctrine, a battle plan should be based not upon the enemy's assumed intentions, but upon his capabilities, and must guard against the most dangerous course of action open to him. If Nimitz deployed his carriers at Midway, the wily Yamamoto might slip around the end to again blast Pearl Harbor. King's caveat and War College doctrine would then place the cross squarely on Nimitz's shoulders, and he had his predecessor's example to forewarn him that he would be the first to be crucified.

It was impossible to cover all the bases. All available American forces concentrated at Midway were less than adequate to defend it. To hold Midway and risk the unexpected was the only hope for victory. Nimitz, the resolute man with the white hair and the very blue eyes, never faltered. Early in May he flew out to Midway to confer with Commander Cyril T. Simard, U.S. Navy, the island commander, and Lieutenant Colonel Harold D. Shannon, commanding the Marines, and assure himself that everything possible was being done to help them defend the island. On 20 May he let Simard in on the secret that Japanese plans to take the atoll were known. Additional patrol planes and Marine Corps fighters were sent to

Midway. Patrol craft were stationed along the route as aircraft-rescue ships, and two seaplane tenders were stationed at French Frigate Shoal. The Marines were reinforced, and dug in for battle. Every available submarine was pulled back to Hawaii to be refueled and restationed for the Midway battle. Nimitz persuaded General Delos C. Emmons, Hawaii's commanding general, to reduce Oahu's defenses and send to Midway eighteen of his B-17s, as many as that small atoll could accommodate.

Nimitz was committed to fight for Midway before FRUPac found new evidence to confirm the identity of AF, but perhaps that confirmation did some good. Finnegan never gave up his frantic research, and slept very little in the month of May. One morning he, Dyer, and I chanced to be at Rochefort's desk when the subject came up again. I had never been to Midway, but at the University of Hawaii I was in charge of the Materials Testing Laboratory and participated in an investigation of the effect of using coral and salt water in mixing concrete for construction on Midway, so I was familiar with some of Midway's problems. I suggested to Rochefort that fresh-water supply was a constant problem at Midway, and a breakdown of its new fresh-water distilling plant would be a serious matter. The Japanese held Wake and many other fresh-water-starved atolls in the Pacific, so they would be sensitive to that problem. Since there was a cable connecting Oahu and Midway, communications could be carried on in strict secrecy without committing anything to the air waves. Finnegan grinned and remarked that if the Japanese discovered that Midway was short of fresh water, the Wake radio intelligence unit would surely report it to Tokyo. Rochefort looked at him thoughtfully and said "That's *all right*, Joe." From Rochefort, that was high praise.

That was the last I heard of the matter until after the war. In March 1949, J. Bryan published in *The Saturday Evening Post* an article entitled "Never a Battle Like Midway," which disclosed that AF had been identified as Midway through the Japanese reporting the interception of a radio message about a distilling-plant breakdown. I wrote to Rochefort asking him if he knew where the story came from. So far as I knew, the idea had never gone beyond a private discussion in the basement.

Rochefort replied that Bryan had his facts straight, although Layton and Nimitz had accepted the identification of AF long before the incident. Some time after our discussion, Rochefort talked it over with Admiral Bloch who, as Commander, Fourteenth Naval District, was also Commander, Hawaiian Sea Frontier. With Nimitz's approval, they concocted a scheme to send a coded message by cable to Simard at Midway directing him to send to Commander, Hawaiian Sea Frontier, a plain-language radio message that the distilling plant had broken down and Midway was in danger of a fresh-water shortage. Bloch replied, also in a plain-language radio message, that a bargeload of water would be sent immediately. This exchange of messages was kept secret.

The Japanese took the bait like hungry barracuda. The next day, Wake radio intelligence reported that AF was short of fresh water because of a distilling-plant breakdown. Finnegan decrypted this message and Layton passed it to Nimitz a few hours after Wake had transmitted it. That ended the uncertainty about the identification of AF, but some people were slow to get the word. General Henry H. Arnold, Commanding General, U.S. Army Air Forces, left Washington for a West Coast inspection trip while Washington still considered an objective on the West Coast as a possibility for AF. In accordance with the War College's doctrine of guarding against the most dangerous course of action open to the enemy, Arnold retained on West Coast airfields hundreds of planes that might have been useful defending the Aleutians.

Finnegan continued to milk the Wake radio intelligence reports for information. The Japanese geographic grid remained unsolved, which left us floundering for exact positions whenever the Japanese used the grid. In one message, however, they divulged the bearing from Midway of the point at which the carriers planned to launch their first air strike. Unfortunately, the code group for that bearing was also unsolved. The only other occurrence of that code group that Holtwick's IBM machines could find was in a radio intelligence report from Wake Island. There were great gaps in the readable text in that message, but Finnegan believed it to be an intelligence report of an unidentified radio news broadcast from Honolulu. I soon discovered that none of the news broadcasters kept scripts of their broadcasts, but Finnegan would not let it rest there. Perhaps, if he could see the newspaper story on which the broadcast was based, he would get a clue. He wanted to see all the local papers.

That morning Ensign Donald M. "Mac" Showers, a bright-eyed, eager, and intense youngster, fresh from the mainland and under orders from Captain Mayfield, district intelligence officer, reported for temporary duty with me in the basement. Before he could take off his hat and look around to see into what strange place he had landed, I pointed him back to the District Intelligence Office in Honolulu with orders to get a complete set of all the newspapers published in Honolulu since 7 December. I knew there was no one in that office, except Captain Mayfield himself, who had any idea

Donald M. Showers
Courtesy: U.S. Navy

of what went on in our basement. Nearly anyone Showers approached for help would consider his mission the wildest boondoggle. "Don't you know there's a war on?" Some of the wartime issues of the Honolulu newspapers were already collectors' items. There was no time to equip him with a proper requisition. I simply told Showers not to come back until he had the papers. A more experienced officer than Showers would have asked for more instructions. He said "Aye aye, Sir," in the best tradition, and went on his way. The next day he came back, looking weary, bedraggled, and unshaven, but he had one bound volume of the *Honolulu Advertiser* and another of the *Honolulu Star-Bulletin*. His diligence earned him only the task of scanning them all in an attempt to find something that would satisfy Finnegan.

I cannot remember whether he found anything that was any help, but Finnegan discovered somehow that the planned launching point of the first air attack was northwest of Midway. That information I am very sure was useful. Finnegan jumped immediately from that problem to a premonition that something important was going to happen seven hundred miles due west of Midway. We arranged to have the submarine *Cuttlefish* cover that spot on her way toward Midway from her patrol area off Saipan. She had adventures of her own there, although she never found out what the

Japanese planned to have happen. As for Showers, he spent the entire war in Combat Intelligence and the following twenty years of his life in naval intelligence. Of all the officers and men working in the basement during the Battle of Midway, Showers was the only one eventually to reach the rank of rear admiral.

The newspaper incident cost me my credibility with the chief clerk of the Navy Yard. Two months later he accosted me, shaking in his hand a bill for "binding newspapers."

"Don't you know that regulations require all binding to be done by the Government Printing Office in Washington?"

I did. I did, indeed, but how could I tell him that there had seemed to be a good chance that the Japanese would solve that problem for us before the bill came in?

On 26 May Halsey's Task Force 16 returned to Pearl Harbor from the Coral Sea to refuel and prepare for battle. Halsey was ill and had to be hospitalized. Raymond A. Spruance succeeded to the command of Task Force 16. I met Spruance for the first time soon afterwards. Slonim, who had been Halsey's radio intelligence officer in the *Enterprise*, continued with Spruance. While the *Enterprise* was in port, Slonim spent most of his time in the basement, catching up on things that had happened while he was at sea. My files were useful to him. One afternoon I took to him aboard ship a copy of the latest Japanese fleet organization and some late call identifications. He introduced me to his new boss.

Spruance had a reputation for being cold and reticent, but I did not find him so. He sometimes asked me very probing questions and listened patiently while I tried to frame intelligent answers. I remember a formal reception for a British admiral much later, when Spruance was chief of staff for Nimitz. I had been busy up to the last moment, changed hurriedly into white dress uniform, and arrived at the reception just under the wire. I passed down the reception line, waved along by the aides, until I encountered Spruance, the first admiral in the line. He reached over and buttoned the unbuttoned top button of my blouse, gave it a little straightening pat, and smiled. A cold and reticent admiral would not have done that. Nimitz would have, and made some inquiry about Mrs. Holmes. Hart would have remarked, with a gleam of amusement in his eyes, that the Navy's standard of decorum was slipping when an officer could appear half-dressed at a formal reception. King, who never excused a fault, would have glared his disapproval until he reduced me to crimson confusion.

———

The *Yorktown*, limping along with her below-decks shattered by the bombs she had taken in the Battle of the Coral Sea, her crew secure in the knowledge that they had acquitted themselves well in battle and were bound for three months in a West Coast navy yard, arrived at Pearl Harbor a day and a half behind Task Force 16. As soon as she was within flight range, the repair superintendent and the master shipfitter, with a team of navy yard planners and estimators, flew south to meet her. As she rounded Hospital Point at 1430 on 28 May the big Ten Ten dry dock was ready to receive her. Long before she settled on the keel blocks she swarmed with workmen from the Navy Yard.

I went down to the dry dock that night to see her under the floodlights that turned night into day in blacked-out Hawaii. Every welding machine on Oahu had been marshalled at the dock. There was a story that to supply enough power for the welding machines, the Hawaiian Electric Company had to pull the switch on sections of the residential area of Honolulu in turn. After the war I tried, without success, to verify that story. Lucille Anderson always claimed credit for an unburnt offering to victory at Midway. She had saved a half-dozen rationed eggs to make a cake. Without warning, although her husband was a vice-president of Hawaiian Electric, the power went off when her cake was in the oven. I could well have believed it, as I watched the *Yorktown* blazing from bow to stern with welding arcs. In two days and nights the Navy Yard made repairs that normally required two months and the *Yorktown* was fit for battle again. The *Shokaku*, also damaged by bombs at the Battle of the Coral Sea, was out of action for two months.

Time was running out, and just how long it had to run was a question of vital importance. Estimates, based on plot and assumed speed of advance, varied all the way from the first to the tenth of June. In the undecrypted 10 per cent of the Japanese operation order lay the answer, concealed by the unsolved internal time-date cipher. Only three other occurrences of this cipher could be found, very thin fare to sustain a struggle to break it.

One evening, near the end of a long, twelve-hour shift, Finnegan enlisted Ham Wright's aid in an all-out attack on the time-date cipher. They worked all night and on into the next day, drawing Dyer and Rochefort into the blitz. Admiral Nimitz sent for Rochefort the next morning. Rochefort delayed responding until the cipher had been worked out. Finally, Wright announced that 4 June was the date set for the attack on Midway, and 3 June was the date for the air strike on Dutch Harbor. Rochefort immediately challenged Ham's conclusions. When he was satisfied that Wright had the best answers, he shucked his old red smoking jacket and carpet slippers, changed into a fresh khaki uniform, and reported to Admiral Nimitz.

The rest of us could only stand and wait. I went topside to the fresh air and sunshine of the Administration Building's lanai. I had met William A. New there the day before. He was commanding officer of the *Pike*, and an old friend of my submarine days. The *Pike* was in Manila when the war started. With the other submarines of the Asiatic Fleet, she had been beaten back step by step, first to Surabaya and finally to Fremantle, in the southwest corner of Australia, trying to defend against each successive Japanese landing with torpedoes that failed to function. Ordered to bring his decrepit submarine with her war-weary crew back to the West Coast for repair and refit, Billy New had worked his way across thousands of miles where only the flag of Japan was flying, across the Celebes Sea, the Philippine Sea, and the western Pacific, to Hawaii. There he was sent once more into the breach. With three other submarines, the *Pike* was ordered to take station patrol three hundred miles north of Oahu, to guard against a surprise carrier raid on Pearl Harbor. To New it was an old story, and always the Japanese had been victorious: it would be better to conserve our resources for the defense of California. Only a desk-bound officer who had not borne the brunt of battle could be optimistic enough to believe that this time it would be different.

On the lanai I met another old friend and shipmate who had been in the *Yorktown* through all her tribulations. He was apprehensive about her hurried repairs and, like every other officer and man in her, disappointed that she was not going back to the West Coast. I tried to tell him that the decisive battle of the war was coming, and that the *Yorktown* might get there in time to decide its outcome. I could not reveal the source of my information and it was impossible to convey to him my feeling of urgency.

Just then Dyer came up out of the basement, on his way home at last, after the successful conclusion of the time-date cipher blitz. Under his arm was his old lunch box. His uniform looked as though he had slept in it for three days. He had. He was unshaven and his hair looked as though it had not been cut for a month. It had not. His eyes were bloodshot from lack of sleep, and his gait betrayed how close he was to utter exhaustion. With a seaman's contempt for a landlubber, my carrier friend remarked, "Now there goes a bird who should be sent to sea to get straightened out."

For an instant my blood pressure soared to the bursting point and I nearly blurted out the truth. Dyer was one of the kingpins of the little band of officers whose genius and devotion to duty, over many years, had given us an opportunity to win a victory at last. If he wasted his time on spit, polish, and punctilio, the war would be much longer and cost many more lives. Fortunately, I regained control of myself in time and mumbled something like, "Oh, he's all right," feeling like Peter when he betrayed the Lord. Dyer would have been the first to condemn me if I had broken the secrecy that we all prized much more than any credit or the hope of reward.

Spruance sortied from Pearl with the *Enterprise* and *Hornet*, six cruisers, and ten destroyers, on 28 May. Task Force 17, Frank Jack Fletcher, in the *Yorktown*, with two cruisers, and six destroyers, followed on 30 May. Good fortune was with them. The Japanese had planned to reconnoiter Pearl Harbor with seaplanes refueled by submarines at French Frigate Shoal. This operation was thwarted by the presence at the rendezvous of two American seaplane tenders, already anchored and tending planes. Lines of Japanese scout submarines between Pearl Harbor and Midway were late arriving on station. The American carriers joined forces northeast of Midway on 2 June without having been sighted by the Japanese.

On 1 June the Japanese changed their five-digit code. The main source of American information went out like a snuffed candle. We still had traffic intelligence and direction finders, and we could still read a few minor codes. We already knew the strength of the Kido Butai approaching Midway from the northwest, and the date and approximate position from which it would launch the first attack. We knew the strength of the AF Occupation Force and its supporting transports approaching Midway from the west. We did not know that Yamamoto in the Combined Fleet flagship, *Yamato*, with an armada of battleships, cruisers, destroyers, and the light aircraft carrier *Hosho*, was trailing the Kido Butai, a few hundred miles behind.

On 30 May the *Yamato*'s radio intelligence intercepted a long coded message originated by a U.S. submarine that was directly ahead of the AF Occupation Force. From this, the Japanese assumed that their transports had been sighted. The message was probably from the *Cuttlefish* reporting that she had sighted Japanese planes and had been attacked by bombers. Japanese radio intelligence noted greatly increased radio traffic coming out of Hawaii, a large percentage of which consisted of urgent priority messages, but the Naval General Staff still believed that the U.S. carriers were in the vicinity of the Solomon Islands. On 3 June, however, Tokyo reported that radio intelligence had located an American carrier force at sea in the vicinity of Midway. This message was received in the *Yamato*.

Long after the war, Kuroshima told me that he had advised Yamamoto not to break radio silence to pass that information on to Nagumo in the Kido Butai. Combined Fleet operation orders already required Nagumo to give first priority to U.S. carriers and to be ever alert for an opportunity to attack them. There should be no need to remind him. Furthermore, Nagumo was an addressee on the message from Tokyo and there was a good chance that his flagship, the carrier *Akagi*, had already received it. To open up the *Yamato*'s radio transmitter would reveal their position to U.S. direction finders. Nevertheless, Kuroshima was oppressed by a deep sense of guilt for having advised Yamamoto to maintain radio silence.

Right on the schedule established by Ham Wright's solution of the time-date cipher, the Japanese Northern Force hit Dutch Harbor with a damaging air raid early in the morning of 3 June. Admiral Theobald had been informed that an air attack on Dutch Harbor would be followed by landings at Kiska and Attu, but he believed that this intelligence was based on Japanese radio deception and that the Japanese really intended to seize Dutch Harbor. He therefore disposed his surface forces to cover that more dangerous capability of the enemy, leaving Kiska and Attu to be occupied by the Japanese without opposition.

A patrol plane seven hundred miles west of Midway sighted the AF Occupation Force later in the morning of 3 June. B-17s from Midway bombed the force in the afternoon but caused no damage. Four torpedo planes attacked a tanker that night and one of them scored a hit, which only slowed the Japanese ship temporarily. The next morning the Kido Butai was discovered two hundred miles northwest of Midway. Strikes were exchanged between the Japanese carriers and Midway-based planes. The Japanese air attack did not knock out the shore defenses, but it destroyed Midway's air strength, except for the B-17s and the patrol planes. Only six Japanese planes were lost in this attack. Shore-based planes attacking the carriers got no hits and caused no damage to the Kido Butai.

Next, torpedo planes from the U.S. carriers found and attacked the Kido Butai. They were annihilated by the Japanese defenders and scored no hits. Before the defending Japanese fighters could recover from slaughtering the torpedo planes, however, dive-bombers from all three American carriers were over the Kido Butai. In three minutes, the carriers *Akagi*, *Kaga*, and *Soryu* were in flames and doomed. The *Hiryu* escaped to launch two attacks, which torpedoed and disabled the *Yorktown*. The *Hiryu* survived until five o'clock that afternoon, when it too was disabled by dive-bombers, and sank the next morning. Japan was at the pinnacle of her power in that moment just before the dive-bombers struck the Kido Butai. Much hard fighting remained but, from that instant, the power of Japan declined. The Kido Butai no longer dominated the Pacific Ocean.

With the *Hornet* and *Enterprise*, Spruance controlled the air and the sea in the vicinity of Midway in the daytime, but the Japanese were much stronger than Task Force 16 in gun power. An encounter at night or in low visibility might yet reverse the victory. Calmly analyzing the situation, Spruance refused to be lured into a precipitate pursuit of the fleeing remnant of the Kido Butai. He maneuvered carefully to avoid all chance of a night encounter. On the morning of 5 June, search planes from Midway discovered two Japanese cruisers, the *Mogami* and *Mikuma*, that had been damaged in a collision while maneuvering to evade the submarine *Tambor*. Planes from Midway attacked, and the *Mikuma* was disabled by a Marine plane diving into its after turret. On 6 June dive-bombers from Task Force 16 sank the *Mikuma* and severely damaged the *Mogami*. The crippled *Yorktown* and her attendant destroyer, the *Hammann*, were torpedoed by *I-168* on 6 June. The *Hammann* sank immediately, and the *Yorktown* went down the next day.

After the code change on 1 June it was impossible for FRUPac to follow the Japanese actions. Copies of dispatches received from our own forces came to FRUPac, but their contents were meager and often conflicting. Some information was picked up by an occasional message from Japanese forces in the Marshalls in a code we still could read, but for the rest we were back to educated guesses based on traffic intelligence. Finnegan went around muttering "The big boy is out there," meaning that Yamamoto, with most of the Japanese Combined Fleet, was in the central Pacific hunting for Spruance. Finnegan was right, but he had nothing tangible to go on. Information to confirm his hunch was not available until much later.

Many strategists, amateur and professional alike, have criticized Spruance for not driving to the westward on the night of 4 June to cut off the surface forces of the defeated Kido Butai. Had he done so, he would have probably encountered the concentrated surface force of the Kido Butai and the AF Occupation Force—four battleships, several cruisers, and some destroyers. When it was later learned that Yamamoto with seven more battleships, and additional cruisers and destroyers were also within supporting distance, the criticism was silenced. Fortunately, it was Spruance who was in command and not his critics. On 11 June, Task Force 17, the survivors of the *Yorktown* group, and Task Force 16, with the *Hornet* and *Enterprise*, entered Pearl Harbor, where we anxiously awaited them.

Time molds the shape of the ships man uses as the implements of war, but a name lives on. One hundred and thirty years before, when men waited for an *Enterprise* to make port after battle, they waited for a brig, a cloud of snowy sails above a scrubbed deck, and a hull oak-ribbed and sturdy; a thing of symmetry and beauty. The brig had gone, the sails had gone, and beauty, too, had gone from war, but the *Enterprise* remained. Strangely reincarnate as a steel envelope welded about the machinery that gave her life, she was a temple of pride and an object of affection, but not a thing of beauty. Beneath her ungainly flight deck and her asymmetric island, she had the clean, fine lines of a cruiser's hull, the suggestion of speed, the arrogance of power. Her haughty forefoot cleaved the oily harbor water, and proudly at the peak she flew the ensign she had worn in battle as gloriously as any ship has ever shown those colors.

CHAPTER 10

HONOLULU WAS TENSE with foreboding before the Battle of Midway. The Army went on full alert. Increasing numbers of search planes thundered overhead before dawn each morning. The Navy Yard blazed with lights at night despite hysterical exertions of the Civil Defense authorities to enforce stringent blackout regulations in town. In wartime Honolulu military and civilians were inextricably mixed. Rumors were bound to spread. Fortunately, censorship of mail, and cable, and radio, was rigid and effective. The newspapers cooperated to conceal foreknowledge of impending attack and to maintain an illusion that life in Honolulu was normal. All the big, black headlines were about the war in Europe, and local high-school graduations commanded front-page space. When Roosevelt High School seniors asked permission to leave their gas masks at their seats while they went up to receive their diplomas, it was denied. There was a feeling it could happen any time, but the newspapers dutifully refrained from comment. As did everyone else with dependents in Honolulu, I worried about what might happen to Izzy and Eric, alone in the house on Black Point, if the Japanese made any kind of diversionary attack on Oahu.

Then, on 4 June, the attack on Dutch Harbor was in the news. The military governor recommended evacuation of all women and children from downtown Honolulu as an air-raid precaution. The defenses of the Panama Canal were reported going on full alert. The First Fighter Command, on the West Coast, ordered silence for all coastal radio stations between Canada and Mexico. Next day, headlines screamed:

ENEMY BATTLESHIPS, CARRIERS DAMAGED BY MIDWAY FORCES

That evening, the *Honolulu Advertiser* announced that it "was swamped when the word got abroad of the sweeping victory at

Midway and there was unanimous expression of joy when the news was confirmed."

In our basement it did not make much difference. We knew the Japanese had been decisively defeated, but there was no great moment of exhilaration. Perhaps it was exhaustion, like that of a distance runner collapsing over the tape at the end of a long, hard race, but cryptanalysis was always a manic-depressive business. When we were reading the enemy's current secret messages, everyone was spurred to frantic effort. When darkness suddenly descended, everyone was plunged into correspondingly deep gloom. Each man feared in his bones that we would never again succeed in the long and difficult task of breaking a new code.

Work continued at a dogged pace. Everyone was working about eight hours in every twenty-four. Finnegan disappeared for a few days. I worried that he might have been in an automobile accident in the blackout. In a city that only recently had been considered rife with Japanese and German secret agents, he might have been the victim of some cloak-and-dagger intrigue. I suggested that we send out a search party for him. Rochefort retorted, "I know where Joe is. Relax." Sure enough, Finnegan was at his desk the next day, red-eyed and surly and more demanding than ever. We never held formal muster at FRUPac. Absenteeism was no problem, rather the reverse. There was always danger that some key man would work himself into a nervous breakdown just when he was needed most.

Cryptanalysts turned to the weary task of breaking the new code. Traffic analysts were busy identifying new calls and perfecting their call lists. Lieutenant Drew W. Kohler, a linguist and a Naval Reserve officer, joined the language section. His presence meant that more translator time could be spent on back traffic. Many of the messages in the old code that had been tossed aside to clear the way for urgent work on more promising ones could now be mined for valuable information. It was history, not operational intelligence, but much of it was of strategic importance.

With time no longer so pressing, we could afford to work on intelligence for intelligence officers. Back traffic and better call lists enabled us to improve our estimate of the Japanese naval order of battle. Tables of Japanese fleet organization were refined until we had an almost complete listing of all Japanese naval vessels, down to and including all destroyers and submarines, by name and type and organization. Sometimes we confused names, as when we read

Joseph Finnegan

"Ryukaku" for "Shoho." We dubbed a cruiser whose name we did not know "No Name," and carried it on our list under that name for so long that we pronounced it No-na-me, as though written in *kana*. Probably we frequently interchanged names of destroyers with others in the same division. These were technical errors that interfered little with the strategic usefulness of our order-of-battle information.

With this information, we were able to check back and determine when and where Japanese naval vessels disappeared, and often what had happened to them. This we needed, for future operations, to estimate the enemy's strength and the effectiveness of our own weapons; but it was a grim job. Experience during the attack on Pearl Harbor taught me to downgrade cynically all battle reports of damage to the enemy. In the excitement of battle even the coolest individual hears what he wants to hear and sees what he expects to see. It is a condition common to all men. But I was not prepared for the discouraging regularity with which Japanese ships that had been adjudged sunk turned up in subsequent operations.

Official communiqués and news accounts reported optimistically heavy losses in the Japanese Navy, but a running check of our information on the Japanese order of battle proved otherwise. At the end of April 1942, with the Japanese conquest of Southeast Asia and the

East Indies practically complete, we knew that the enemy had lost no battleships, no aircraft carriers, and no cruisers. The total of all combat ships lost by the Japanese Navy at that time was five destroyers and six submarines.

Japanese naval losses were insignificant until American and Japanese carriers met in battle. At the Battle of the Coral Sea, American losses exceeded Japanese, but communications intelligence was able to confirm immediately that one Japanese aircraft carrier and a destroyer had been sunk. After the Battle of Midway, it required some time to collate conflicting operational reports with communications intelligence and prisoner-of-war interrogation to reach the firm conclusion that four Japanese aircraft carriers and one heavy cruiser had been sent to the bottom by American carrier planes. I remember crossing them off the order-of-battle list. Mac Showers looked at the abbreviated list and remarked, "It makes you feel kind of sad, doesn't it?"

I knew then that I had a true intelligence officer working for me. Showers was more familiar with the names, characteristics, and organization of Japanese ships than he was with the ships of his own navy. The best intelligence officers come to identify more or less with the enemy's organization, and strive to think as the enemy does. Even for me, it was sobering to realize that in one afternoon Nagumo's Kido Butai had passed into history with Napoleon's Old Guard, Nelson's Band of Brothers, and Stonewall Jackson's Foot Cavalry, but I confess that I always felt personally vindictive toward every ship that participated in the attack on Pearl Harbor. I kept a carefully verified list of their names and ceremoniously crossed each name off the list with great satisfaction as we confirmed its owner's sinking.

Before the war we had expected that Asiatic submarine squadrons would take a heavy toll of the Japanese Navy. The immunity of Japanese naval vessels to submarine attack during the Philippine operation was demoralizing. Early in the reworking of back traffic we discovered evidence that at least part of the trouble was defective torpedoes. In December 1941 the *Seawolf* fired four torpedoes at a big Japanese seaplane carrier under conditions that should have ensured four hits. When the Japanese report of that action was decrypted, we learned that two of the *Seawolf*'s torpedoes ran harmlessly under the target, where torpedoes with magnetic exploders were intended to explode, and one made a direct hit. None exploded. Soon we had other Japanese reports of torpedoes running harmlessly under the target, or scoring direct hits without exploding, or exploding prematurely before reaching the target.

There were several reports from submarines of torpedoed Japanese cruisers but none of them checked out, and "prematures" may have accounted for some of these reports that turned out to be false. Our technique of checking individual ships by name did not work for vessels smaller than a destroyer, for marus (transports and freighters), or for some naval auxiliaries that did not appear in fleet organization tables. It did not reveal damage to ships remaining on the active list. We were able to identify by name only one Japanese destroyer and three submarines sunk by our submarines in the first six months of the war. There had been no opportunity to effect a submarine concentration for the Battle of the Coral Sea, but at Midway, timely information and the availability of submarines provided a perfect opportunity to use submarines decisively. I never knew who drew up the submarine plan for the Battle of Midway. At that time the Submarine Force was given very little latitude in planning its operations. It is most likely that the operation orders for the Submarine Force, Pacific, were dictated by CinCPac's War Plans Division. Whoever was responsible for the submarine disposition at the Battle of Midway did not do a good job. Only one submarine got a shot at a Japanese ship: the *Nautilus* scored one hit with a dud torpedo on an already disabled aircraft carrier.

Combat Intelligence received copies of the patrol reports of submarines operating out of Pearl Harbor. In these reports, submarine captains often blamed torpedo failures for their misses. We could rarely find direct evidence to confirm specific claims, but an accumulation of Japanese reports of our torpedo failures supported them. ComSubPac's staff torpedo officer, in his endorsements of patrol reports, ascribed the misses to commanding officers' errors rather than to torpedo failures. He did not seem ready to initiate a rigorous investigation of torpedo depth control and torpedo exploders.

Captain John Wilkes, who was my commanding officer when I was engineering officer of the *Barracuda*, was Commander, Submarines, Asiatic. Many incidents of torpedo failure were reported in his command and he did everything in his power, under difficult circumstances, to discover the causes. I had a chance to compare notes with him when he came through Honolulu. I went to my friend and classmate Captain Tom B. Hill, then fleet gunnery officer, and told him about Japanese reports of our torpedo failures. There was little he could do directly, but through CinCPac he began to put pressure on the Bureau of Ordnance for a thorough investigation of torpedoes.

Admiral Charles A. Lockwood, who relieved Wilkes as Commander, Submarines, Southwest Pacific, in February 1943, after the

Charles A. Lockwood
Courtesy: Pacific Submarine Museum

Asiatic Fleet was disbanded, continued to work vigorously on torpedo problems. When he reported tests demonstrating that torpedoes ran ten feet deeper than set, the Bureau of Ordnance was apathetic until Admiral King intervened and directed the bureau to recheck all the tactical data on torpedoes. About 1 August 1942, the bureau confirmed that the torpedoes did indeed run ten feet deeper than set, and practically admitted that the depth-control mechanism had been incompetently designed and inadequately tested by the Newport Naval Torpedo Station. Unfortunately, depth control was only one of a series of defects in the torpedo. The magnetic exploder designed to explode the torpedo under the bottom of the target was erratic. It failed if the torpedo ran too deep, and often exploded prematurely if the torpedo ran shallow. When the torpedo made a direct hit, the impact often caused the exploder to collapse before it functioned.

As might be expected, information wrested from enemy sources and observations made during the stress of battle were conflicting and incomplete. U.S. submarines had actually sunk four large naval auxiliaries and more than fifty marus in the first six months of war, in addition to the combat ships which we credited to them. Japanese naval planners were seriously concerned about what submarine warfare was doing to their logistics. On 25 June, the *Nautilus* torpedoed and sank the *Yamakaze* and took excellent periscope pictures of that Japanese destroyer disappearing beneath the waves. Mark 14 torpedoes and Mark 6 exploders functioned—sometimes—but the Submarine Force was greatly handicapped by poor torpedoes until late in 1943. Had American torpedoes been anywhere near as effective as Japanese torpedoes, the war would have been over much sooner at much less cost in blood and treasure.

In early 1940, long before we entered the war, German submarines had experienced a strangely parallel concatenation of torpedo defects—erratic depth control, magnetic exploders running harmlessly under the target or exploding prematurely, and failures of the contact exploders. Personnel of the German Torpedo Experiment Station were court-martialed, but for a time German submarines were severely crippled, and it was not until December 1942 that all defects were corrected. When I learned about the German experience I found it difficult to believe that the similarity was just coincidental. Between the two world wars, there was a marked tendency for our submarine designers to copy anything German. Had we somehow learned about German magnetic exploders and copied them blindly? In 1968, however, a correspondence with Henry W. Gottfried made me consider that there might be another explanation.

In the summer of 1941, Mr. Gottfried, a U.S. Naval Reserve officer, was sent to Newport Torpedo Station for a four-week training class in torpedoes. A week after his arrival he was closely questioned by representatives of the Office of Naval Intelligence. He heard that Naval Intelligence had already uncovered two sub-lieutenants of the German Navy enrolled in the torpedo class. They had enlisted in the U.S. Navy six months earlier at Great Lakes. Because of Mr. Gottfried's Germanic name, suspicion fell on him also. Could it be that German spies had copied the magnetic-exploder design from Newport? If they did, Great Britain owes a deep debt of gratitude to the incompetence of Newport Torpedo Station. German submarines came close to winning the Battle of the Atlantic. If they had not had the handicap of the faulty magnetic exploder, history might have been very different.

Combat Intelligence assisted, at least to some extent, in confirming defects of submarine torpedoes. It was completely ineffective in getting across to the U.S. Army Air Forces the fact that high-altitude bombing was small threat to Japanese naval vessels under way and able to maneuver. After six months of war, and after the Battle of Midway was over, our check showed that the Army Air Forces had not yet sunk a Japanese naval ship as large as a destroyer. Whether secrecy inhibited this information from reaching the high command of the Air Forces, or whether it just went in one ear and out the other, I will never know.

The *Honolulu Advertiser* of 8 June and also the *Honolulu Star-Bulletin* carried accounts of a speech by General Arnold, claiming that in the first six months of war the Air Forces had sunk "33 Japanese warships and 44 Japanese transports, freighters and tankers." Postwar examination of Japanese records revealed that the Army Air Forces sank only two small minesweepers and six marus during that period. *Time* magazine of 15 June 1942, reporting the Battle of Midway under "World Battle Fronts," said: "In the Japanese Fleet of battleships, cruisers, destroyers and submarines, the capital ship was the aircraft carrier. That fleet, built around sea-borne air power, had to retreat before U.S. air power in a still mightier form: the land-based airplane, now come into its own as a dominant weapon of naval warfare. . . . On a hugely swollen scale, the Battle of Midway was a repetition of the earlier rehearsal in the Coral Sea when Douglas MacArthur's bombers from Australia took the play from the Navy." This was the news that greeted the carrier pilots when they arrived at Pearl Harbor on 11 June, after sustaining grievous losses to win the Battle of Midway.

The Army Air Forces had indeed bombed Japanese ships in the Coral Sea and at Midway, and ships of the U.S. and Australian navies as well, but they made no hits on the ships of any navy in either of those two battles.

Admiral Nimitz issued a communiqué: "Through the skill and devotion of the armed forces of all branches in the Midway area, our citizens can now rejoice that a momentous victory is in the making." He quietly passed the word down the line that he would tolerate no criticism of the Army Air Forces. His was the statesmanly policy that cooperation would win the war soonest, and interservice bickering would only delay the victory. Since I was researching Japanese ship losses, I was among the first to get Nimitz's message. In almost daily communiqués, "Douglas MacArthur bombers" were reported to have sunk Japanese ships. If they had used intelligence sources to verify their claims, Southwest Pacific Air Forces might have changed their bombing tactics earlier and had a greater effect on the war.

Progress on the five-digit code that the Japanese had been using since 1 June 1942 was slow. It was August before any light began to dawn. That same month, the code, having been in effect only a little more than two months, was changed again. Right after the Battle of Midway, the *Chicago Tribune* published, under sensational headlines, a story that naval intelligence knew Japanese plans and details of their strength and dispositions before the battle. Any informed reader could only conclude that Japanese codes had been broken.

The connection between the *Tribune*'s story and the quick code change seemed obvious to the cryptanalysts. Painfully maintained security, essential to their success, had been flagrantly broken by someone and an irresponsible newspaper had valued sensational headlines higher than national strategic advantage. Postwar information has failed to disclose that the Japanese learned of the *Tribune*'s improbity. The code change in August appears to have been purely fortuitous, but the *Tribune* incident was another blow to the cryptanalysts' already-battered morale. There was nothing to be done but to start all over again at the beginning. The quick change of code effectively safeguarded the Japanese Navy's most important communications all during the summer and fall of 1942, while the U.S., Australian, and Japanese navies battled it out in the Solomon Islands.

I blamed the faulty air-conditioning in the basement for a flare-up of my arthritis. I would not go to the Navy Yard doctor for fear he would have me relieved from active duty. In a previous attack, while I was at the university, an orthopedist designed for me a contraption of steel rods and leather to hold my spine immobile and suppress muscle spasms. It was grotesque worn under a uniform, but in the basement it was all in the family and nobody cared what anybody wore. Then someone told me about Dr. Bowers, a Naval Reserve doctor on duty at the hospital, who was a specialist in arthritis. He discovered that I had an infection, for which he gave me a new antibiotic. In a few days I could discard my back brace and kick myself for not having gone to him sooner.

One morning, as Rochefort left for lunch at the yard officers' mess, he instructed me to write up an answer to the dispatch lying in the top drawer of his desk. It was a message from the chief of naval operations to the Fourteenth District requesting recommendations for awards to radio intelligence personnel for the Battle of Midway. I knew that Rochefort, like many of the old-timers, believed that no such awards should be given during the war because public recognition for radio intelligence would be public admission of success, and would jeopardize security. I am sure he did not expect to dispose of the problem by simply tossing it over to me as a routine administrative matter.

In my earlier appraisal I had judged radio intelligence specialists to be hard workers—devoted, even clever; some of them a little eccentric, but, as a group, lacking in the real genius essential to cope with the stupendous task they had undertaken. In encounters with the naval selection boards, many of them had accumulated scars that curtailed their professional careers. Events had demonstrated that both the naval selection boards and I had underestimated them. Years of difficult and exacting labor, intentionally conducted in obscurity, by the whole radio intelligence organization had now paid off, and between the attack on Pearl Harbor and the Battle of Midway, FRUPac had spearheaded one of the great naval intelligence successes of history. Well-earned commendations and awards could do much to rectify old injustices and strengthen the organization for the hard work ahead. When Rochefort came back from lunch I asked him for a little time to think about it.

The next morning I presented him with a typewritten memorandum, in which I recommended that any awards that were to be made should go to the veterans who had long years in radio intelligence. I listed them by name, remarking that Dyer's work and service had been outstanding. Not only had the old-timers, as individuals, contributed most by reason of their skill and experience, but without the groundwork they had laid we would have gotten nowhere. It was most important that all of them be continued in radio intelligence work for the duration of the war and not be distracted from it by more glamorous or more rewarding opportunities. A little generosity in awards right then would make it easier to accomplish this.

I told Rochefort I thought he ought to seek other opinions. He directed me to talk it over with Holtwick, who was one of the veterans, and with Tom Steele, who was the senior among the recent recruits. The three of us met several times. We were all agreed on the philosophy of rewarding the old-timers. I then proposed that we should start by recommending Rochefort for the Distinguished Service Medal. We agreed on this also, and drew up a message with that recommendation in reply to the request from the chief of naval operations. This I took to Admiral David W. Bagley, who had relieved Admiral Bloch as Commandant, Fourteenth Naval District, for approval and release of the message. Because of his limited acquaintance with the radio intelligence organization, Admiral Bagley was understandably hesitant about signing it. As I remember, he consulted Admiral Nimitz, who concurred in the recommendation. About a week later we received a message that CominCh had decided not to give any awards for radio intelligence work until after the war was over. I was very naive then, and believed that only security considerations had prevailed, but there was much more to it than that, as I learned later.

The First Marine Division landed on Guadalcanal and Tulagi in the Solomon Islands on 7 August 1942. Two days later, in a night surface attack, the Japanese sank one Australian and three American cruisers. I remember the dispatch from Commander, South Pacific, reporting this stunning defeat. Rochefort hid it in his desk for hours, too heartsick to show it to anybody. The Solomon Islands were under the jurisdiction of Commander, South Pacific, who had headquarters at Auckland, New Zealand. Like Commander, North Pacific, he was under Admiral Nimitz, Commander in Chief, Pacific Ocean Area. Of course, General MacArthur, Supreme Commander, Southwest Pacific Area, was independent of CinCPac. FRUPac passed all radio intelligence to CinCPac's fleet intelligence officer, who was responsible for exchanging intelligence with MacArthur and with keeping ComSoPac, ComNorPac, and seagoing task forces informed.

Until the Battle of Midway, communications intelligence completely dominated combat intelligence, but when the action shifted to the Solomons there was also a change in the nature of combat intelligence. The Japanese, being now on the defensive and having their forces concentrated in Rabaul, no longer needed to transmit plans by radio and this, together with the change in their code, made it impossible for radio intelligence to determine specific details of their dispositions and timing. We could still read some minor codes, including the local one used in the Marshalls and Carolines. The port director at Truk continued to use that code to report arrivals and departures of combat vessels. With this information and traffic analysis, it was frequently possible to detect a buildup of Japanese naval strength at Truk or Rabaul, which usually preceded a naval move against Guadalcanal. Although ComSoPac received radio intelligence from CinCPac, he had to rely primarily on reconnaissance, coast-watchers, and aerial photographs. For this he built up an intelligence organization at his headquarters.

When the Japanese occupied Kiska and Attu, ComSubPac sent

several large fleet submarines from Pearl Harbor to the Aleutians to reinforce the old S-boats already there. Charts, maps, and other information on the Aleutians were woefully lacking at Pearl Harbor. Some of the submarine commanders came to me for help. I knew that a surveying expedition had gone out from Pearl Harbor to the Aleutians a few years before. A search disclosed a collection of aerial mapping photographs marked "confidential" and tucked away in a safe. I had a number of these photostated and distributed to submarines going north. It was pitifully inadequate intelligence service. In August, when the Marine Corps' Second Raider Battalion, which was under Lieutenant Colonel Evans F. Carlson and was known as Carlson's Raiders, embarked in the submarines *Nautilus* and *Argonaut* for a raid on Makin Island, the task force commander, Commander J. M. Haines, came to me for information on the Gilbert Islands. I had practically nothing to give him. Yet the Aleutians had been American territory since the purchase of Alaska in 1867, and the Gilberts had been a British crown colony since 1892. Somewhere, there was information on the hydrography, topography, and physical oceanography of these islands. We needed an organization to collect such information (and much more) and make it available on demand.

Carlson's Raiders brought back a captured Japanese chart of Tarawa Atoll in the Gilberts; clear proof, we thought, of Japan's long-range preparations for conquest of the Gilberts. I was ready to rush it to the photostat for copies when it struck me as vaguely familiar. A translator soon told me why. Only the title and the written descriptions were in Japanese. Otherwise, it was an exact duplicate of the U.S. Hydrographic Office chart of Tarawa in our own portfolio. Rochefort reminded me that when the Tokyo earthquake of 1923 destroyed the plates of the Japanese Hydrographic Office's charts, the U.S. Hydrographic Office gave the Japanese duplicate plates of its charts of the Pacific. What we had captured was a perfectly legal Japanese edition of one of our own charts, complete with all the inaccuracies of the original surveys made in the mid-nineteenth century, without a jot of new information.

Radio intelligence had been highly successful in strategically defensive operations. For offensive operations additional intelligence services were required. The commandant of the U.S. Marine Corps, in a letter to Admiral King on 24 March 1942, suggested the formation of a joint intelligence center at Pearl Harbor. His plans called for 81 officers and 121 men of the Army, Navy, and Marine Corps, with a U.S. Navy commander or captain as officer-in-charge, to collect, collate, and disseminate intelligence to all forces operating in the central Pacific area. These plans were well in advance of anyone else's at that time. In July, Commandant, Fourteenth Naval District, was directed to establish the Intelligence Center, Pacific Ocean Area (ICPOA) as a shore establishment, primarily for service to the fleet. It was to be a naval operation, with liaison to the Army and Marine Corps, rather than a joint operation. The diagram below shows the new administrative establishment. The organization and flow of the intelligence handled in Pearl Harbor was so complex that it is impossible to present a satisfactory diagram. At the time, security demanded a certain blurring of the lines.

ComFourteen bucked the job of officer-in-charge of ICPOA to Rochefort, who was already overworked in Communications Intelligence. One morning, late in July, Rochefort dropped a mass of papers on my desk and told me to find some space to put the new organization. I was relieved to discover that only seventeen officers and twenty-nine men had been ordered to ICPOA by Washington, but even that number created problems.

FRUPac had expanded to fill all available space in the basement. The cryptanalysts were justly concerned that bringing a number of new people into the basement would erode the security essential

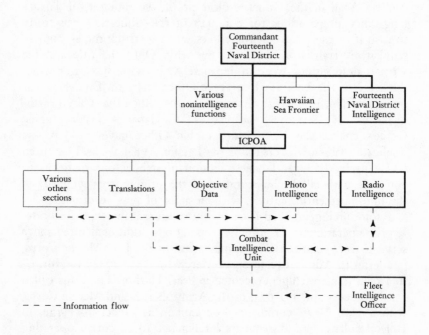

for their work. My section of the old Combat Intelligence-FRUPac organization became the Combat Intelligence Unit (later the Estimate Section) of ICPOA. With its charts, and files, the hectograph, and the scrambler telephone to the fleet intelligence officer, it was moved to the far end of the basement. This provided space for a few desks in the Combat Intelligence Unit for the earliest ICPOA arrivals and isolated them somewhat from the production areas of radio intelligence. Fortunately, these newcomers filled urgent needs in the Combat Intelligence Unit itself.

The first to report was Lieutenant Richard W. Emory, a tall, good-looking, Harvard-educated lawyer, whose keen legal mind enabled him to become an outstanding naval air intelligence officer. Shore-based air organizations were important elements of Japanese naval strength, and the names and radio call signs of air fleets and air squadrons appeared often in their naval communications. We had been able to keep general track of their geographic distribution, but we knew little about their strengths, their capacities, or their assigned tasks. It was fortunate that Emory joined us when he did. He sorted out the information into a Japanese naval air order of battle that added greatly to the value of our weekly estimates of the distribution of Japanese naval strength. He also gave us valuable liaison with the Naval Air Station on Ford Island.

When Major Thornton M. Hinkle, the Marine Corps liaison officer, joined ICPOA he had his work cut out for him. It took a Marine to unravel the order of battle of the Japanese Naval Special Landing Forces which, as already mentioned, were roughly the counterpart of the U.S. Marine Corps. Lieutenant George Leonard, who like Emory was an ex-lawyer, became ICPOA's Objective Data Section and started collecting and collating information on the islands of the central Pacific, through which we would have to fight our way.

In September 1942 Captain Roscoe H. Hillenkoetter, U.S. Navy, reported to ComFourteen for duty as officer-in-charge of ICPOA, relieving Rochefort of this extra-duty assignment. Hillenkoetter was an experienced intelligence officer. His experience in France presaged his early transfer to the Atlantic, but in the short time he was with ICPOA he was able to get that organization well started. On 25 September he moved it into the Navy Yard's new supply building.

For a time, ICPOA was largely a paper organization. The Photographic Reconnaissance and Interpretation Section Intelligence Center (PRISIC) was already functioning on Ford Island with some personnel ashore and some afloat in the carriers. It became a part of

Richard W. Emory

ICPOA but remained where it was and continued to function as before. FRUPac also became a nominal part of ICPOA, as the Radio Intelligence Section, but it remained in the basement with Rochefort in charge. It continued to make reports directly to CinCPac and to the radio intelligence network and to take direction from Op-20-G. My own Combat Intelligence Unit remained with Radio Intelligence in the basement, and through it passed most of the information from Radio Intelligence to CinCPac and ComSubPac. Emory and Hinkle continued to work with us, each contributing his special information to the weekly estimates. John Morris and Sidney J. Legendre, inseparable brothers, both lieutenants in the Naval Reserve, joined ICPOA to run its Administrative Section. They became justly famous for their ability to obtain any equipment, supplies, space allocations, or personnel that might be required. Their arrival ended most of my administrative responsibilities to ICPOA.

In the fall of 1942 very little information was coming into ICPOA, other than the highly classified intelligence originated by Radio Intelligence and passed to a very small number of individuals. There were few captured documents, few prisoners to interrogate, and very few aerial photographs of enemy-held territory to interpret. The Bishop Museum and the library of the University of Hawaii were sources of background information on the small is-

lands near the equator known as the "line islands." At this time also few demands were being made to ICPOA for information, but the organization was quietly preparing for the future.

Lieutenant Colonel Joseph J. Twitty became the Army liaison officer. He had been a Japanese-language student in Tokyo but, of more immediate importance to ICPOA, he was an experienced topographer and cartographer. Through him, the resources of the U.S. Army's 64th Topographic Company became available to ICPOA. Captain William B. Goggins, who had been severely wounded while executive officer of the cruiser *Marblehead* in the Java Sea, was ordered from Washington as executive officer of ICPOA and prospective relief for Captain Hillenkoetter.

In October Rochefort received temporary duty orders to the Office of Naval Operations in Washington. It would be an opportunity for him to gather up some of the loose ends of our relations with Op-20-G. We needed more trained cryptographers, more translators, more *kana* radio operators, more communication and radio direction-finding equipment, and Washington was our only source of supply. Hard work and the bad air-conditioning in which we all worked had Rochefort down physically. He had a persistent bronchial cough and had lost a lot of weight. At that time, the air trip to the mainland was an ordeal but he might get a few days' leave to spend with his family as he passed through California. Dyer would be in charge. I could continue doing routine paper work for the organization. Hillenkoetter would fight our battles with Com-Fourteen and the CinCPac staff while Rochefort was gone. Before he left, Rochefort turned over to me a package of personal papers and the keys to his desk. I somehow got the feeling that he anticipated being away longer than we expected, but I did not even suspect that I would not see him again until long after the war was over.

A couple of weeks after Rochefort's departure, Hillenkoetter came down into the basement with Captain Goggins, whom I then met for the first time, and who brought into the musty basement a breath of the sea and a sense of the reality of the war. After being wounded in the *Marblehead*, Goggins had made an almost miraculous escape from Java just before it fell. When Hillenkoetter introduced him as "your new boss," I thought he was referring to his own expected relief as officer-in-charge of ICPOA. It was not until he handed me the written orders from the Office of Naval Operations that I realized Captain Goggins was relieving Rochefort as officer-in-charge of the Radio Intelligence Section. I immediately took him to the back room and presented him to Dyer, who was as surprised as I had been.

Rochefort had been summarily relieved as officer-in-charge of Communications Intelligence in Hawaii. It was another blow to our morale. Communications Intelligence fell in a no-man's-land between the Communications Division and the Intelligence Division of the Navy Department, subject to the pressures, jealousies, and petty politics of both divisions. Had an Engineering-Mathematics Department in a university been involved, it would have been just as vulnerable to the same sort of infighting. The only probable explanation of what happened to Rochefort is that he became the victim of a Navy Department internal political coup. He wrote me a long letter, dated 16 November 1942, at Pasadena.

When Rochefort arrived in Washington, he learned that he was not going to return to Pearl Harbor. Informally, he was accused of "squabbling" with CinCPac staff, opposing the organization of ICPOA, and not keeping CominCh informed on intelligence matters. All these charges could have been easily disproved but, instead of being decorated or given a spot promotion to captain for the greatest intelligence achievement in the Navy's history, he was relieved of duty in radio intelligence, and ordered to sea. For more than a year his unsurpassed technical qualifications and his exceptional analytical ability were lost to radio intelligence at a time when the Navy needed them badly.

In the last paragraph of his letter to me, Rochefort sent "best regards to all" and "sincere regrets on leaving under such circumstances." He expressed his gratitude "to the entire crew for your unselfish and tireless work which resulted in the best damn Intelligence Organization the U.S. Navy or any other navy has ever seen." We were assured that Captain Goggins had nothing to do with the events in Washington, and Rochefort hoped we would "all be as loyal to Goggins as you have been to me."

I showed this letter to the old-timers in our section, many of whom had a better understanding than I did of what had happened. The last paragraph of Rochefort's letter facilitated Goggins's smooth take-over of an organization that had been badly shaken. Fortunately, Goggins was an able administrator and an expert in naval communications. He and I became close and enduring friends. I had no difficulty carrying out Rochefort's last instructions to me— to give Goggins my undivided loyalty. His knowledge of communications and his good relations with CinCPac staff were very important to FRUPac just when its own communication network had to be expanded and improved.

I regret that I did not take Rochefort's letter to Admiral Nimitz. Several years after the war, when I visited the admiral at his home in Berkeley, he told me he had heard rumors that there had been injustices in recognition of the excellent work that had been done by Radio Intelligence, and he asked me if I knew anything about it. At his request, I prepared a typewritten memorandum and sent it to him. He attached to my memorandum a long holographic letter to the Secretary of the Navy requesting that Rochefort be awarded the Distinguished Service Medal. Some time later, he sent me a carbon copy of his letter and a copy of the reply from the Assistant Secretary of the Navy. The time for consideration of World War II awards had expired and could not be reopened.

Admiral Nimitz was then near the end of a life of devoted and distinguished service to the Navy. I was sorry that the Navy had so perfunctorily turned away his request, but I was grateful to him for the demonstration of his lifetime loyalty to those who served him well. It was not the individual for whom the bell tolled but the Navy died a little.

CHAPTER 11

WORK ON THE FIVE-DIGIT CODE continued to receive highest priority. Practically all of the time of Dyer, Wright, Finnegan, Lasswell, and most of the cryptographers, was occupied with that code. Holtwick gave it first precedence in the machine room. Despite the code changes made by the Japanese, there were short periods when some of the five-digit messages could be read. I cannot remember, and did not always know, what messages were in what codes but, with few exceptions, messages of highest security classification and broadest distribution—particularly those concerned with important Japanese operation orders—were in the five-digit code.

Code changes were causing the Japanese considerable difficulty. Their forces were spread out over the western Pacific, and communications with some detachments were difficult and uncertain. Before the code could be changed, code books and enciphering tables had to be delivered to all holders. Occasionally, a major message would have to be encrypted in some minor code because an addressee did not hold a more secure one. Sometimes, to the cryptanalyst's delight, a message would be transmitted in a superseded code.

I remember one message that must have been decrypted early in July 1942, when we were reading very little, if any, current messages in the five-digit code. It might have come from back traffic, or it might have been in a minor code, or it might even have been encrypted in a superseded version of the five-digit code. However it came about, we were able to read all of a Japanese message planning a land attack on Port Moresby.

A Japanese Army force planned to land near Buna on 21 July 1942 and cross the Owen Stanley Range to attack Port Moresby from the rear. For anyone with an elementary knowledge of the jungles of New Guinea, this plan was unbelievable. Even more improbable, by 18 September 1942, the advanced echelon of this force had actually reached a point only thirty-two miles from Port

Alva B. Lasswell

Moresby before it was turned back by the Australians and annihilated in retreat. I do not know how the intelligence reached MacArthur, but Samuel E. Morison, the historian, reports that MacArthur's headquarters knew of Japanese plans to cross the Owen Stanley Mountains even before their forces landed near Buna. That information, which played an important part in the defense of Port Moresby, must have come from the decrypted message.

While the land attack was being turned back, a Japanese amphibious approach to Port Moresby, by way of Milne Bay, was being just as decisively defeated by the Australians and Americans. After these two failures, the Japanese turned their major attention to Guadalcanal. Their Army continued its desperate and tenacious defense of its Papuan beachheads, but the bulk of reinforcements was diverted to the Solomon Islands.

Christmas 1942 was not as grim in Honolulu as Christmas 1941 had been. The news from the Solomon Islands was far from reassuring, but there was no longer the threat of impending disaster that overwhelmed us the year before. In appreciation of the privilege of being allowed to stay on in Honolulu, Izzy decided to have as many of our homesick friends to Christmas dinner as she could possibly manage. That Christmas she managed about fifteen guests—all male.

Honolulu still observed a blackout, and dinner had to end before sunset. Military police and civil defense wardens roamed the streets looking for blackout and curfew violators. I had heard that some of my university friends had been investigated for singing nostalgic German Christmas carols. When Finnegan stood up and led the language officers in an emotional rendition of "Kaigun Kōshin Kyoku," the Japanese Navy song, in Japanese, his Irish tenor must have been heard to the uttermost limits of Black Point. I thought we might all end up in jail for the night.

Before the end of 1942 we began to receive some captured documents from the Solomon Islands. In the southwest Pacific, captured documents went to MacArthur's headquarters to be translated by the Allied Translator and Interpreter Section (ATIS). In the South Pacific, documents and prisoners of war were first sent to Commander, South Pacific, in Nouméa, and when they were no longer of value to him, the documents were sent to ICPOA at Pearl Harbor.

There were a few nuggets of pure gold among the documents captured at Guadalcanal. One such nugget was a chart of Palau. According to our most recent Hydrographic Office charts, Malakal Passage, to the eastward, was the main channel to the anchorage at Palau, and submarines picketing Palau had consistently patrolled off that passage but made no contacts. The captured chart revealed that big Japanese ships used Toagel Mlungui, or West Passage. When the *Seawolf* arrived off Palau, in November 1942, she was directed to watch Toagel Mlungui. The first day on station, she sighted an aircraft carrier coming out of that channel. She was unable to get in an attack, but the riddle had been solved, and from then on the patrol area off Palau produced many contacts.

ICPOA had no translation or interrogation section until the first contingent of twenty graduates of the Navy's language school arrived, in February 1943. These young reserve officers had received eleven months of intensive instruction in Japanese at the language school in Boulder, Colorado. None of the regular Navy Japanese-language officers at Pearl Harbor, who had spent three years in Tokyo studying the language, believed that after only eleven months of instruction anyone could have any useful knowledge of Japanese. The Japanese themselves considered that their difficult and enigmatic language was an effective safeguard for their written secrets, and security provisions for such materials were primitive. I was invariably frustrated by the Japanese language, and never acquired a knowledge of more than the *katakana* syllabary and a few special Chinese characters, or *kanji*. Had the U.S. Navy been dependent on people like me, Japanese secrets would have been safe; but it was not. It handpicked a number of collegiate scholars to study Japanese. In a relatively short time the success of that project was amazing.

No one had any experience in organizing a translation and interrogation center, and Lieutenant F. R. Biard, a FRUPac language officer, was put in charge of the first contingent of "Boulder Boys" to arrive at Pearl Harbor. The language training of these officers had been nonspecific, and their knowledge of ships and the sea and the Navy was rudimentary. Much of the material that would have to be translated in the future was bound to be highly specialized. In addition to a general knowledge of the language, Navy translators had to become familiar with Japanese place-names, Japanese ships' names, the Japanese naval order of battle, and with the *kanji* peculiar to naval technology. Available dictionaries were general and most of them were obsolete. The first tasks were to compile word-lists and gazetteers, and to invent methods and organize procedures for identifying, sorting, and classifying large quantities of documents. It was fortunate that documents to be translated and prisoners to be interrogated were few in number at this preparatory stage.

What captured documents fell into our hands before the translation section of ICPOA became functional were exploited by Layton or his assistant, Lieutenant Robert E. Hudson, in the Fleet Intelligence Office, or by the overworked translator-cryptanalysts in FRUPac. Layton gleaned the first real information on the size and strength of the Kido Butai from a fragment of a radio call list picked up from a Japanese plane that was shot down during the Pearl Harbor attack. Dr. Denzel Carr, one of my university friends, then a Naval Reserve lieutenant commander and one of the Navy's best linguists, was on duty with the District Intelligence Office in Honolulu. He could lend assistance in emergencies, but he was normally very busy with matters in his own office.

The two-man midget submarine sunk inside Pearl Harbor on 7 December was so badly battered that nothing of intelligence value could be recovered from it. However, another one grounded off Bellows Field and was captured intact. From it was recovered a chart of Pearl Harbor showing the annotated track of a submarine through the long entrance channel, around Ford Island, along Battleship Row, and back out the channel again.

This chart passed through many hands before it reached Rochefort's desk, a day or two after the attack. The FBI in Honolulu examined it and translated the notations. It was impossible to determine whether these notations were in past, present, or future tense. The FBI considered them to be positive evidence that a submarine or submarines had scouted the Pearl Harbor anchorage at least once before 7 December. The track and the notations on the chart reminded me of the safe courses and turning points my navigator in the *S-30* inked on the Pearl Harbor charts we used in entering and leaving port. That was what the Japanese submariner had done. He had prepared his charts in advance, and inked in his courses, turning points, and bearings to assist him in navigation when he might be otherwise distracted. Nevertheless, his submarine never came near the Pearl Harbor channel. Its gyrocompass failed and it went around Diamond Head rather than to the entrance buoys. This was reaffirmed much later when all the information on the Pearl Harbor attack was collated.

The chart was a photographic copy of one furnished to the dredging contractor working at improving the Pearl Harbor channel. Stamped "confidential" in big letters, it apparently had been copied or stolen from the contractor's office. The channel alignment on that chart was the one originally proposed. However, during the progress of the work, the planned alignment was changed. Had the submarine actually followed the track laid down on the chart, it would have grounded on the bank in Pearl Harbor channel, rather than on the reef off Bellows Field.

Ensign Kazuo Sakamaki, the commander of the Bellows Field submarine, was the first Japanese prisoner of the war and the only survivor of the ten men who manned the five midgets that took part in the Pearl Harbor attack. Although he later wrote a book about his experiences, he was deeply chagrined at finding himself a prisoner of war soon after his submarine stranded. He refused to answer any questions, and demanded only that he be shot. The next group of Japanese prisoners to be interrogated in the Hawaiian area were from the aircraft carrier *Hiryu*, sunk at the Battle of Midway. They were not quite so gung ho.

Most of the survivors of the *Hiryu* were taken off the ship by Japanese destroyers, but some thirty-five men of the engineer's force, including the chief engineer, were forgotten and left below decks. These abandoned survivors came up on deck just as their ship was going down. They were fortunate to swim off and find an empty life raft. Two weeks later they were rescued by a U.S. seaplane tender from Midway. The questioning of thirty-five prisoners overwhelmed interrogation resources. Lieutenant Robert E. Hudson was flown out to Midway to take charge of the prisoners who, having been left behind on a sinking ship, were reasonably cooperative with their rescuers. Hudson's interrogations disclosed many facts and details clarifying our knowledge of the Battle of Midway.

Several years after the war was over, a squadron of the Japanese Self-Defense Force visited Pearl Harbor, and the Commandant, Fourteenth Naval District, held a garden party in their honor. As Captain Robert E. Hudson, then the district intelligence officer, and I were standing together reminiscing about the war, a Japanese Self-Defense officer came over and greeted Hudson like a long-lost brother. The two officers were obviously glad to see each other in that peaceful setting. When the sputter of excited Japanese died down they reverted to English and I could understand. The Japanese officer was one of the *Hiryu*'s survivors. He lost most of his clothes in the *Hiryu* and, before interrogating him, Hudson outfitted him in work clothes from small stores. "Best pair of shoes I ever owned," the ex-prisoner told me. It was not necessary for a prisoner of war and his interrogator to be forever mortal enemies, even in that war of many atrocities.

The first documents to reach Pearl Harbor from Guadalcanal included a number of Japanese propaganda leaflets—"surrender" leaflets—in bad English, illustrated with crude pornographic pictures. I remember a "bride's book," in full color, with complete anatomical details, that must have been the personal possession of some love-sick Japanese bridegroom. Somebody swiped it off Rochefort's desk before I could evaluate it fully.

A steady stream of captured personal diaries began to appear in early 1943. These presented another problem for the harassed translation section because they were written in *sōsho*, the Japanese cursive script, in which the Boulder Boys had received little instruction. Japanese soldiers and sailors were addicted to keeping diaries. Some of them had real literary merit. Sometimes they provided intelligence of considerable value, and occasionally they were evidence of war atrocities. For years I kept, in my attic, photostatic copies of one diary describing the punishment meted out to two American prisoners who tried to escape. A Japanese surgeon cut their livers out to see how long they would survive. I was sometimes tempted to produce those diary pages when my academic friends were loud in the cry of "mea culpa" about the atom-bombing of Hiroshima.

One item picked up in the Solomons was of great interest to me.

It was a partially burned chart, picked up from a Japanese search plane that had been shot down. On it was drawn a series of lines that appeared to be part of the Japanese grid which, for so long, had resisted my efforts at solution. Several instances of the use of grid coordinates, referring to the Solomon Islands, had occurred in back radio traffic. With that chart and these grid coordinates, we worked out the principles upon which the grid was based. It was an ingenious system, by means of which a small area anywhere in the world could be secretly designated.

Even after the basic system had been discovered, I could not convert grid coordinates into longitude and latitude because I did not know the *kana* sequence used. Lasswell had taught me the *kana* syllabary in the A-Ka-Sa-Ta sequence, but I could not reshuffle the *kana* to be consistent with the known grid coordinates. Watching me sweat over the problem, he suggested that I try the sequence Japanese children used in learning the *kana* syllabary. It seemed that Japanese school kids learned it by reciting a little poem that went I-Ro-Ha-Ni. . . . Lasswell rearranged my *kana* cards in that sequence and the grid fell into place like a Marine platoon at the bugle's call. The Japanese grid system had one major fault. If it was recovered for any one area, the whole worldwide system was compromised. We never again had much trouble with the Japanese grid.

———

On 29 January 1943 the Japanese submarine *I-1* was sunk by two New Zealand corvettes, the *Kiwi* and *Moa*, close to shore near Guadalcanal. Most of the crew of the *I-1* escaped to shore, taking with them current code books but leaving behind call lists, old code books, and charts. Allied divers salvaged a treasure trove of valuable secret documents. The submarine's escaping crew landed behind American lines on Guadalcanal. For fear of disclosing their position in the jungle they buried the codes they had brought ashore, rather than burn them. When news of the loss of the *I-1* under such conditions reached Tokyo, there was consternation in the communications security section, and strenuous efforts were made to destroy or recover the lost code books. The *I-1* was carrying not only the current codes, but copies of reserve editions scheduled to go into effect before the submarine returned from its mission. More than 200,000 secret documents, widely distributed across the broad Pacific, had been compromised and had to be replaced. It was months before the mess was cleaned up, and many of the compromised items had to remain in service for some time.

By the time the red-covered, five-digit code book and the additive tables retrieved from the *I-1* reached FRUPac, the code had been changed, but to Dyer and Wright that code book was as precious as a moon rock to an astronomer. For many long hours they had puzzled and schemed to work out the meanings of those five-digit code groups. Now they could turn the pages and verify their recoveries, reliving old triumphs and rationalizing old mistakes. With superseded call lists Huckins, Williams, and Leigh could verify the Japanese fleet organization and check the names of new ships and stations. In a thin pamphlet, also red-covered, were all the two- and three-letter area designators. Sure enough, AFG was French Frigate Shoal and AF was Midway—or rather Otori Shima (Big Bird Island), the name the Japanese had given to Midway in expectation of its capture.

One man from the *I-1* was captured. He was sent to Pearl Harbor for interrogation. Biard was then head of the translation-interrogation section of ICPOA. After the formal interrogation had been completed, he and I had a session with the prisoner because I wanted to ask a few questions about torpedoes. The prisoner was wary at first, but when he realized he was talking to another submariner he loosened up. No submariner could be anything but sympathetic with the predicament of the *I-1* during its last battle and, as the prisoner's story unfolded, his gestures and facial expressions made it almost unnecessary for Biard to translate what he said. When I thought we had reached adequate rapport, I had Biard slip him the question I had come to ask. Did Japanese submarines have difficulty with torpedoes that exploded prematurely? "We don't, but you do," he answered with a smirk. I conceded that he had made his point, and it must have given him great satisfaction.

When the new year (1943) began, FRUPac was again reading many Japanese messages in the five-digit code. For most of these messages, the Combat Intelligence Unit of ICPOA served as a middleman between FRUPac and Fleet Intelligence, but when we had information that might enable a submarine to make contact with a Japanese aircraft carrier or a task force, I went directly to the chief of staff of ComSubPac and delivered it orally. I did not tell him how the information was obtained, but he must have guessed. We kept no records. If I had a position in latitude and longitude, I wrote the figures in ink on the palm of my hand, and scrubbed my hands after I had delivered the message. Results were disappointing. In 1942 the most important Japanese combat ship sunk by submarines was the heavy cruiser *Kako*, and Ultra information was not a factor in that sinking.

Very early in 1943 a series of developments, the most important of which was the breaking of the maru code, led to different arrangements for delivering intelligence to ComSubPac. American submarine operations had forced the Japanese to organize freighters, tankers, and transports (that is, marus) in convoys, which were formed at the points of departure and routed to their destinations by divergent tracks. Each convoy was assigned positions through which it was scheduled to pass at definite times. The escort commander, the convoy commander, the port director at the port of arrival, and other interested parties were informed by radio of the route and schedule of each convoy, in order that proper escort and air cover could be provided, or the convoy diverted, if necessary. Convoy routing messages were often transmitted in a special code we came to know as the "maru code."

The breaking of the maru code multiplied the business we had with the submarine force. About that time Commander Richard G. Voge became operations officer of ComSubPac. He was an old friend, and together we worked out a system of handling submarine intelligence. The semidetachment of the Combat Intelligence Unit of ICPOA from FRUPac, incidental to the organization of ICPOA, gave Voge and me a place where we could meet without intruding on the cryptographers, but where we could discuss Ultra information in security. Each morning, about nine o'clock, Voge came over to the Combat Intelligence Unit. With him he brought a copy of a thin-paper plotting chart of the western Pacific on which he had plotted his best estimate of the positions of all his submarines on patrol. While he read through the "book" of all the intercepted Japanese messages that had been decrypted in the previous twenty-four hours, we added to the submarine situation plot the tracks and routes of all known Japanese convoys at sea, and any other pertinent enemy information. Our daily conference became the basis of almost perfect coordination between operations and intelligence for ComSubPac.

Whenever Voge discovered a message that routed a convoy within reach of a patrolling submarine, we researched Combat Intelligence files for additional information, and referred back to the translator to verify critical details. The files of submarine situation plots were always available to translators and cryptanalysts. Work on messages for convoys out of reach of patrolling submarines could be deferred in order to concentrate on more urgent

Richard G. Voge
Courtesy: U.S. Naval Academy Alumni Association

messages. Voge kept us informed of any communications from submarines. This feedback helped both parties.

A Japanese maru, encountering hostile submarines, broadcast a standard emergency coded signal giving its position, and a single code group meaning "submarine sighted" or "torpedo attack" or "I am sinking" or some similar short-form message. Quick exchange of information between FRUPac and ComSubPac solved this simple system. Submarines on patrol were taciturn for fear that enemy direction finders would fix their positions. Often the earliest and best information Voge had on the whereabouts of his submarines came from Japanese transmission of these short signals. We put in a private direct telephone line between the Submarine Operations Office and the Combat Intelligence Unit, with old-fashioned, hand-crank magneto ringers, to avoid going through any switchboards. There was an officer on watch at both ends of this telephone line twenty-four hours each day. Whenever a submarine reported an attack on a convoy, we carried the news back to the translators and the cryptographers immediately, and we all felt personally involved in the submarine war.

The maru code was a four-digit one with some kind of superimposed cipher. I do not know who made the first break in it. It was probably a joint effort involving the whole communications intelligence network. Lieutenant Commander Henry M. Anthony, a U.S. Coast Guard officer and a skilled cryptanalyst who had been on duty with FRUPac since the war began, was an expert on merchant-ship communications. The maru code was his primary interest. Ordinarily, the messages came in, were identified in a routine scan, then decrypted and translated by whichever one of three language officers, Benedict, Roenigk, or Bromley, was on watch. At intervals the Japanese changed the cipher key, and occasionally this caused trouble that made the convoy messages unreadable for two or three days. When that happened, one of the expert cryptanalysts, Dyer, Wright, or Anthony, had to take a hand to get production back on the track again.

Some veteran cryptanalysts and others considered that giving Ultra information to submarines was not warranted. Each person admitted to the secret of Ultra eroded its security. In his testimony before the Army Pearl Harbor Board, General Marshall quoted security regulations requiring that no action be taken on Ultra information, regardless of any temporary advantage that might be gained. He stated that there had been cases when convoys in the Atlantic, routed into known German wolf packs, were not diverted because, if they had been, the Germans might deduce that their codes had been broken. He was apprehensive that Japanese ships in the Pacifiic were being sunk by our submarines through the use of Ultra information.

There was justification for this opinion during 1942 when the Ultra information passed to submarines mainly concerned Japanese aircraft carriers and came from the five-digit code. The Japanese might well suspect that submarine contacts with carriers were too frequent to be by chance. Aircraft carriers were priority, but very difficult, targets for submarines. Carrier task forces usually steamed at high speed. In the majority of contacts, a submarine's slow submerged speed relegated her to the frustration of watching carriers speed by outside torpedo range. Torpedo failures were an additional factor. There was a general belief that the proportion of torpedo failures in attacks on Japanese heavy warships was greater than it was in attacks on the slower and lighter-built marus. Whatever the causes of this difference, in the first two years of the war American submarines sank no aircraft carriers, and the Ultra information on carrier movements that we gave to submarines was all risk for no gain.

Or loss. Until the Battle of Midway, Japanese aircraft carriers dominated the war in the Pacific. For half a year after that battle, the balance of power between carrier forces determined the direction in which the war would move. The potential gain from a submarine sinking a Japanese aircraft carrier was, therefore, much greater than "a temporary advantage."

Breaking the maru code introduced new factors. The specific information contained in convoy-routing messages made it possible to direct submarines to mid-ocean contacts, eliminating long and frequently fruitless searches. Once in contact with a slow convoy on the open sea, a submarine had a wide choice of tactics and often could attack repeatedly. Moreover, by 1943 the Japanese were being forced to a defensive strategy. The sea, which had been a freeway for the Kido Butai's aggressive operations, was becoming a barrier separating the parts of Japan's island empire from each other. The convoy routes bound the separate components together. Over the sea the marus carried Japanese men and weapons to the fighting fronts and brought back essential raw materials from the fabulous Indies. Each maru that sank weakened the threads that bound the Japanese Empire together. The submarine war on the marus was a direct attack on Japan's life-support systems.

There were nights when nearly every American submarine on patrol in the central Pacific was working on the basis of information derived from cryptanalysis. The Japanese might surmise from the frequency and location of submarine attacks that the maru code had been compromised but, if they did, there was small chance it would cause them to suspect that the more sophisticated five-digit code had also been broken. Messages of strategic importance were transmitted in that code, and their decryption sometimes yielded information of inestimable value—as it did at Midway. Messages in the maru code concerned only the movements of marus. The limited risk taken in allowing submarines to use liberally information from the maru code was justified by the large potential gain. Intelligence, like money, may be secure when it is unused and locked up in a safe. It yields no dividends until it is invested.

CHAPTER 12

In April 1943 FRUPac and ICPOA moved from the Navy Yard, Pearl Harbor, to a two-story wooden building that had been built for them on the rim of Makalapa Crater, a short distance from CinCPac headquarters. FRUPac grew rapidly after the Battle of Midway. The machine room, in particular, was bursting at the seams and, since it had to be air-conditioned, a building designed for FRUPac had to be constructed. FRUPac had been administratively tied to ICPOA since the inception of the latter, whose preemption of prime space on the second floor of the new Fourteenth Naval District's supply building had never been popular with the supply officer. FRUPac's move to Makalapa was a golden opportunity for the Fourteenth Naval District to get ICPOA, too, out of the crowded Navy Yard. The new building was isolated on a dead-end road and surrounded by a high chain-link fence, with a Marine sentry always posted at the gate. Everybody was happy with the move.

The fortunes of ICPOA had waxed and waned during its nine-month existence. FRUPac and the Combat Intelligence Unit continued to supply most of the information concerning the enemy because, until the second half of 1943, operations in the central Pacific were defensive. No large-scale offensive operations were yet being planned in detail and ICPOA, therefore, had few assigned responsibilities. Seventeen of the officers originally ordered to ICPOA had drifted away to other and more urgent assignments by February 1943, when the first group of twenty language officers arrived. Hillenkoetter had been detached and the administration of ICPOA and FRUPac was again united, with Captain Goggins as officer in charge of both. ICPOA then consisted of the Objective Data Section, under Lieutenant George Leonard; the Language Section; and the Combat Intelligence Unit, which was nominally a part of ICPOA but functioned as a part of FRUPac. PRISIC, continuing as a semiautono-

William B. Goggins

mous part of ICPOA, had moved from Ford Island to the second floor of the Kodak Hawaii Building in Honolulu.

By the time the move was made to Makalapa, the Objective Data Section (which later became the Enemy Bases Section) was becoming an important depository for strategic information on the islands of the Pacific. Information collected from libraries, the Bishop Museum, ONI publications, submarine patrol reports, and a few aerial photographs, was collated and filed geographically by atolls and islands. This led to an early assignment for ICPOA, to which I at first objected.

During the Battle of Midway, CinCPac's War Plans Division discovered to their embarrassment that they had sent more B-17 bombers to Midway than that island could hold. A senior officer in War Plans insisted that it was the function of intelligence to keep his division informed of the facilities of our own bases as well as of those of the enemy. I believed that job belonged to the Operations Division, which should have better and more accessible sources of such information than any intelligence unit. The wee small voice of one very junior officer was lost, but the argument ended when the big transport *President Coolidge* hit a mine in one of our own defensive mine fields at Espiritu Santo and sank. The Objective Data Section was better organized to compile the necessary information, and they got the job. Lieutenant John Park Lee and two yeomen were assigned to what later became the Allied Bases Section, and later still became the Hydrographic Section. Lee organized the production and distribution of *Secret Sailing Directions* for Allied bases in the Pacific. I still think I was right. It was a job that the Operations Division should have done. The success of *Secret Sailing Directions* was due mainly to the exceptional ability of John Park Lee.

The Combat Intelligence Unit had grown along with FRUPac. Our plotting facilities, with their expanded collections of charts and maps, required more space. The manifold file of hectographed Japanese messages, a basic source of information for the Japanese naval order of battle, grew to occupy more space than had originally been allotted to the entire unit. Even the card file of place-names had grown to more than twenty thousand cards. Multiple names of many places, Japanese secret area designators, and our own secret code names used in operation orders, made that file an essential tool for cross reference.

About the time we moved to Makalapa, our group was expanded by the addition of Lieutenants John A. Harrison, Paul T. Yardley, and Elden S. Chapman. With Mac Showers, we now had enough lieutenants to stand a continuous watch and, in addition, to assign to each officer a separate project of his own. I no longer stood a night watch, but I spent seven days a week in Combat Intelligence. During the critical stages of an operation I slept in a bunk room across the hall. When I went home to sleep I was always on telephone call by the watch officer. After Admiral Lockwood became ComSubPac in February 1943, our relations with the submarines grew even closer. Combat Intelligence performed most of the intelligence services for Submarine Force, Pacific. I proudly wore the submarine insignia I had earned before the war, and Admiral Lockwood treated me as one of his own staff. Sometimes I thought he believed that producing intelligence for submarines was our only function—but it was not.

Each week the Combat Intelligence Unit turned out an estimate of the distribution of Japanese naval forces. It was mainly based on Japanese naval radio communications. We might have been misled by radio silence or radio deception but it was the best information we had. This estimate was classified "Top Secret Ultra." We delivered several copies to Captain Layton, who forwarded them, with his comments, to top commanders to be used as the basis for strategic planning. In March 1943 we estimated that the Japanese naval combat strength in the North Pacific was one heavy cruiser, the *Nachi*, one light cruiser, the *Tama*, and four destroyers.

In the Aleutians, we had a task force that consisted of the heavy cruiser *Salt Lake City*, the light cruiser *Richmond*, and four destroyers. This force, which was under the command of Admiral Charles H. McMorris, exactly balanced the estimated Japanese forces at Paramushiro, in the Kuriles. When FRUPac decrypted messages indicating that the Japanese were about to send a convoy from Paramushiro to Attu with reinforcements, McMorris with his task force put to sea to intercept it. About one hundred and eighty miles west of Attu, on the clear morning of 26 March, the lookouts of his scouting line sighted the convoy. Secure in the knowledge that his force was equal to any covering force the convoy might have, McMorris went after it. Then, over the horizon, loomed a Japanese force of four cruisers and four destroyers.

The Japanese had sent an additional heavy cruiser and a light cruiser to beef up their Northern Force, without the courtesy of a radio message to announce their intentions—or at least FRUPac never received its copy. McMorris, whose wisdom even in his Naval Academy days had earned him the nickname "Soc" (for Socrates), could not have been more surprised than I was, but his amazement was punctuated by 8-inch shells falling on his task force. In a long-range engagement that lasted more than three hours, against an enemy nearly double his strength, McMorris succeeded in blocking the reinforcement of Attu, while inflicting about as much damage on the Japanese as his own task force received. He then withdrew without losing a ship. Soc McMorris had been on CinCPac's staff for the first four months of the war, and after June 1943 he was CinCPac's chief of staff. I got to know him well and to enjoy a sense of security while he was chief of staff. He must have known where the estimates of Japanese strength in the Kuriles originated, but he never said anything to me about the Battle of the Komandorski Islands, and I certainly never brought up the subject.

In the South Pacific the Japanese were trying to stabilize the situation after the evacuation of Guadalcanal. Their first effort, to reinforce Lae, in northern Papua, by six thousand troops in a convoy of eight transports and eight destroyers, ended in the decisive Battle of the Bismarck Sea on 2 March 1943. Bombers of General George C. Kenney's Fifth Army Air Force sank all eight transports and four of the destroyers, ending forever Japanese attempts to supply Papua by surface ships.

Imperial headquarters then decided that Allied bases in Papua and the lower Solomons should be hit with massive air attacks, in order to give the Japanese time to prepare new defense lines in the upper Solomons and New Guinea. Admiral Yamamoto moved his headquarters to Rabaul to direct this operation. The elite carrier pilots and their planes operated with the Eleventh Air Fleet from shore bases at Rabaul and in the central Solomons. Some of the carriers were used to ferry planes from Japan to Truk, whence they were flown down to Rabaul.

From decryption of messages to the carriers, as well as from arrival and departure reports originated in a minor code by the port director of Truk, we knew about this traffic. Truk was closely picketed by submarines. On 8 April FRUPac decrypted a message scheduling the arrival of a task force, including three aircraft carriers, at Truk in the early morning of 10 April 1943. For some reason, probably to arrange for extra escorts to join up, this message specified the position of the task force for the evening before its arrival. Voge got off a message to John A. Scott, commanding the submarine *Tunny*, which was patrolling southwest of Truk.

Scott used all his information and his new SJ radar to fullest advantage and moved out to make a night contact on the surface. With consummate skill, he maneuvered the *Tunny* into perfect position between two columns of Japanese ships. In quick succession, he fired both bow and stern tubes, ten torpedoes, at two aircraft carriers at ranges between six hundred and eight hundred yards. Diving deep, to avoid escorts, Scott heard seven torpedo explosions at the proper intervals.

There was high elation in FRUPac when that news came in over the telephone from ComSubPac, but the rejoicing was short-lived. The next day, FRUPac picked up and decrypted a message from Truk's port director reporting the safe arrival of all three Japanese carriers. The damned torpedoes had "prematured."

The first strike of the big Japanese air blitz hit the Guadalcanal area on 7 April with more than 170 planes, the biggest air strike in the Pacific since Pearl Harbor. Yamamoto then turned his attention to Papua and hit Oro Bay, Port Moresby, and Milne Bay with massive air strikes. Japanese aviators claimed that in their one-week blitz they sank one cruiser, two destroyers, and twenty-five transports, and shot down 175 Allied planes. Yamamoto believed that the Battle of the Bismarck Sea had been avenged and any planned Allied offensive disrupted. Actual Allied losses were one destroyer, one corvette, one tanker, and two transports sunk, and about 25 planes shot down. Japanese plane losses were nearly double those of the Allies.

Overestimates of enemy losses are dangerous. They are apt to lead commanders into making unsound tactical decisions. Such estimates were not peculiar to the Japanese or to aviators. Submarine commanders, too, working under great stress and with limited opportunity to observe, frequently believed that they saw and heard things that did not happen. One of the most thankless, but necessary, tasks of intelligence units was the deflation of inflated battle reports. From the nature of aerial combat, aviators' reports generally were exaggerated greatly, but some organizations were worse than others. Communiqués from "MacArthur's Headquarters," based on claims made by the Fifth Army Air Force, frequently reported devastating raids on Rabaul. Fortunately, Japanese naval air bases had a routine system of reporting their air strength by radio, and they also promptly reported their battle losses to headquarters. These messages were readily identified, and Dick Emory became expert at interpreting and analyzing them. Often, before glowing reports of the bombing of Rabaul made the headlines, we knew that little impression had actually been made on the Japanese air strength. The Combat Intelligence Unit's weekly reports of the enemy's naval air order of battle were reasonably accurate. Yamamoto, however, had no comparable service.

———

Admiral Isoroku Yamamoto, with members of his staff, planned a visit to the advanced Japanese airfields in the upper Solomons for 18 April 1943. These plans led directly to his death. So many different accounts of this episode have been published, and so many of them are pure fiction, that I no longer have confidence in my memory of even my own minor involvement in the part communications intelligence played. Traffic analysis had soon discovered the move to Rabaul of the commander in chief of the Combined Fleet. There were never enough intercept facilities to copy more than a fraction of all Japanese naval communications, but the Rabaul traffic was being closely monitored. Several days before Yamamoto's departure from Rabaul there were indications of his special interest in the airfields around the southern end of Bougainville Island.

There were great holes of unreadable text in many messages. Despite this difficulty, Ham Wright recovered the code groups for a few area designators. These were identified as the names for satellite airfields near Buin, and Dick Emory found them on the chart. Then, on 13 April, Lasswell pulled out a message detailing the schedule for Yamamoto's inspection party. As I recall, it was a comparatively short message, but Lasswell had worked it out in every minute detail before he showed it to me. I read it to Layton over the secure telephone, and then, so that there could be no mistake about it, Lasswell and I walked over to CinCPac headquarters with a copy of the message. When we left Layton, he was on his way to confer with Admiral Nimitz. Both Lasswell and I were glad to have it out of our hands.

The decision about what action to take was difficult. Bougainville was at the extreme range of the best U.S. Army fighter planes on Guadalcanal. Successful interception required precise timing, careful planning, and a skillful and daring attack, with the odds in favor of failure. There were questions whether or not the elimination of Yamamoto would be in the best interest of the Allies. He had planned the attack on Pearl Harbor, but he had also planned the Battle of Midway. It was agreed by everyone, however, that Yamamoto was the outstanding Japanese naval officer and there was no one his equal to step into his shoes. His loss would be a tremendous blow to the morale of Japan. But last and not least, the cryptographers feared that an attempt to intercept Yamamoto's plane would tip off the Japanese that their communications were insecure.

Sixteen Army fighters took off from Guadalcanal on 18 April, made a flawless interception, and, in a terrific air battle, shot down the two bombers carrying Yamamoto and members of his staff. One American plane and its pilot were lost. Yamamoto was killed in the action. As we had expected, his loss was a tremendous blow to Japanese morale. The apprehensions of the cryptographers were amply justified, however, because security for handling Ultra information on Guadalcanal was woefully inadequate, and too many people learned about it.

It became an item of widespread interservice gossip that the dramatic interception of Yamamoto's plane had been contrived through broken Japanese codes. It was a minor miracle that the story did not break in American newspapers. Had Japanese intelligence been as omniscient as it was reputed to be before the war, the Japanese surely would have learned the truth, but their smug confidence in the security of their communications was unshakable. Eventually the U.S. Army developed a sound system for handling Ultra information, but until the war ended the U.S. Navy vacillated between dangerous exposure of Ultra and overrestrictive distribution of it.

Yamamoto was a gambler. Another turn of the cards might have brought up another Pearl Harbor—or another Midway. Admiral Mineichi Koga, who became commander in chief of the Combined Fleet, was a conservative, defensive strategist, which made him difficult to destroy, but he was never the equal of Yamamoto.

By the middle of 1943, assisted by Ultra, the submarines had doubled their 1942 rate of sinking marus, but aircraft carriers were still elusive and submarines were still plagued by torpedo defects. On 11 May 1943 the U.S. North Pacific Force landed the Army's 7th Infantry Division on Attu. Koga responded by departing from Truk for Tokyo on 16 May with a strong force of battleships and cruisers and the aircraft carrier *Hiyo*. It was his intention to join forces with carriers and cruisers at Yokosuka and overwhelm the U.S. forces in the Aleutians. He arrived at Tokyo on 22 May. Before his relief expedition could get under way, all Japanese resistance on Attu ended. On 10 June, Japanese carriers started to leave Yokosuka for maneuvers and for training pilots in the Inland Sea.

Combat Intelligence had missed the reinforcement of the Japanese Northern Force prior to the Battle of the Komandorskis but, in May and June, FRUPac had early and accurate information on Koga's movements. Lockwood alerted his submarines but, just outside Tokyo Bay, Koga, at high speed, slipped by the *Sawfish* and *Trigger*, beyond the range of their torpedoes. The *Trigger* and *Salmon* next had frustrating radar contact at long range with two of the carriers en route to the Inland Sea. On the night of 11 June, however, the *Trigger* was patrolling off Tokyo Bay when the aircraft carrier *Hiyo*, with two destroyer escorts, came zigzagging down the bay at 21 knots. This time, Roy S. Benson, in the *Trigger*, succeeded in maneuvering to within twelve hundred yards of the speeding carrier. He fired six torpedoes and heard four explosions, but three of them were "prematures," and only one functioned properly. That one nearly accounted for the *Hiyo*. She barely made it under tow to Yokosuka's dry dock.

The *Trigger* arrived at Pearl Harbor on 22 June, elated in the conviction that she was the first submarine to sink a Japanese aircraft carrier. FRUPac had already learned, however, about her malfunctioning torpedoes and had read the Japanese message reporting the *Hiyo's* arrival at Yokosuka Navy Yard. A few weeks before, Dudley W. "Mush" Morton in the *Wahoo* had arrived at Pearl Harbor from a patrol off the Kuriles. He had been assisted by several Ultra messages and the *Wahoo* had sunk three ships on that patrol. Morton, one of the best submarine skippers in the business, was hospitalized for a couple of weeks and I went up to the hospital to talk to him. He was irate about torpedo performance. He was positive, in colorful language, that the *Wahoo* would have sunk three more ships on that patrol, had his torpedo exploders not failed. The experiences of the *Wahoo*, *Trigger*, and *Tunny* convinced both Lockwood and Nimitz that the magnetic exploder was unreliable. On 24 June 1943 Nimitz issued an order to inactivate the magnetic exploder on torpedoes in all ships and planes under his command.

Torpedo experts were still unconvinced. Nimitz's decision to inactivate the magnetic exploders was immediately protested by the Bureau of Ordnance. Admiral Ralph W. Christie, Commander, Submarines, Southwest Pacific, decided to continue using the magnetic exploders in his submarines. It is possible that Nimitz and Lockwood were more sensitive to torpedo defects because of their close association with radio intelligence. They stuck by their decision to inactivate the magnetic exploders. The Combat Intelligence Unit watched closely, expecting an immediate climb in the number of ships sunk by submarines. It did not happen. The July and August sinkings were twenty-three and twenty-one, respectively, about the same rate as before. The reason was not long unrevealed. It was discovered that the contact exploder, which was designed to act on impact of the torpedo with the target, was also incompetently designed and inadequately tested. The torpedo shops at Pearl Harbor modified the exploder, which greatly improved its performance, although it still produced some duds. It was the end of September 1943 before submarines, departing from Pearl Harbor on war patrol, had reasonably dependable exploders. In November 1943, submarines sank forty-five marus.

On 28 July 1943 the Japanese withdrew all their forces from Kiska without being detected, but it was not until 15 August that a large force of American and Canadian troops stormed what turned out to be a vacated island. The Aleutians were then secure. In the South Pacific, Allied forces were moving up the Solomons, step by step, and in the southwest Pacific, MacArthur was preparing to advance along the north coast of New Guinea. The Central Pacific Force had been heavily reinforced in preparation for offensive operations in the Gilberts and Marshalls, scheduled for November 1943. Admiral Spruance was detached as chief of staff to Admiral Nimitz and on 5 August 1943 assumed command of the Central Pacific Force. On 20 August Admiral Richmond Kelly Turner was ordered to command the Fifth Amphibious Force and directed to plan and conduct landings in Micronesia. These events brought about great changes in ICPOA.

There are many islands in Micronesia and not much was known about them. Submarines had reconnoitered the Marshalls and adjacent islands. They had made periscope observations of many atolls and discovered naval activity and airfields at Kwajalein, Maloelap, Wotje, and Mili, but a periscope view of an island disclosed little

Ralph W. Christie
Courtesy: U.S. Naval Academy Alumni Association

about developments ashore. The early carrier raids had produced
a few photographs. The Seventh Army Air Force had made photo-
reconnaissance flights over the Gilbert Islands and Nauru, which
the Japanese had fortified and developed since taking them from
the British. Airfields had been constructed on Tarawa and Nauru,
and Makin had a seaplane base.

Enemy Bases Section of ICPOA had the task of assembling and
preparing information bulletins to assist CinCPac's War Plans Division in selecting objectives for the first offensive. The texts of early
bulletins were mimeographed. Ground pictures and periscope pictures were reproduced by PRISIC. In spite of the reconnaissance
flights, there were still comparatively few aerial photographs available. Enemy Bases Section was shorthanded, but fortunately PRISIC
had a temporary surplus of officers. Someone in the Navy Department had foreseen the need, and started a school for photographic
interpreters at Anacostia, D.C. Graduates of that school arrived at
PRISIC in Honolulu before there were many photographs to interpret, and were reassigned by PRISIC to the aircraft carriers and
patrol squadrons of the Pacific Fleet and to the North Pacific and
South Pacific forces. Nevertheless, in the summer of 1943, PRISIC
still had a surplus of people, some of whom were assigned to Enemy
Bases Section.

George Leonard, chief of Enemy Bases Section, made each of his analysts responsible for assembling all available information on a specific small area, and producing a preliminary bulletin. Candidates for the photo-interpreter school had been selected from geologists, foresters, architects, and others familiar with aerial photographs. They were intelligent, well-educated, adaptable young men, and they soon became familiar with the areas assigned to them, even though they had never visited them. As the War Plans Division narrowed its interest down to specific areas, the analyst concerned and his files were sometimes temporarily moved to CinCPac headquarters to work directly with the planners. This served very well.

The Joint Chiefs of Staff issued a directive for Operation Galvanic, dated 1 September 1943, for CinCPac to retake the Gilberts and Nauru from the Japanese. The choice of objectives for Galvanic had been dictated largely by the necessity for intensive and systematic photographic reconnaissance before an amphibious assault on a fortified beachhead could be conducted. The Marshall Islands were beyond the range of land-based aircraft, but from advanced bases at Funafuti, in the Ellice Islands, long-range planes could reconnoiter and photograph the Gilberts and Nauru.

On 7 September 1943 the intelligence section of Admiral Nimitz's staff was reorganized to cope with the increased work load. As explained earlier, although the acronym FRUPac has been used throughout this narrative, there was not actually any such organization until this time. What happened was that the Radio Intelligence Section was separated from ICPOA and transferred to the U.S. Pacific Fleet as the Fleet Radio Unit, Pacific (FRUPac). Captain Goggins remained with the unit as officer-in-charge. ICPOA was placed directly under the assistant chief of staff for intelligence (J-2), Joint Staff, Commander in Chief, Pacific Fleet, and Commander in Chief, Pacific Ocean Area (CinCPac-CinCPOA), and was renamed Joint Intelligence Center, Pacific Ocean Area (JICPOA). Joseph J. Twitty, now a brigadier general, was appointed J-2 and officer-in-charge of JICPOA. Captain Layton remained fleet intelligence officer. The Combat Intelligence Unit of ICPOA became the Estimate Section of JICPOA. I remained chief of the Estimate Section and became also deputy officer-in-charge of JICPOA and a member of the joint staff. I had been promoted to the rank of commander in June 1943.

Early in September I went over to PRISIC to get acquainted and learn something of the problems of a photo-interpreter. They were working a sixteen-hour day in two eight-hour shifts, not because of the volume of work, but because there were not enough desks and work space for more than half of them to be on duty at one time. They kept busy reworking old photographs of the Aleutians and the Solomons, but their morale was low because they felt left out of the current action. I told them that they would soon be up to their ears in urgent work. A group of four or five of PRISIC's young officers specialized in producing three-dimensional terrain models of objectives on various islands. They made a plaster-of-paris model of the island of Kiska, but it was so heavy it would have been difficult to take to sea. I knew that a bombardment of Wake Island was being planned. I let them in on the secret and asked them to prepare a terrain model of Wake. They turned out a beautiful piece of work, in full color, about three feet by four feet, on plywood. At that scale, a thick coat of paint exaggerated the maximum elevation of Wake's terrain, but the airfield, the buildings, and the new Japanese installations were conspicuous. I do not know whether the task force's gunnery officers found it useful, but it admirably served my purpose, which was to improve the morale of the model-builders, and that paid off handsomely.

As soon as primary objectives of Operation Galvanic had been designated, the model-makers began preparing terrain models of Nauru and the island of Betio, on Tarawa Atoll. Betio was easy. Like Wake, it had little elevation and there were good low-oblique pictures available so that the airfield, the buildings, and other installations could be identified and positioned properly. Nauru was different. There were fewer photographs and the only maps we had were small-scale. Nauru had an elevation of more than two hundred feet and the contour lines on the map were wide apart. Fortunately, the Fifth Amphibious Force arranged to bring to Honolulu a party of British officials who had lived in the Gilberts before the war. They arrived about the time the models were completed and were brought up to the Enemy Bases Section for consultation.

They viewed the model of Betio with nostalgia, pointed out the houses where they had lived, and deplored the Japanese slit trenches that zigzagged across the tennis courts. When I asked them about the reef and the height of the tides on the beach, they were vague and ill informed. I was exasperated until I recalled that I had lived eight years within a few hundred yards of Kahala Beach and knew less about the reef and the tides there than the Britishers knew about the beaches of Betio. I was relieved when I learned that the Fifth Amphibious Force had found an authority on tides in the Gilbert Islands who would answer just such questions.

The model of Nauru was different. Around it gathered the model-makers and a tall, dour Scotchman, who viewed their efforts with contempt and frankly stated that Nauru was not like that at all. He was the engineer of the phosphate works on Nauru and he knew the six square miles of that island like the palm of his hand. Moreover, he had completed a survey just before the Japanese landed and he had brought along with him a large-scale map, with close-contour intervals. Within an hour, the model-makers had scrapped their old model and were busy cutting out contours for a new one.

The planners had never been too happy with the selection of Nauru for amphibious assault, and they followed the construction of the new model closely. It was frightening. Nauru was built like a hard straw hat. Its flat brim, a few hundred yards wide and a few feet above sea level, was twelve miles in circumference. On it were the phosphate works and the settlement. The crown rose precipitously from the brim to a plateau, two hundred feet high. The plateau, where phosphate rock had been mined, was pocked with excavations and coral spikes, making an almost impenetrable terrain. On the brim, the Japanese had built an airfield, protected it with coastal batteries and antiaircraft guns, and dug in for an obstinate defense.

The paint had not yet dried on the model when Admiral Nimitz and the Fleet Marine officer came up to see it. They asked only a few questions. It was a model to speak for itself. Admiral Nimitz, with those penetrating blue eyes, looked straight at his companion and asked, "General, how would you take that island?" The general grimly answered, "A straight frontal assault is the only way." They both then walked silently away. A short time later, the chief of staff directed us to move the model to the briefing room next to Admiral Nimitz's office.

A few days after that, on my way to lunch at the BOQ, I encountered Admiral Nimitz and Admiral King walking down the road to CinCPac headquarters. Admiral Nimitz stopped and introduced me. Admiral King did not remember me, but I remembered him. Nearly twenty years before, he was commander of the Submarine School at New London when I was a student there. Some of my fellow students dated one of his daughters and reported that she defended her father's strict discipline and exacting demands with the statement: "He is the most even-tempered man in the Navy. He is always in a rage." King was tough but I was confident that he made sound decisions. I was glad the model of Nauru was still on display in the briefing room. On 27 September the Joint Chiefs of Staff approved Nimitz's recommendation to substitute Makin for Nauru as the second objective of Operation Galvanic. The 27th

Army Division had an easy time at Makin. Had they assaulted Nauru, there would have been few survivors.

Accumulation of information on the Gilbert Islands accelerated. Army, Navy, and Marine Corps shore-based planes made reconnaissance flights from Funafuti and the Canton islands. On 19 September a carrier task force raided the Gilberts and made many low-oblique photographs of Tarawa. The *Nautilus* began an eighteen-day surveillance and photographic reconnaissance of the beaches of Tarawa, Makin, and Abemama on 25 September, during which she took two thousand photographs of the beaches. She also discovered that, on the charts of Tarawa, the island of Betio was aligned eleven degrees out of its correct orientation. The *Nautilus* did not return from that mission until late October. PRISIC worked night and day to process and interpret the photographs and compile mosaics and maps, so that the Fifth Amphibious Force could incorporate the new information into operation plans and distribute it to far-flung operational forces.

The excellent work of the *Nautilus* established a standard for submarine photographic reconnaissance for future operations in the central Pacific. Periscope photography presented a perspective of the beaches similar to that of the coxswain of a landing craft. The Fifth Amphibious Force requested detailed submarine reconnaissance before each operation. JICPOA and the Submarine Force worked in close cooperation on these missions. JICPOA prepared preliminary information on charts, tide and current tables, beach defenses, radar, and mines. PRISIC frequently detailed photographer's mates to submarines on reconnaissance patrol, and when the submarines returned, reproduced the photographs, collated them with aerial photographs, and disseminated the product.

The work of preparing the final information bulletin fell mainly on the Enemy Bases Section, and a large share of the basic information was derived from aerial photographs and photo-interpretation. The Estimate Section had only a small, but sometimes important, part to play. Captain Goggins charged me with the responsibility for passing Ultra information to the Enemy Bases Section in a sanitized form that could be used in the confidential bulletins. Most important of that information was the estimate of the strength of the Japanese garrison.

There was an amusing story that photo-interpreters computed the size of the island's defense force by counting the privies the Japanese erected on the lagoon beaches. They then multiplied the number of privies by the estimated ratio of Japanese military men per privy and produced an accurate estimate of the strength of the garrison. Certainly an increase in the number of privies would be suspicious, but I believe that the privy-count theory came out of a Nouméa barroom, originated by the fertile mind of a certain South Pacific intelligence officer. The Estimate Section of JICPOA calculated the strength of Betio's garrison by more orthodox methods.

Ever since he joined ICPOA in the fall of 1942, Hinkle had prepared estimates on the strength of the garrisons of Japanese bases in Micronesia for the weekly "Estimate of Japanese Strength" put out by the Combat Intelligence Unit (now the Estimate Section). At first, these estimates were little better than guesses but each week they were refined, as information accumulated. There were few Japanese army troops in the Marshalls and Gilberts. Those islands were defended by special naval units, whose communications went out over naval radio circuits in naval codes. Hinkle collected order-of-battle information on these special naval defense forces in the same way that Emory followed the shore-based air flotillas, Showers kept track of carriers and battleships, and Yardley checked off Japanese destroyers each week. Traffic intelligence would sooner or later locate each unit. A decrypted message or a captured document or an indiscreet entry in a captured diary would eventually reveal the table of organization and, consequently, the strength of a unit. Thus, when Hinkle located the Sasebo 7th Special Naval Landing Force, the 3rd Special Base Force, the 111th Pioneers, and a Fourth Fleet construction unit on Betio, he had an accurate estimate of the total strength of the garrison. Of course, he may have checked out the privy count with the photo-interpreters, but I have no recollection of it.

This order-of-battle method was usually reliable but it was subject to errors if the Japanese slipped in an uncommunicative unit at the last moment—as they did the extra cruisers at the Battle of the Komandorskis. There had been no major reinforcement of Betio, however, since May of 1943. That month FRUPac decrypted a message revealing that a couple of marus were en route to Tarawa. One of them had a cargo of four 8-inch coast-defense guns, captured from the British at Singapore and destined by the Japanese to defend the once-British island of Betio. When Voge read that message in the morning FRUPac "book," we conspired to consign those guns to the bottom of the sea. The submarine *Pollack* was patrolling in the Marshalls. Voge ordered her to run down to the vicinity of Jaluit and waylay one of the Tarawa-bound marus. She sank the *Bangkok Maru* on 20 May 1943. Unknown to us, the *Bangkok Maru* was not carrying the big guns for Betio, but did have on

Paul T. Yardley

board twelve hundred troops intended to reinforce that island's garrison. Most of them were rescued and taken to Jaluit, where they stayed until the end of the war. We were disappointed that the guns got through, but the trade-off of twelve hundred men for four big guns on Betio was in our favor.

We were fortunate that Joe Twitty was an expert topographer. No one else at JICPOA had any appreciation of how many ground maps, beach maps, gridded bombardment maps, air support charts, and anchorage charts would be required, or of the technical difficulties that were involved in producing them. Twitty coordinated the work of PRISIC and the U.S. Army 64th Topographic Company so that the thousands of maps needed were produced on time and reflected the results of the latest reconnaissances. Shortly before the Fifth Amphibious Force departed Pearl Harbor, JICPOA distributed a map of Tarawa, scaled 1 : 10,000, showing nearly all the defense installations of that island. Among the many field guns, antiaircraft guns, and coast-defense guns, the map showed two two-gun batteries considerably larger than the others. The JICPOA information bulletin identified them as "20-centimeter coast-defense guns," thus sanitizing our Ultra-derived knowledge that they were 8-inch coastal guns from Singapore. Two of those guns were knocked out

Joseph J. Twitty
Courtesy: U.S. Army

by a carrier strike on 18 November. The other pair opened up on the battleship *Maryland* on D-day but were silenced by the fire of that battleship's 16-inch guns.

While the South Pacific Force under Halsey was continuing its difficult campaign to push the Japanese out of the Solomons, the Central Pacific Force under Spruance was preparing for its first offensive, against the Gilberts. Halsey's intelligence organization provided nearly all the intelligence for his operations, but both the intelligence and the operations relating to one area often affected what went on in the other. In October, Koga learned of a shipping buildup when a reconnaissance plane, launched from the submarine *I-36* on a one-way suicide mission, flew over Pearl Harbor. Convinced by the buildup and by carrier strikes on Wake on 5 and 6 October that Nimitz was preparing to retake that island, he brought the Japanese fleet from Truk to Eniwetok. No sooner had he arrived there than the situation became critical in the Solomons and he returned to Truk, but too late to send reinforcements south before the Battle of Empress Augusta Bay.

On 1 November 1943, SoPac forces landed on Bougainville Island. The next night, in the Battle of Empress Augusta Bay, a Japanese cruiser force was defeated while it was attempting to attack the American transports, losing one cruiser and a destroyer. The Americans lost no ships in that battle, but in the confusion of the night action the Japanese were convinced that the Americans had suffered crippling losses, and Japanese intelligence had no way of correcting optimistic battle reports. Koga thought he saw a chance for another Battle of Savo Island. He sent the powerful cruisers of the Second Fleet from Truk to Rabaul to be within easy striking distance of Bougainville. South Pacific surface forces, under Halsey, had been seriously depleted by transfers to the Central Pacific Force, under Spruance, for the Gilberts operation, so despite the American victory at Empress Augusta Bay, the Japanese cruisers were a serious threat to the Bougainville expedition.

Messages decrypted at FRUPac disclosed Japanese plans for the southward movement of the Second Fleet cruisers. There was a possibility that some of the surface forces recently detached from ComSoPac could be returned to him in time to meet the threat, but only at the expense of delaying the Gilberts operation—and to that Spruance objected. When shore-based air forces spotted the Japanese cruisers coming south, Halsey ordered his two available carriers, the *Saratoga* and *Princeton*, to make a daring strike on Rabaul Harbor on 5 November, timed for the arrival of the Japanese cruisers. The Japanese were surprised by the strike. Only one destroyer, and none of the cruisers, was sunk, but the Second Fleet suffered such severe bomb damage that it was out of action for the next three critical months. Consequently, the Gilberts operation encountered no opposition from Japanese surface forces.

Izzy's Christmas dinner of 1942 was such a success that we planned to double up in 1943 by having as many JICPOA-FRUPac men as the house would hold for Thanksgiving dinner, and a different group for Christmas. By stretching out the extended dining-room table with the library table and card tables, we seated about twenty guests for Thanksgiving, but the party was sober and subdued. Tarawa had been stormed on 20 November by the Second Marine Division, which had won a great victory over a bitter Japanese defense, but at terrific cost. Our estimate of four thousand seven hundred Japanese on Betio was within one hundred of being correct, and only about one hundred and fifty of them survived the battle, but by the time the island was secured one thousand Marines had been killed and two thousand wounded. The Fifth Amphibious Force had obtained good information on the tides but, in the compromise to get the best combination of moon, surf, and tide, it had encountered an unpredictable "low dodging tide." This factor was responsible for many Marine casualties, and left an unfortunate impression that intelligence had done a poor job on beach information.

I felt bitterly hypocritical about that Thanksgiving. ComSubPac had several submarines strategically disposed for Operation Galvanic. One of these was the *Sculpin*, under command of Fred Connaway, patrolling between Truk and Ponape. Riding in her was Captain John P. Cromwell, Commander, Submarine Division Forty-Three. He was in the *Sculpin* so that he could, on radio orders from Lockwood, form a wolf pack to coordinate an attack by several submarines, in case the Japanese fleet sortied from Truk. When he was at Pearl Harbor, Cromwell took turns standing top watch at ComSubPac headquarters, and I sometimes passed information to him over the private phone line. Izzy and I had been close friends of the Cromwell family for years. A few days before the *Sculpin* departed from Pearl Harbor, Izzy went shopping with John to buy Christmas presents for his wife, Margaret, and two children in Palo Alto. He left the gifts with Izzy, to mail just before Christmas.

About 16 November FRUPac decrypted a Japanese message detailing the route of a convoy that would pass in the *Sculpin*'s vicinity. I called Voge on the private telephone immediately. There were indications that it was an important convoy. Both Voge and I were elated that the *Sculpin* would have an opportunity to attack. That night Voge sent out the information to Connaway. Of course, the message was not acknowledged but we did not have long to wait for confirmation that it had been received. Early in the morning of 19 November, a Japanese ship transmitted a short-form message reporting a submarine attack about where the *Sculpin* would have met the convoy.

Some eight hours later, the Japanese destroyer *Yamagumo* reported sinking a submarine in the same vicinity. This was not too alarming. Nine times out of ten, when Japanese escort vessels made such reports, the submarine had successfully evaded. We were more concerned when we did not hear from the *Sculpin* during the next night. For a few days, we buoyed our hopes by imagining conditions that would cause her to maintain radio silence. On 29 November Lockwood ordered Cromwell to form his wolf pack. Still, nothing was heard from the *Sculpin*. Lockwood canceled that order and directed the submarine to reconnoiter Eniwetok and report. When the *Sculpin* still remained silent we knew that she had gone.

I was acutely aware that John Cromwell was dead when Izzy joyfully mailed his Christmas presents to his family who, in ignorance, might have a merry Christmas, but who most certainly would not have a happy new year. It was a burden I had to bear in secret. Izzy and Margaret did not know until 30 December, when the Navy announced that the *Sculpin* was overdue and presumed lost.

The whole story was not known until after the war ended. The *Sculpin* made contact with the convoy but she had been sighted at dawn and forced down by the escort. Some hours later, when she came up for a periscope observation, the *Yamagumo* caught her with a well-placed depth-charge attack and forced her to the surface where she was destroyed by gunfire. Forty-two of the *Sculpin*'s men were picked up by the *Yamagumo* and rushed to Truk for questioning. Cromwell rode the *Sculpin* down in her last dive, refusing to abandon ship and be captured by the Japanese, because "he knew too much." Some of the *Sculpin*'s men survived Japanese prison camps and told the story when they were repatriated. Cromwell was awarded the Congressional Medal of Honor. He was cited for sacrificing his life to protect the secrets of Operation Galvanic and the location of submarines patrolling in the central Pacific. Those were ephemeral secrets that in a week or two would have little value to the Japanese. But Cromwell knew too much about the intimate connection between submarine operations and radio intelligence. He chose to die to protect the Ultra secret.

CHAPTER 13

THORNTON HINKLE, who calculated the strength of the garrisons of Japanese bases in Micronesia for the Estimate Section, was also chief of the Enemy Land Section of JICPOA, whose job it was to study Japanese defense methods and defense installations. The fact that Carlson's Raiders, in their early raid in the Gilberts, had been forced to defend themselves with captured Japanese rifles and machine guns emphasized the necessity for a systematic study of the operation of Japanese weapons of all kinds. By November 1943 the Enemy Land Section consisted of two Navy language officers, both of whom had Army reserve officer training and were specialists in documents concerning land forces; two photo-interpreters who specialized in shore-defense construction; and two Marine officers who specialized in Japanese weapons. All these people needed an opportunity to make firsthand observations in combat. In Operation Galvanic they got it.

JICPOA fielded two intelligence teams to accompany the assault forces, one to go with the Marines to Betio, and the other to land with the Army on Butaritari Island, in Makin Atoll. Each team consisted of a language officer, an officer from the Enemy Bases Section, a photographer, a ground-study officer, and an enlisted man. Because they needed to be right behind the assault waves and there is little room for noncombatants on a contested beach, the teams had to be kept small. They were, in fact, too small to achieve all their objectives. The lone language officers were kept busy with the operational requirements of the combat commands, almost to the exclusion of their intelligence functions, and the teams had to rely mainly on the combat forces' normal salvage operations to collect enemy equipment. Combat salvage teams, however, had little interest in preserving enemy equipment for intelligence purposes. Souvenir-hunters destroyed or "liberated" more intelligence material than the teams could collect. One sailor picked up a Japanese

Thornton M. Hinkle
Courtesy: U.S. Marine Corps

code book as a souvenir. That code remained in use in the Marshalls for several weeks after Tarawa fell but, much to Dyer's disgust, it had been superseded by the time the code book was discovered in a barracks inspection back at Pearl Harbor. Nevertheless, like everyone who had anything to do with Tarawa, the JICPOA intelligence teams learned a lot from the experience, and they proved their worth to both combat forces and the intelligence organizations.

Intelligence teams became larger and better organized with each succeeding operation. U.S. Army nisei enlisted men joined them for the duration of each operation to assist in the interrogation of prisoners, and more language officers were added to the assault divisions. Explosives intelligence units, specializing in Japanese mines and aerial bombs, were eventually added, also. CinCPac issued a directive establishing an inspection system for all captured enemy equipment and documents. "Souvenirs" retained by individuals had to be inspected and stamped by an intelligence officer. Souvenir-hunters could exchange items of intelligence value for other items, and the stamp enhanced the value of the souvenir. To some extent, they then assisted in the collection of intelligence materials, but special salvage squads were later added to the JICPOA intelligence teams.

When the intelligence teams returned to Pearl Harbor from the Gilberts, JICPOA published and distributed their studies of the defenses of Betio and Butaritari islands. The photographs, sketches, and descriptions of Japanese installations in these reports, coordinated with interpretations of aerial photographs of the same islands taken before the operation, greatly improved the accuracy of photo-interpretation of similar construction in the Marshalls. JICPOA's primary responsibility was the preparation of intelligence for CinC-Pac, but it produced much material for direct distribution to intelligence officers in all echelons. By the end of 1943, more than seventy JICPOA bulletins on subjects from "Performance Tests on Captured Zero" to "Japanese Amphibious Operations" had been prepared and distributed. Printing and reproduction facilities were taxed beyond their limits, and the plant in the Kodak Hawaii Building was no longer adequate for PRISIC. Early in 1944 plans were made for a new three-story JICPOA building next to FRUPac, on the rim of Makalapa Crater.

With the arrival of captured documents and prisoners of war at Pearl Harbor, directly from the Gilberts operations, it became necessary to divide the Language Section into the Translation Section and the Interrogation Section. A stockade to hold prisoners of war for interrogation, before turning them over to the Army for transportation to the mainland, was built at Camp Catlin. Two lieutenants, Frank B. and David Huggins, brothers who were born and educated in Japan, took over the task of interrogation. Fortunately, a group of twenty more officers from the language school at Boulder arrived at this time.

Large quantities of captured documents generated the problem of what to translate first. This question could never be resolved to everyone's satisfaction, but the Japanese gave us welcome assistance in one aspect of it. They, like other maritime peoples, issued a series of "Notices to Mariners" concerning changes in lights and buoys, hazards to navigation, chart corrections, and similar items of interest to navigators. A number of these publications fell into our hands at Tarawa. They would all have been set aside for translation after items concerning the Marshall Islands had been exploited, had it not been that some of them had conspicuous red borders. Immediate attention was given to the latter, and they turned out to be classified "secret." Almost invariably a red-bordered notice marked the limits of a Japanese defensive mine field—an area "closed to navigation" for Japanese shipping—information of the utmost importance to our submarines operating in Japanese waters.

In 1942 and early 1943, the area between northeast Honshu and Hokkaido had been a happy hunting ground for submarines. Japanese shipping was plentiful and their antisubmarine forces in those waters were weak. The submarine *Pickerel* was sent into the area in March 1943. FRUPac picked up a report of the sinking of a Japanese submarine chaser by a torpedo that could have been fired only by the *Pickerel* on 3 April. On 7 April two marus sank in the *Pickerel*'s area but it was not clear from the decrypted message what had sunk them. The *Pickerel* was due to leave her hunting ground and start homeward at sunset on 1 May 1943, but nothing was ever heard from her. The submarine *Runner* left Midway on 28 May for the same area. She also disappeared without a trace. After that, Lockwood decided to give the area a rest for a while.

The submarines that had been scheduled to patrol northeast of Honshu were rescheduled to enter the Japan Sea, which until then had been free of submarine operations. This was a project Lockwood had been planning for a long time. Tsushima Kaikyo, the southern entrance to the Japan Sea, was known to be heavily mined. Tsugaru Kaikyo was narrow and difficult of navigation. La Pérouse Strait, the remaining entrance, was used by Russian shipping plying between the United States and Vladivostok, carrying lend-lease material to Russia. The Russians gave us no information, but their use of that strait indicated that a surfaced submarine could go through at night without undue risk of hitting a mine. Three submarines were scheduled to run La Pérouse on the night of 4 July 1943, operate four days in the Japan Sea, and come back out the way they went in. The *Narwhal*, which carried two 6-inch guns, was to bombard Matsuwa, in the Kuril Islands, as a diversion while the three submarines made their exit from the Japan Sea via La Pérouse.

For this operation, JICPOA prepared an information bulletin "Sea of Okhotsk and Sea of Japan," and the model-makers went to work on a model of Matsuwa To. All four submarines returned safely from their patrols, but their achievements were not proportional to the risks they had taken. In August the *Wahoo* and *Plunger* entered the Japan Sea and found plenty of easy targets but, because many of their torpedoes were defective, they sank only two ships. Mush Morton then took the *Wahoo* back to Pearl Harbor to reload with the new electric torpedoes. At his request, the *Wahoo* was scheduled to go back into the Japan Sea in September.

Morton was hospitalized while his submarine was moored at the Submarine Base. I went up to the hospital to talk to him about his runs through La Pérouse and to discuss the preparation of any special charts and information he might need for his next venture. He was very much interested in the big Japanese train ferries that plied Tsushima Kaikyo, so JICPOA supplied him with all the information it could collect about the ferries' characteristics, routes, and schedules. When the Japanese announced that one of these ferries, the *Konron Maru*, had been sunk on 5 October we knew that Morton had achieved his objective. We knew also from Japanese sources that, after her perilous transit of La Pérouse, the *Wahoo* had run the full length of the Japan Sea and penetrated the waters of Tsushima. We never heard from the *Wahoo*. She probably was destroyed in one of the many antisubmarine actions the Japanese reported in the Japan Sea. Captain Atsushi Oi, a Japanese antisubmarine planner, told me after the war that an American submarine's presence at Tsushima disrupted traffic with Korea and threw Japanese antisubmarine headquarters into confusion.

In August 1943, after the area off northeast Honshu had been given three months' rest, Willis M. "Tommy" Thomas in the *Pompano* was sent there. We know from Japanese reports that a submarine sank a maru on 3 September and damaged the heavy cruiser *Nachi* three days later, but we heard nothing directly from the *Pompano*. The night she was due to leave her operating area, her marker on the big magnetic wall chart in ComSubPac's operations office was turned to point for home. Each morning thereafter, her magnet was advanced a day's run toward Midway. These movements were faithfully copied on the submarine situation chart in the Estimate Section.

We in the Estimate Section were so closely related to ComSubPac's operations office that the loss of a submarine was as agonizing to us as it was to them. Ordinarily, a few days after leaving her operating area, homeward bound, the *Pompano* would have originated a radio message reporting her estimated time of arrival at the perimeter of Midway's aerial search sector, in order to minimize the chance of a surprise encounter between friendly forces. When this message was not forthcoming, apprehension deepened into gloom, as each day the *Pompano*'s silent marker bravely marched across the chart's white paper.

We attempted to conceal our anxiety from each other by elaborate pretenses. When Voge finished reading the FRUPac "book" in the morning he casually inquired, "Anything happen in northeast Honshu?" He knew we had searched the day's traffic and researched the back traffic fruitlessly, and that if we had discovered anything it would have burned the wire to ComSubPac's operations office. I shook my head. "Hear anything from *Pompano*?" I knew if any such message had come in he would have let me know immediately. Even if I had been home in bed, he would have telephoned to announce nonchalantly "We heard from Tommy Thomas," knowing I would sleep better for the rest of the night. Lockwood requested Midway to extend their air search to the maximum distance on the *Pompano*'s bearing, in hopes that she might be still alive, but had a damaged radio and was unable to communicate. The magnetic marker advanced to the air-search perimeter and desperately clung there until the Navy Department announced "*Pompano* is overdue and presumed lost."

Overdue-submarine procedures, repeated for three submarines sent to operate off northeast Honshu in the summer and fall of 1943, were doubly frustrating to the Estimate Section. Did the Japanese have some new antisubmarine device of which intelligence was ignorant? Sometimes, in an emergency, the Japanese announced a new mine field by radio. In late 1943 FRUPac picked up a message bounding a small area closed to navigation, near the Pacific end of Tsugaru Kaikyo. Was it a mine field? It was outside our submarine operating areas and in water we thought to be too deep for moored mines. We picked up a few other messages reporting marus mysteriously sunk in areas off northeast Honshu, when we had no submarines operating there. Could it be that these marus had blundered into their own defensive mine fields? Occasionally, we heard a maru report sighting mines floating off northeast Honshu. All this pointed to the existence of mine fields there. When the red-bordered "Notices to Mariners" were discovered, we tore through captured documents looking for more. Intelligence teams in the field were instructed to watch out for anything with red borders or red covers. We needed someone in the Estimate Section who knew more than we did about Japanese mines and their capabilities.

Early in 1944 Commander, Mine Force, Pacific, whose headquarters were also at Makalapa, sent Lieutenant Edward McC. Blair, a mine-warfare intelligence officer, to work with JICPOA. We put him in the Estimate Section where he would have access to Ultra as well as to captured documents, and where he could work closely with submarines. When captured documents from Kwajalein started coming in, this special attention to Japanese mines soon showed results.

Chart overlays of Japanese mine fields in areas where submarines were operating were prepared and issued to submarines, and bulletins on other information of Japanese mining practices were distributed. We learned that in the fall of 1942 the Japanese had laid a thin line of mines to seaward of the maru routes off northeast Honshu.

These mines sank only marus until the *Pickerel* apparently had the misfortune to run into one, in the spring of 1943. About that time the Japanese reinforced those mine fields with more than three thousand mines. Although U.S. mines were rarely laid in water of more than 60 fathoms, in deference to the possibility that the Japanese laid them deeper, the *Runner* was cautioned to stay outside the 100-fathom curve. As our knowledge of the fields northeast of Honshu accumulated, we learned that the Japanese were laying anchored mines there in 250 fathoms. It was probably our ignorance of this that doomed the *Runner* and the *Pompano*. We later learned that the Japanese sometimes laid moored mines in water more than one mile deep.

At Kwajalein we captured documents that revealed Japanese plans to build a huge mine barrier from Kyushu to Formosa, behind which maru traffic would be protected from submarines. Fortunately, we had learned about the plans by the time the first mines were laid in February 1944. Voge kept our submarines out of the East China Sea until additional information, received a few months later, revealed the extent of the barrier and the gates our submarines could use to pass safely through it. Captured documents were not always that helpful, and sometimes JICPOA's copy of secret Notices to Mariners did not get through on time. In 1944 we lost three more submarines in mine fields, and two other "missing" submarines were probably mined. But, considering the magnitude of the Japanese mining effort, there can be no doubt that, had it not been for Ed Blair's efficient research, the list of missing submarines would have been longer. As the U.S. fleet pushed westward, the demand for mine-warfare intelligence expanded beyond the Submarine Force. A separate Mine Warfare Section of JICPOA, with Blair as its chief, was established to coordinate all mine-warfare intelligence in the Pacific. The final bulletin that section issued consisted of charts, reduced to convenient size, showing the limits of all Japanese mine fields and annotated with essential information concerning mines and mine lines in each field. When the Japanese surrendered and turned over complete information on their mine fields, there was little new information to add to that bulletin. The Mine Warfare Section's information was as good as the Japanese information.

Dick Emory's long and patient work with FRUPac's decryptions of Japanese naval air force messages prepared him to profit from the translations of captured documents, and to refine his basic knowledge of the Japanese naval air order of battle and of their procedures for air search. Air Squadron 24 was based on Kwajalein. Many of its planes had been lost down the Solomons' sinkhole and in air attacks on American task forces in the Gilberts operations, but about 25 November forty bombers from Hokkaido and thirty-six fighters from Rabaul were flown in as reinforcements. Newly installed American radio direction finders and radio-intercept stations were favorably situated for monitoring Kwajalein radio traffic. This enabled Emory and Chapman to work out a detailed plot of Japanese air searches in the Marshalls. Since the Japanese could not maintain a full-perimeter search with the planes they had available, they left the northern sectors vacant and concentrated their searches to the south and southeast, from which directions they expected an attack. Kwajalein, the heart of Japanese defenses in the Marshalls, was at the center of a web of Japanese bases.

In planning his approach to attack Kwajalein and Wotje, Admiral Charles A. Pownall, commanding a task force of six carriers, ten cruisers, and eleven destroyers, took full advantage of Emory's excellent intelligence concerning Japanese air searches. The large task force came in from the northeast and, at dawn on 4 December 1943, reached its strike position without having been sighted by the Japanese. This performance, against a war-experienced enemy expecting an attack, was more remarkable than was the Kido Butai's undetected approach to Pearl Harbor during an uneasy peace, almost exactly two years before. The strike, however, achieved only moderate success, sinking four ships and destroying fifty-five Japanese planes.

After this carrier strike, the U.S. Seventh Army Air Force and land-based Navy planes, flying from new air bases in the Gilberts, took over the air preparation for Operation Flintlock, the conquest of Kwajalein and Majuro, in the Marshall Islands. Each day the Japanese naval air squadrons reported to Tokyo by radio. FRUPac intercepted and decrypted these routine messages, so Emory was able to keep close track of their air losses and air strength in the Marshalls, and of the weather reports from Japanese air bases. U.S. land-based air forces were not very successful in reducing Japanese air strength or destroying Japanese defense installations, but their thorough reconnaissances and aerial photography produced information supporting the decision to make a direct assault on Kwajalein Atoll and Majuro, bypassing strong Japanese bases on Wotje, Maloelap, Mili, and Jaluit.

Consolidation of intelligence and close cooperation between JICPOA and CinCPac's Plans and Operations Division paid big dividends. The lessons of Tarawa were rapidly assimilated into plans for

Operation Flintlock. The results of aerial and submarine reconnaissance and photography arrived promptly at JICPOA, where photointerpreters, educated by the Tarawa operation and the subsequent study of Japanese defenses there, quickly identified similar installations on Kwajalein. This intelligence was incorporated into the thousands of maps, charts, bombardment grids, and air target folders then in preparation for the forthcoming operations.

The resistance of Japanese defense positions on Tarawa to bombing and to naval gunfire had been somewhat in the nature of a tactical surprise. U.S. naval ordnance had not been adequately tested in peacetime and, in general, was designed for use against ships. In 1941 the Navy took over Kahoolawe, a small uninhabited island near Maui, in the Hawaiian Islands, for use in testing live ammunition and for training pilots and gun crews in bombing and bombardment under simulated battle conditions. On Kahoolawe, the Marines built duplicates of the Japanese defense installations of Tarawa. Live bombs from planes and live ammunition from ships were tested against these installations and the results closely studied to devise the best method of attack.

About the end of 1943 JICPOA began issuing information bulletins and air target folders on each of the major atolls in the Marshalls. Air target folders were classified "restricted" and information bulletins were classified "confidential," except for the Kwajalein bulletin, which was kept "secret" until D-day when it, too, was downgraded to "confidential." All the bulletins and folders carried a standard yellow cover, which became JICPOA's trademark throughout the Pacific.

The intelligence annex to the Gilberts operation order consisted of twenty or thirty mimeographed pages, supplemented by maps, charts, and air target folders, separately distributed. I was appalled to discover that as many as five hundred copies of the basic intelligence text had been distributed. Each one was a potential source of disclosure of the operation's objectives. One of my first actions, when I acquired greater responsibility for JICPOA, was to create a Distribution Section, whose duty it was to withhold critical information from the merely curious, but to expedite delivery of all JICPOA publications to those who needed them. I believed that distribution based strictly on a "need to know" principle would greatly reduce the number of copies issued. However, the complexity and size of expeditionary forces grew so rapidly that for each organization eliminated from the distribution list several others had to be added. As a consequence, from Operation Flintlock on, information bulletins were distributed in the thousands rather than the hundreds.

Classification of intelligence material was a matter of delicate balance. The wealth of intelligence we distilled from captured Japanese documents was a constant reminder of the perils of lavish distribution. Underclassification was impossible to correct, and usually brought down the wrath of the top brass on the easily identified culprit. It was hard for a timid administrator to resist the temptation to overclassify, but overclassification limited and slowed the flow of information downward, and information that did not reach those who needed it was useless.

Intelligence derived from decryption of enemy radio messages was classified "Ultra" or "Top Secret Ultra," and was not handled by the Distribution Section. Practically everything produced by the Estimate Section was classified "Ultra," and was distributed by the fleet intelligence officer, or directly by the Estimate Section in accordance with the fleet intelligence officer's directions. Distribution was extremely limited. FRUPac was segregated from JICPOA, and only the Estimate Section and a few other JICPOA officers had any knowledge of how it worked or the intelligence it produced. Information closely connected with plans, or with operations in progress, was generally classified "secret" regardless of origin, and that too had limited distribution.

We believed the Japanese were not aware of the amount of intelligence we derived from captured documents. Better Japanese security provisions could drastically cut down this source, so we classified intelligence from captured documents as "confidential," permitting relatively broad and flexible distribution, while retaining reasonable security against compromise.

Since air target folders, most of whose information was derived from aerial reconnaissance and photographs, had to be flown in combat over enemy territory, they were classified "restricted," and every effort was made to exclude from them any information that might cause serious damage if it fell into enemy hands.

By the end of 1943, JICPOA had available large quantities of information that could be classified "confidential" or lower and given broad distribution. Every man who entered the combat zone needed basic information on the characteristics of the enemy he might encounter, on the terrain over which he would fight, on the flora and the fauna he might encounter, and on the identity, nature, and culture of any noncombatant natives he might meet. Information on Japanese weapons and how to operate them also needed the broadest possible distribution.

Until after Operation Flintlock JICPOA did not have the personnel or the facilities to mass-produce this type of information, and it was not distributed widely enough. The sole exception was the *Castaway's Baedeker*. This was a handy little booklet on how to survive on an uninhabited island in the South Pacific or adrift in a rubber boat. It antedated JICPOA, having been compiled by PRISIC and ICPOA, with the assistance of Dr. Kenneth Emory of the Bishop Museum, before JICPOA was organized. The total of its many editions and reprintings must entitle it to a place among the best sellers of the war years.

Castaway's Baedeker was the forerunner of the "Guides" series. The first work in that series was an unpretentious little booklet, *Guide to Pacific Islands*, and the last official one was an elaborate, illustrated pamphlet on slick paper, *Guide to Japan*, edited by John Park Lee. At the end of the war, an unofficial *Guide to the United States* was put out in a very limited edition by the Advanced Intelligence Center on Guam. It featured such useful information for returning veterans as: "The practice of marketing and sometimes cooking eggs in their shells may at first be repugnant but it is not actually unsanitary. Scrambled eggs in the United States are not unpalatable although they may lack the delicate green color so familiar to all ranks of all services in the Western Pacific."

We discovered very early that, to be effective, intelligence had to be properly presented with emphasis appropriate to its importance. After the Tarawa landing in November 1943, General Holland M. Smith, U.S. Marine Corps, irately and vigorously complained that the impact of 8-inch shells among loaded transports, in a presumably safe anchorage, was his first information that the Japanese had 8-inch guns on Tarawa. General Smith was known as "Howling Mad" Smith not merely because his initials were H. M., and his protests commanded attention. At first I was indignant.

These were the guns whose delivery to Tarawa Voge and I had tried to sabotage in May. We had sanitized our Ultra-derived knowledge of them by referring to them in the JICPOA information bulletin as "20-centimeter coast-defense guns," and that is how they were labeled on maps of Tarawa's defense installations. Then I realized that in the intelligence annex to an operation order more than a foot thick, the only reference to them was a couple of mimeographed lines buried in a long descriptive paragraph, and I had to concede that the general had a point. We decided that information bulletins, which henceforth served as part of the intelligence annex to operation orders, should make maximum use of annotated maps and sketches, diagrams, tabulations, and photographs, and leave as little as possible to text. This trend was noticeable in the information bulletins for Operation Flintlock, and continued until text all but disappeared from such publications. That, too, had its pitfalls, as we discovered much later.

Traffic analysis and the decryption of Japanese naval messages by FRUPac, in cooperation with the worldwide naval communications intelligence network, supplied daily information enabling the Estimate Section to keep reasonably current and accurate estimates of the location and movement of Japanese fleet units. Decryption of messages supplied information upon which the disposition of our submarines was based, and almost nightly produced detailed route points of convoys to guide submarines into contact.

One evening, about the first of December 1943, a particularly important message came in. It was fragmentary and garbled, but identification of the Japanese carrier *Zuiho* and two escort carriers, the *Unyo* and *Chuyo*, among the addressees attracted the attention of Lieutenant David A. Ward, a translator-cryptanalyst on watch. Despite the garbles, the coordinates of a few positions were solid. Ward consulted the submarine situation chart in the Estimate Section and noted that the *Sailfish* might be able to intercept if she received the necessary information promptly. He worked on that message, to the exclusion of all others, for his whole watch.

The senior translator on watch wanted to wait in the hope that a later interception of a duplicate of the message might come in to clear up the garbles and he thought that the message needed more work. Ward, however, aware that delay might make it impossible for the *Sailfish* to make contact, wrote up the fragment his hard labor had produced and left it in the Estimate Section when he went off watch. I had it earmarked in the daily "book" for Voge's immediate attention when he came up for the morning conference. Voge was elated.

"Here is where we get a carrier," he gloated.

I remarked sarcastically that we had produced similar information many times before, still no submarine had yet sunk a Japanese aircraft carrier. Modern fleet submarines armed with Mark XIV torpedoes had sunk only marus, naval auxiliaries, destroyers, and obsolescent light cruisers. This time it would be different, Voge argued. Defects in the torpedo exploders had at long last been corrected. The *Sailfish* was Voge's old command. He knew her and her crew, including Robert E. M. Ward, her new skipper. He would like to make a little bet.

"O.K.," I replied. "I will cover one dollar of your money, and hope to lose the bet."

Early on the morning of 3 December FRUPac intercepted a standard Japanese short-form message reporting the position of a submarine attack. We knew that the *Sailfish* had made contact. What we did not know was that she and the Japanese task force were in the middle of a raging typhoon that taxed the seamanship of both friend and foe; a circumstance that those who fought the war on a chart's smooth paper were too prone to forget. Bob Ward, the *Sailfish* and her crew, and the torpedoes, met every test and, in three successive attacks that stretched out over ten hours of battling the sea and the enemy, sank the *Chuyo*. The *Sailfish* became the first U.S. submarine to sink a Japanese carrier.

I paid my bet to Voge with a check two and a half feet long, suitably decorated by JICPOA sketch artists and annotated, "On *Sailfish* account." I told Voge that when the check cleared through the Bank of Hawaii I would keep it as a souvenir marking the end of the immunity of Japanese heavy combat ships to submarine torpedoes. Voge thwarted me by not cashing it. He had it framed, and hung it in ComSubPac's operations room. When Voge died, shortly after the end of the war, his widow, Alice, returned the check to me and it is now displayed in the Submarine Museum at Pearl Harbor.

———

On 29 January 1944 four fast carrier groups of the U.S. Pacific Fleet made the first of a series of strikes on Japanese airfields on Maloelap, Wotje, Roi, Kwajalein, and Eniwetok islands. By the time the first troops landed on Kwajalein on 31 January, Japanese air forces in the Marshall Islands had been completely annihilated. Not one of the 297 vessels of the Marshall Islands Joint Expeditionary Force, carrying 54,000 troops, was attacked by Japanese aircraft during the whole operation. By 6 February 1944, Majuro and the entire atoll of Kwajalein were securely in American hands. Kwajalein Atoll was defended by about 8,700 Japanese, who had plenty of time to prepare their well-designed and strongly constructed defense positions. At Tarawa, which was defended by less than half that number of Japanese, 1,000 Marines had died in the assault. Kwajalein cost the assault forces 372 lives. This great improvement was due to many factors, not the least of which were effective use of good intelligence and the knowledge gained by the bombardment with live ammunition of mock-up Japanese defense structures on Kahoolawe.

CHAPTER 14

THE CONQUEST OF KWAJALEIN ATOLL yielded a wealth of intelligence material. Kwajalein was the repository of many important Japanese documents, and the JICPOA teams were better organized to collect and preserve intelligence material of all kinds than they had been in previous operations. The first and most important item to reach JICPOA was a portfolio of about seventy-five secret charts of the lagoons and harbors of Micronesia. These charts were in a patrol vessel that was forced ashore on Gehh Island in the Kwajalein Atoll early in the operation. When Gehh Island was taken on 1 February 1944 the red-bordered charts were recovered and rushed to JICPOA.

The importance of this find was immediately recognized and, before the charts were sent to the Hydrographic Office in Washington, which indicated that it would take months to translate, reprint, and distribute them, they were all photographed by PRISIC. Joe Twitty had the 64th Topographic Company run off a large number of copies on their offset presses, while the Translation Section prepared JICPOA Bulletin No. 24-44, "Explanatory Notes on Japanese Captured Charts." The charts and the bulletin were then issued to the fleet in time for Operation Catchpole, the conquest of Eniwetok. The notes and legends in the charts were in Japanese and the soundings in meters. I have no doubt that many navigators cursed them fluently while acquiring a Japanese vocabulary limited, like my own, to cartographic terms picked up from JICPOA bulletins. But, despite the inconvenience of having to dig for it, the new information in these charts was of great value in the Eniwetok operation, and the alacrity with which JICPOA reproduced and distributed the makeshifts demonstrated again the importance of close association and cooperation between intelligence, planning, and operations.

Since it had not been necessary to commit the reserves of the Marshall Islands Joint Expeditionary Force to the assault on Kwajalein, they were restructured as the Eniwetok Expeditionary Group and assigned to the assault on Eniwetok. The airfield of Eniwetok and all the visible Japanese installations were on Engebi Island, at the northern end of the atoll. To protect the Kwajalein operation, a fast carrier task group struck Engebi on 31 January 1944, destroying all the Japanese planes there. Carrier strikes were repeated several times in the first two weeks of February. Air strikes and naval gunfire bombardment preceded the landing on 17 February, and on 18 February Engebi was reported secured. JICPOA produced Bulletin No. 3–44, "Eniwetok Information Bulletin" in preparation for this operation, but its contents were meager. More timely intelligence was produced by aerial photographs taken during the carrier strikes.

Eniwetok is only 669 miles from Truk, where the Japanese had more than three hundred and fifty planes and a strong contingent of surface forces from the Combined Fleet. Before leaving Pearl Harbor for the Kwajalein operation, Admiral Spruance drew up plans for Operation Hailstone, a carrier strike on Truk, in order to protect Eniwetok from Truk-based air raids. He also anticipated attacks by Japanese surface ships on his vulnerable expeditionary forces, but Admiral Koga was so frustrated by the complications of his new defensive status that he resorted to inaction.

When Operation Hailstone was scheduled, Dick Emory repeated his feat of plotting the pattern of Japanese air searches, so I was confident that Admiral Marc A. Mitscher's carriers could make an undetected approach and a surprise attack on Truk. I expected that this would bring on a fleet action between Spruance's Fifth Fleet and the Combined Fleet surface forces at Truk. I said as much to Admiral McMorris, CinCPac's chief of staff. He shook his head in disagreement. Truk was within bombing range of Bougainville and Kwajalein, both then in American hands, and its supply lines were constantly harassed by submarines. It was no longer a safe base for the Japanese fleet. Wise old Soc McMorris predicted that Koga would get the major Japanese fleet ships to hell out of there before the planned carrier strike. Soc was right.

A plane from Bougainville made a reconnaissance flight over Truk on 4 February 1944 and counted many destroyers and submarines, ten cruisers, two carriers, and one battleship, but the exodus of large combat ships had already started. Continuously informed by the Estimate Section of the many ships of all kinds at Truk, ComSubPac had spread a net of ten submarines around the atoll to catch any ships that left Truk to fight or flee. The *Musashi*, Koga's flagship, departed for Japan soon after the Bougainville reconnais-

Charles H. McMorris
Courtesy: U.S. Naval History Division

sance flight. The rest of the fleet's combat ships retreated to Palau,
leaving behind light forces, auxiliaries, and many marus. The *Agano*
was the last fleet cruiser out of Truk. It departed on 16 February
and was torpedoed and sunk by the submarine *Skate* the next day.
The other ships headed for Palau managed to get through the submarine net.

Profiting from Emory's studies of Japanese air searches, Mitscher's carriers did make an undetected approach, as I had foreseen.
The first fighter sweep, launched from the carriers before dawn on
17 February 1944, caught Truk's defenders by surprise and disabled
their air defenses. Although by then the combat ships of the fleet
had fled, as Soc McMorris predicted, in two days of repeated strikes
the carriers destroyed most of the seaplane carriers, submarine tenders, and marus that had been left behind.

Truk continued for some time as a staging stop for air and submarine forces, but it never again became an important Japanese
naval base. Bypassed Rabaul, without support from Truk, withered
on the vine and became more of a liability than an asset to Japan.
At Pearl Harbor, on 7 December 1941, Kimmel lost his battleships.
Had he, by some miracle of divination, anticipated the Japanese attack, he might have saved the battleships by the same tactics of re-

treat that Koga used. Had he done so, and Pearl Harbor's fuel and facilities been destroyed instead of the battleships, the war would have been longer and the criticism of Kimmel more acrimonious.

Spruance, commander of the Fifth Fleet, in the battleship *New Jersey,* led a task group in a circumnavigation of Truk Atoll, sinking one light cruiser, a destroyer, and some smaller vessels. In the evening of 17 February FRUPac intercepted a message from Pis Island, on the rim of Truk's atoll, reporting that a landing was in progress; good evidence that the Japanese were just as jittery as we were on the 7th of December 1941, with our reports of paratroops landing on Ewa Plain. Some wag from the Estimate Section suggested that the landing the Japanese reported might be Spruance going ashore for his evening constitutional.

The Estimate Section knew that a Spruance hike could be a grueling military maneuver. Spruance liked to walk for physical exercise while thinking out his problems, and would do so on board ship, if necessary, but preferably on shore. Frequently he asked an officer whose views he wanted to probe to walk with him. He and Nimitz once invited Dyer to go on a long hike with them, a significant selection because Dyer was one of a small group of officers (Dyer, Wright, Rochefort, Finnegan, Lasswell, Huckins, and Holtwick) whose passion for anonymity concealed their genius from all but the most discerning. That group founded the Combat Intelligence Unit, which became FRUPac, which spawned ICPOA, which blossomed into JICPOA. For Dyer, who spent the war years working long hours at a desk under fluorescent lights or in the air-conditioned machine room, the all-day hike was an ordeal. He spent the following two days in the hospital recovering from sunburn.

The initial landings at Eniwetok proceeded simultaneously with the carrier strikes on Truk. It had been expected that, after the capture of Engebi Island on 18 February 1944, only mopping-up operations would be required to complete the conquest of Eniwetok. During the fighting on Engebi, however, Ensign Donald M. Allen of the JICPOA team discovered and translated a document which revealed that both Parry and Eniwetok islands, near the southern end of the atoll, flanking the passes that afforded entrance to the lagoon, were heavily defended. Our aerial reconnaissance had not picked up any sign of this activity. Plans for the remainder of the operation had to be hastily revised. The capture of Eniwetok Island required three days of hard fighting, during which other documents disclosing Japanese plans for the defense of Parry Island were discovered and translated by a JICPOA team. This on-the-spot exploitation of captured documents was the happy result of a combination of alert language officers, good luck, and good management. Even without the confusion of combat, it was a difficult task to sort out captured documents according to their importance and priority.

In early 1944 groups of about thirty officers were arriving at regular intervals from the language school at Boulder. Most of them went to the Translation Section, until there were more than 200 language officers at JICPOA. The section was headed by Commander John W. Steele, a retired naval officer, and Major Lachlan M. Sinclair, an Army officer, was the executive. All the rest were Naval Reserve officers, specially recruited for instruction in the Japanese language.

To process the mass of documents arriving from the Marshalls, the Translation Section was reorganized into *han*, or subsections, which eventually numbered fifteen. Each *han* specialized in translating documents on a particular subject. There was a *han* for documents relating to Japanese aviation, another for land forces, one for radar and sonar, one for ordnance, one for ships and shipbuilding, and so on. This organization permitted a language officer to acquire an extensive knowledge of the Japanese *kanji* dealing with his subject. It also encouraged many of them to take courses in radar, visit ship-repair yards, and to increase their general knowledge in their particular fields. This type of organization, however, required a group of exceptionally skilled and experienced officers to separate and classify documents when they first arrived at JICPOA. That group became known as the Sparrows, for their ability to scratch through a mound of horse manure and select the few grains of potentially important information.

From the end of 1943 on, it was impossible to translate every document that came to JICPOA. We were inundated with material from Kwajalein and in one shipment from Saipan we received fifty tons of Japanese documents. Items of low intelligence value or of interest only as background information were shipped on to the Washington Document Center, which Goggins called the Over the River Burial Association. JICPOA concentrated on documents of direct importance to operations in the Pacific. Many of these required only identification and indexing slips. Others were partially translated and the information transmitted directly to the JICPOA section concerned; for example, a red-bordered Notice to Mariners went directly to the Mine Warfare Section. Keeping track of the documents, in order to avoid loss of important ones and duplication within JICPOA and with the Allied Translation and Interrogation Section of the Southwest Pacific Command, required a complex filing system.

JICPOA issued thirty-nine volumes of CinCPac-CinCPOA translations and interrogations and about ninety special translations. Some of them were works of immense strategic importance, such as *1944 Japanese Army Mobilization Plans, Hypothetical Defense of Kyushu, Kagoshima Defense Battle Plan, Digest of Japanese Naval Air Bases,* and *Manual of Anti-Aircraft Defense.*

Naval language officers were recruited from the nation's postgraduate schools and from Phi Beta Kappa lists, so it is not surprising that JICPOA turned out such scholarly works as *Japanese Place Names Arranged by Characters* and *Japanese Military and Technical Terms.* It is not surprising either that, with their academic background, many language officers found it difficult to adjust to a military routine. No relationship has ever been established between punctilio and military effectiveness, as attested by Washington's ragged Continentals, Sherman's Bummers, and Stonewall Jackson's foot cavalry or, for that matter, some of FRUPac's outstanding regular Navy cryptanalysts. When some of my Procrustean colleagues protested the unmilitary attitude of the Translation Section, I advised them to "relax, we have always won our wars with a bunch of damned civilians in uniform anxious to get back to their own affairs, and we will win this one the same way."

JICPOA's Translation Section operated in three shifts, each shift eight hours a day, seven days a week. The language officers called it the "Salt Mines," or the "Zoo Section." It was often difficult for them to discern any connection between their work and operations in progress. As the war moved westward, however, more and more of them were assigned to temporary duty with combat units, with civil governments of occupied territories, and with JICPOA teams. Sometimes they were pitched into combat situations without adequate training or practice in the use of the weapons they were given to defend themselves. Respect for language officers and appreciation of their value increased with each succeeding operation. Eighty-four translators were sent out with the Okinawan campaign. It was a privilege to serve with the Navy language officers. They contributed their fair share to the victory in the Pacific and in the years of peace since then, many have achieved distinction in the judiciary, in diplomacy, and in academic circles.

On 23 February 1944, only five days after they had blasted Truk, Mitscher's carriers struck Guam, Rota, Tinian, and Saipan, in the Marianas. Except for Guam, very little was known about those islands, and one of the purposes of Mitscher's strike was to obtain photographic coverage of them. Having been detected during the run in, the task force had to beat off repeated torpedo and low-level bombing attacks. However, the strike destroyed 168 Japanese planes and produced the much-needed photographic intelligence. Submarines, strategically stationed for that purpose, sank six marus fleeing from Saipan.

The Joint Chiefs of Staff on 12 March issued a directive that determined the course of the war in the Pacific for the next six months. MacArthur was directed to occupy Hollandia by 15 April, while Nimitz was to keep Truk and the other Caroline Islands neutralized and furnish MacArthur with fast carrier support. Nimitz was also directed to occupy Saipan, Tinian, and Guam, starting 15 June, and Palau starting 15 September. Of course, in our lowly echelon, we did not see that directive but we soon learned that Saipan was our next target, and we were grateful for the three-month lead time. Saipan presented new intelligence problems that required time for solution.

On 30 March Spruance with a large part of the Fifth Fleet hit Palau, thirteen hundred miles west of Truk. The carriers were detected four days before they struck and the Japanese fleet abandoned Palau in a hurry, but more than 100,000 tons of marus and about 150 Japanese planes were destroyed. The harbor was mined by carrier planes and, again, valuable photographic intelligence was obtained. As the fleet flagship *Musashi* pulled out of Palau, the *Tunny* hit it with one torpedo, but did only light damage to the biggest battleship ever built. Koga was not aboard his flagship. He and most of his staff had embarked in two planes and left Palau for the Philippines the day before the strike.

On 13 April 1944, only seven days after its return from the Palau strike, Mitscher's Task Force 58, which consisted of the fast carrier groups of the Fifth Fleet, sortied from Majuro to support MacArthur's landings at Hollandia. Between 21 and 24 April it bombed Japanese positions in western New Guinea. On its way home it hit Truk again on 29 April. In all these carrier strikes in the Carolines and New Guinea, Japanese submarines tried, without success, to intercept the carrier task forces.

Since the *I-175* sank the escort carrier *Liscome Bay* on 24 November 1943, Japanese submarines had accomplished very little, and twenty-five of them, including the *I-175*, had been lost. In addition,

Admiral Takeo Takagi, commander of the Sixth Fleet (Submarine Force), had lost his flagship, the submarine tender *Heian Maru*, and his other big tender, the *Rio de Janeiro Maru* in the first carrier raid on Truk. It is not surprising that he was unable to mount an effective submarine attack against carrier task forces. The major factor in the high loss rate of Japanese submarines was their lack of radar. The Estimate Section, mainly through radio intelligence from FRU-Pac, was able to make reasonably accurate estimates of the activity of enemy submarines in each of their operating areas, but Japanese radio messages rarely pinpointed submarine positions in sufficient detail to guide antisubmarine forces into contact. There were exceptions.

When the *I-32* was sent on a supply mission to Wotje, FRUPac picked up and decrypted the message setting up the operation in time for antisubmarine forces to be sent to intercept it. The *I-32* was sunk off Wotje on 24 March 1944 by the destroyer escort *Manlove* and the submarine chaser *PC 1135*. Supply missions to the by-passed Solomon Islands employed many Japanese submarines, and radio intelligence, forwarded to ComSoPac, assisted in intercepting some of them. By the middle of May, however, Admiral Takagi had collected together enough submarines to form a scouting line designed to trap any future U.S. carrier operation off Palau or western New Guinea. His operation order designated this line as the "NA line," which stretched across the eastern mouth of the cul-de-sac between New Guinea and the Caroline Islands.

Seven RO-class submarines left Truk on 15 May 1944 and, without our knowledge, took positions sixty miles apart on the NA line. The next day, the *I-176*, on a supply mission to Buka, was sunk by a group of U.S. destroyers. It had been spotted by a patrol plane whose radio reports brought the destroyers to the contact. Japanese radio intelligence followed the entire action by intercepting the radio communications of the destroyers. Accordingly, when it picked up a patrol plane's report of sighting the *RO-104* on the NA line, the Japanese submarine command reacted quickly. By radio, it ordered the entire NA line to move sixty miles to the southeast and assigned specific positions to each Japanese submarine on the new line. FRU-Pac intercepted that message.

As received at FRUPac, the message could be recognized as an operational directive from Commander, Sixth Fleet, to submarines in the Truk-Rabaul area, but it was essentially unreadable because very few of the code groups were recovered. When Lieutenant Alex Johnson, the newest officer in the Estimate Section, who had recently been assigned the task of preparing weekly estimates of Japanese submarine locations, brought the message to me it looked hopeless. Together we plotted out on the chart what information we had. I cannot remember whether the positions given in the message were in latitude and longitude or in Japanese secret grid coordinates, but it would have made little difference because we had learned to convert readily from one system to the other. I asked Finnegan to look at what we had plotted, and he was soon "hooked" on the problem. It was the kind of thing at which Finnegan was a genius, involving research of back traffic, plugging holes in old messages with newly recovered cipher numbers, and confirming or rejecting guesses derived from the plot. In a day or two, Johnson had a plot of the new NA line that passed every test for consistency and probability.

This all happened at a very opportune time. A short while before, a commander had joined CinCPac's Operations Division for the specific purpose of coordinating antisubmarine operations, particularly the formation of hunter-killer groups to search out and destroy Japanese submarines before they were encountered by the antisubmarine screens of operating forces. This commander was familiar with the quantity and quality of the information the Estimate Section was furnishing submarines and he could not understand why it could not do as well for his antisubmarine group. In vain we tried to convince him that radio intelligence is a weapon of opportunity and, in the last analysis, the enemy had to furnish that opportunity. Then, at last, there came an opportunity he could exploit. In the Solomons there was a hunter-killer group of three destroyer escorts, the *England*, *Raby*, and *George*, ready to go. Prepared with the positions Johnson and Finnegan had worked out, the group was ordered to attack the NA line. En route they encountered the *I-16* on a supply mission from Truk to Buka. The *England* attacked with hedgehogs and sank it, getting the operation off to an auspicious start. Three days later the hunter-killer group reached the northern end of the NA line and began working southward, sinking five of the seven RO-boats on the line. The *England* made all the kills, sinking six submarines in twelve days in the most brilliant antisubmarine operation in history.

A two-pronged Allied advance in the summer of 1944 created a dilemma for the Japanese. If MacArthur continued his advance from New Guinea to the Netherlands East Indies, Japan's oil supply would be cut off. If Nimitz won the Marianas, her sea communications would be crowded against the coast of China, and Tokyo itself would be within range of B-29s, the U.S. Army's new big bombers.

The Japanese made frantic efforts to bolster their defenses against both these threats. For the first time in the war, they began to pull army divisions out of Manchuria, where they were deployed to prevent the Soviet Far Eastern Army from moving to the Soviet-German battle front. Before reinforcements from Manchuria could reach either New Guinea or the Marianas, however, they had to be transported across seas infested with U.S. submarines. How this problem would be solved became the subject of bitter debate between the Japanese Army and Navy.

The Army troops were crowded into transports, which were organized in larger-than-usual convoys and protected by the Grand Surface Escort Force and the newly organized Air Squadron 901. Troop convoys to New Guinea were routed through the South China Sea, where Admiral Christie's Southwest Pacific submarine force patrolled. Christie made good use of communications intelligence in assigning submarines to patrol areas and directing their operations. In April 1944 a convoy of nine transports embarked two Japanese army divisions at Shanghai and departed for New Guinea. In its first encounter with a submarine, northwest of Manila, one transport was torpedoed and sank so quickly that an entire army regiment was lost. Three other transports in this convoy were sunk and, because of the risk of further losses to submarines, the remainder of the troops were disembarked in Halmahera, in the Moluccas, far from their destination. Very few of them reached New Guinea before the issue there was decided.

Christie's submarines, often assisted by communications intelligence in finding targets, were concurrently conducting a systematic campaign against tanker convoys from the East Indies to Japan. Also, when communications intelligence provided early information of a Japanese fleet concentration at Tawi Tawi, in the Sulu Archipelago, they picketed that anchorage, harassing the Japanese fleet and providing strategic intelligence on all of its movements.

Troop convoys to the Marianas had to traverse the patrol areas of Admiral Lockwood's Pacific submarine forces. In April, five special troop convoys were sent to the Marianas with Japanese army reinforcements. Communications intelligence decrypted many messages concerning these convoys, and the information was collated by the Estimate Section and passed on to ComSubPac. Six transports from these convoys were torpedoed and sunk, but many got through to Saipan.

In May and June 1944 cooperation between the Estimate Section and ComSubPac was at its most efficient. Submarines went out on two-month patrols, and the area to which they were assigned had to be decided well in advance. The mine-field barrier between Kyushu and Formosa kept them out of the East China Sea until we could determine safe routes for them through the barrier, which was not until the middle of June. This reduced the areas for submarine operations, and this reduction, together with the larger convoys, made the organization of wolf packs profitable. Voge wanted to send wolf packs into the open sea between Nansei Shoto and the Marianas. If he could count on decryptions of the maru code to continue giving him convoy route points to guide his submarines into contact, that would be the best place for them to be. Once contact was established, the submarines would have a wide choice of tactics and could make repeated attacks on each convoy. Without good information, however, a submarine could patrol the open sea for weeks without making contact with a convoy. Under such circumstances it would be better for the submarines to be close in to Saipan, but Japanese antisubmarine operations were concentrated there and a submarine could attack only once before the convoy reached safety.

We could give Voge no assurance. A code change could black out our sources of information like blowing out a candle. ComSubPac decided to risk the open sea. It was the correct decision. In the last hectic weeks before the American landing on Saipan, several convoys ran the gantlet from Japan to Saipan, incurring heavy losses from submarines. The last Japanese convoy lost five of its seven ships.

Not all the enterprises between the Estimate Section and ComSubPac were successful. The Japanese Navy made a scheduled change in the five-digit code, starting the cryptanalysts all over again at the beginning of the long, laborious task of breaking a new code. Then FRUPac intercepted a message from Wake Island. It was in the old code, and reported that their new code books had not arrived. Japanese supply lines to Wake had been cut off by the capture of Eniwetok, so the cryptanalysts became very much interested in the situation. FRUPac carefully watched radio communications with Wake to learn what Tokyo's solution to this problem would be.

In late April 1944, Tokyo sent out the *Tajima Maru*, an 89-ton picket boat, loaded with supplies and carrying the new code books for Wake, apparently in hopes that the inconspicuous little ship would escape detection. In a message encrypted in the old code, Wake was informed of the *Tajima Maru*'s mission, its route points, and its schedule. This message, also, FRUPac intercepted and decrypted.

ComSubPac had two submarines traversing the route of the *Ta-jima Maru*, the *Haddock* returning from patrol off Okinawa, and the *Tuna* just starting out to patrol Palau. Voge and I cooked up a plot to capture the picket boat and solve the new five-digit code by what Dyer called "the direct method." Dyer was apprehensive. The capture of a code book sometimes evoked changes in enemy communications that turned a coup into a cryptanalyst's disaster, but it did not seem probable that the loss of a small picket in an exposed area would arouse suspicion.

ComSubPac sent radio orders to both the *Tuna* and *Haddock*, directing them to capture a Japanese trawler, whose route points were given, and search it for important documents. Unfortunately, it was impossible adequately to explain the situation in a radio dispatch and neither submarine commander realized that he was on a mission that might be more important than sinking a Japanese battleship. The *Tuna* made first contact, on 4 May 1944. Rather than attempting a capture, she blasted the *Tajima Maru* with her 5-inch gun, then made a cursory inspection of the wreck. The *Haddock* arrived soon afterward but was able only to recover some worthless papers and two prisoners whom the *Tuna* had overlooked. The code books evidently went to the bottom of the sea with the *Tajima Maru*.

All this took place 172 miles north of Wake, but the Japanese knew when and where the *Tajima Maru* had been destroyed by submarine gunfire. The picket boat had evidently been able to communicate with Wake during the attack. The risk we took was much greater than I anticipated, and the only gain was that Wake had to go on using the old code. The Japanese never suspected that we knew the *Tajima Maru* was carrying the precious new code books. We should have sent an experienced language officer—one who was thoroughly familiar with the situation and who could recognize a code book when he saw one—to join the *Tuna* at Midway. Since that could not be done, we should not have attempted a capture at all.

The intrusion of the Japanese Army into the central Pacific changed things for the Estimate Section. FRUPac worked exclusively with Japanese naval codes. We had little knowledge of the Japanese Army's organization and order of battle, and the information we gleaned from Japanese naval communications was insufficient to support our estimates of the strength of the defenses of the Marianas. Four Army officers from the War Department's Military Intelligence Service joined the Estimate Section and were welcomed with open arms. Lieutenant Colonel John W. Fager, the officer in

John W. Fager

charge of the group, took over the estimates of enemy strength on Saipan and Guam, and Captain Gordon Hamilton assisted Emory in making estimates of air strength. Hinkle, who had made estimates of enemy garrison strength in the Marshalls and Gilberts, advised Fager on Japanese naval shore units, but he was mainly occupied with captured enemy equipment, for which JICPOA had become a central depository.

Cooperation between the Army and the Navy in the Estimate Section was ideal. By the summer of 1944 the Army had a system of special liaison units, which controlled the dissemination of Ultra information more efficiently than the Navy did. Army codes and communications were then at least as secure as the Navy's, and often more convenient to use. The Army contingent of the Estimate Section, which eventually grew to number fifteen individuals, set up a communication center which connected us with all the intelligence centers in the Pacific and in Washington. The Army's Signal Intelligence Service did not process Japanese intercepts in Hawaii but, through the Special Liaison Unit at Fort Shafter and Lieutenant Colonel Fager, it made all the intelligence it produced available to the Estimate Section which, in turn, gave SIS access to any intelligence it received from FRUPac or JICPOA.

The Mariana Islands, the next objective for CinCPOA, have some fairly rugged terrain and this had to be mapped by aerial photography. It was a far more difficult job than mapping flat coral atolls, for it involved many sorties of specially equipped photographic planes, expert photo-interpretation and cartography, and rapid production and distribution of great quantities of maps to different scales and charts for many different purposes. Fortunately, Joe Twitty, my boss at JICPOA, was exceptionally well qualified and in the best position to effect the cooperation of JICPOA, Army and Navy air services, the photographic processing and interpretation of PRISIC and its subsidiary InterpRon Two at Eniwetok, the 64th and the 30th Topographic Companies of the Army, the Army Map Service, and the Navy Hydrographic Office in Washington to get this essential job done on time.

The new building for JICPOA was completed 16 May 1944. Except for the Estimate Section, JICPOA moved from the FRUPac building into the new one. Because of the security requirements for the Ultra material it filed and the necessity for its close cooperation with FRUPac, the Estimate Section remained on the first floor of the FRUPac building. As chief of the Estimate Section, I retained my desk in the old building, and as deputy officer-in-charge of JICPOA, I acquired an office alongside Twitty's in the new building. It was fortunate for me that my two offices were so close together.

Photographic laboratory facilities having been incorporated into the JICPOA building, PRISIC moved into them from the Kodak Hawaii Building in Honolulu. PRISIC itself ceased to exist and its functions were reorganized into the Photographic Interpretation Section, the Photographic Laboratory, and the Model Shop. For the first time, photographic intelligence was under the same roof as the rest of JICPOA. Photo-interpretation was the major source of information available to the Enemy Bases Section in producing the yellow-covered information bulletins on the Mariana and Caroline islands. It became equal with communications intelligence and translations as a primary source of intelligence. While it existed, PRISIC functioned as an officer pool to provide photo-interpreters to carriers, amphibious forces, and InterpRons One and Two. JICPOA continued this function. In 1942 there was a surplus of photo-interpreters, and many graduates of the photo-interpreters' school were diverted to other intelligence jobs in which they became very valuable and where their skills as interpreters were frequently useful. In 1944 the demand for photo-interpreters greatly exceeded the supply. The number on duty at JICPOA varied from fifteen to more than ninety.

JICPOA (left) and FRUPac (right) photographed from the top
of the Makalapa Administration Building
Courtesy: U.S. Naval History Division

Tokyo announced the appointment of Admiral Soemu Toyoda
as commander in chief of the Combined Fleet on 5 May 1944. There
were strong rumors that the plane in which Koga left Palau at the
end of March crashed in the Philippines and he was killed. Consequently, there was much speculation at CinCPac headquarters as to
who, in that case, his successor might be. Layton had collected a file
of information on Japanese flag officers but the pressure of his job
caused him to turn it over to Lieutenant John Harrison, a language
officer in the Estimate Section. From captured documents Harrison
expanded Layton's file until we had, at JICPOA, the best collection
of Japanese naval biographies anywhere outside Japan. In appoint-
ing Toyoda, the Japanese Navy jumped over all the seagoing tacticians who had fought the great carrier actions and the battles in
the Solomon Islands to pick a Tokyo administrative officer. Harrison was able to produce a photograph of Toyoda and a short biog-
raphy, and JICPOA published Bulletin No. 57–44, "Changes in the
Japanese High Command," which we distributed widely.

Toyoda never commanded the Combined Fleet at sea, as both
Yamamoto and Koga had done, and he made no change in the basic

John A. Harrison

Japanese strategy of seeking a decisive fleet action under favorable conditions. Koga was thwarted by his loss of carrier planes and pilots but he had formed a plan to overcome this handicap. The plan was the legacy he left to Toyoda and, as it turned out, to us. A copy of his "Z" plan, from which Toyoda's "Sho-Go" plan was developed, was in one of the two planes that crashed in the Philippines.

When first I saw this plan it was as a translation of a captured document we received in an exchange with ATIS in the Southwest Pacific Area. It was labeled "Secret. Not to be copied or reproduced without permission of General MacArthur." Perhaps it was the label that first attracted my attention. We classified captured documents as "confidential" and labeled them "May be copied or reproduced for official purposes with or without credit provided classification is maintained." It was apparent that here was a document requiring rapid and wide distribution to the fleet. I took it down to Layton with the recommendation that we run off a hundred copies and distribute it immediately. Layton was more diplomatic, pointing out that it had been translated by someone unfamiliar with Japanese naval terminology, and that it needed editing, which he would do himself. In the meantime he would send a dispatch from Nimitz to MacArthur asking permission to distribute the translation to the fleet. In a couple of days, it was cleared by MacArthur, edited, reproduced, and on its way to fleet commands.

In short, Koga planned to concentrate Japanese shore-based air forces and to operate his carrier planes from shore bases when the Americans attacked the Philippines, Palau, or the Marianas. There was nothing particularly new about that, but Koga also intended to use some of his empty carriers as a diversionary attack force to draw off American carrier forces while the Japanese surface fleet fell upon and destroyed the American expeditionary forces.

This document reached Spruance before he sailed for Saipan. It undoubtedly influenced his tactics in the Battle of the Philippine Sea, which have evoked discussion among tacticians ever since. It also reached Halsey's staff. It did not influence Halsey's tactics in the Battle for Leyte Gulf, but it should have.

CHAPTER 15

THE ALLIED EXPEDITIONARY FORCE under the supreme command of General Dwight D. Eisenhower landed in Normandy, France, on 6 June 1944. On that same date Task Force 58, the fast carrier force under Admiral Mitscher, sortied from Majuro, in the Marshall Islands. Admiral Spruance, commanding the Fifth Fleet in his flagship, the heavy cruiser *Indianapolis*, joined Task Force 58 on 9 June at the first fueling rendezvous. The Joint Expeditionary Force under Admiral Turner, with a total of 535 combat ships and auxiliaries carrying 127,500 troops, followed in their wake. Their mission: conquest of the Marianas in order to cut air and surface communications between Japan and the south, provide advance bases for U.S. surface and submarine operations, and prepare airfields from which B-29s would be able to bomb Japan. A landing in the Marianas was expected to bring on a decisive fleet engagement.

JICPOA had supplied the Fifth Fleet and the Joint Expeditionary Force with literally tons of maps and charts, air target folders, information bulletins, photographs, estimates, and translations. Radio Intelligence had located the Japanese Mobile Fleet, under Admiral Jisaburo Ozawa, at Tawi Tawi, in the Sulu Archipelago, where it was being picketed by Christie's submarines. The Estimate Section had given Spruance an accurate appraisal of Ozawa's strength but, after the Fifth Fleet left the Marshall Islands astern, the forces afloat were dependent upon their own resources for information on the movement of the Japanese Mobile Fleet.

On board the *Indianapolis* FRUPac had a small team under Commander Gilven Slonim, who acted as Spruance's radio-intelligence and language officer. By means of a special code, FRUPac kept Slonim informed of Japanese radio call signs and other technical information, but Ozawa's radio silence reduced almost to zero the amount of information that could be derived from his communications. The mid-Pacific strategic direction-finders, under FRUPac's supervision, listened intently for any Japanese fleet transmissions. On the night of 18 June 1944, the eve of the Battle of the Philippine Sea, Ozawa did open up his radio transmitter once to alert the Japanese airfields on Guam, and this allowed the direction finders to fix his position quite accurately. Air searches and submarine scouts, however, were Spruance's main sources of information on Ozawa's movements.

On 13 June, Ozawa with the Japanese Mobile Fleet departed from Tawi Tawi for the Marianas and a battle with the American Fifth Fleet under Spruance. Submarines reported Ozawa's departure and, three times during his passage, reported the positions of Japanese major forces. On 19 June the submarines *Cavalla* and *Albacore* sank two big Japanese carriers, the *Shokaku* and *Taiho*, successes to which the Estimate Section had contributed by supplying early information that helped to station the submarines advantageously.

After three days of preliminary bombing and bombardment of the island, the Joint Expeditionary Force landed on Saipan on 15 June 1944. The Japanese put up a strong defense on the beach and in depth. For several days the landing force was dependent on supplies and reinforcements being landed from the transports, and on support of naval gunfire.

Ozawa correctly deduced that Spruance would stay within supporting distance of the landing forces. On 19 June the Japanese attacked the Fifth Fleet with repeated air strikes, launched at long range, and lost three-fourths of their carrier planes and pilots. The next day American carrier planes sank the carrier *Hiyo* and two tankers, and damaged several other Japanese ships. Ozawa had no recourse but to retreat and leave the Marianas to their fate, although he saved most of his ships as a "fleet in being" for future operations.

On the night of 18 June, Mitscher had urged Spruance to allow Task Force 58 to speed westward so that, at dawn, it would be in position to attack the Japanese fleet. Had he been permitted to do so, a larger part of the Japanese fleet would probably have been destroyed. Spruance, however, not convinced that all the Japanese forces had been located, held Mitscher close to Saipan to cover the Joint Expeditionary Force. There is no doubt that Spruance, influenced by the captured "Z" plan we had sent to him, believed that Ozawa intended to draw Task Force 58 away from a covering position and then attack Turner's vulnerable Joint Expeditionary Force astride the Saipan beachhead. Spruance's tactics were thus designed to counter what he estimated to be the enemy's intentions—and so was Nimitz's strategy at the Battle of Midway.

The battle ashore on Saipan progressed slowly against stiff Japanese resistance. There was little the Estimate Section could do but plot the battle lines each day and add up the enemy casualties. The sum of the "body counts" reported exceeded our estimates of total strength of the Japanese garrison. We discounted these gruesome statistics. Historians accuse intelligence of having underestimated Japanese numbers on Saipan, but my undocumented recollection is that the Estimate Section predicted a total strength of 25,000 military defenders, which compares reasonably with the 23,811 enemy buried plus 1,780 taken prisoner.

Admiral Takagi, Japanese submarine force commander, and all his staff were killed at Saipan. Seventeen of the twenty-two Japanese submarines he threw into the battle for the Marianas were sunk. It was some time before either Admiral Shigeyoshi Miwa, who replaced Takagi, or the Estimate Section could confirm the extent of Japanese submarine losses, but the latter soon confirmed that three aircraft carriers, the *Taiho*, *Shokaku*, and *Hiyo*, had been sunk. Of the six Japanese aircraft carriers that had taken part in the attack on Pearl Harbor, the *Shokaku* was the fifth to be sunk. We had long since identified all the ships of the Kido Butai that had attacked Pearl Harbor, and their silhouettes were pasted on the wall in the Estimate Section. It gave me an unprofessional vindictive satisfaction to check off each of those ships as it was sunk. I told Voge I would give a bottle of Scotch to any submarine skipper who sank one of them. Voge was careful to present every qualifying skipper for his bottle, but I never saw Herman J. Kossler, the captain of the *Cavalla*, after he sank the *Shokaku*. Kossler was the only submarine captain to sink a capital ship of the Kido Butai, and I still owe him a bottle of Scotch.

Organized Japanese resistance ceased on Saipan on 9 July 1944, and on Tinian on 1 August. It was 10 August before the fighting ended on Guam. The Marianas were then securely in American hands. Most Japanese strategists knew that they had lost the war, but it required another year of hard fighting and two atom bombs to overcome the doctrine of suicide before surrender, deeply embedded in the Japanese military credo, and the *Yamato-damashii* of war leaders, inspiring them to bring down the Japanese nation, its culture, and economy, in one colossal holocaust rather than face up to defeat. In the Marianas we took some prisoners who elected surrender rather than suicide. They appeared to be convinced that early surrender was a better course for Japan than the death and destruction that further resistance would entail. From ostensibly patriotic motives, they were willing to work with JICPOA's new Psychological Warfare Section in writing leaflets urging surrender. Millions of these leaflets were dropped on Japan with no discernible effect.

During the Marianas campaign, the Pacific Fleet was reorganized. The South Pacific command, then of diminished importance, remained at Nouméa. Admiral Halsey became Commander, Third Fleet, and moved to the central Pacific. The Third Fleet was made up of the same ships as the Fifth Fleet. While the Fifth Fleet, under Spruance, was engaged in one operation, Halsey and his staff, at Pearl Harbor, planned the next operation. When Halsey took over to command the operation he had planned, the Fifth Fleet became the Third Fleet, and Spruance went to Pearl Harbor to compile new plans. The chameleonlike ability of the fleet to take on the color of its commander was remarkable. When it went to sea under Spruance, it refused to be distracted from its objective, and we could read its schedules and confidently plot the locality of all its forces at any hour. When it went to sea under Halsey, whose staff were splendid opportunists, neither the Japanese nor the Estimate Section knew what to expect next.

When Halsey came north to Hawaii, he brought with him a number of bright young intelligence officers, who were ordered to JICPOA. Among them were Lieutenant Commander Logan H. Jenkins and Lieutenant John C. Goodbody, who had been involved in the production of a series of "Know Your Enemy" publications in the South Pacific. Both Captain Layton and I were aware that our production of confidential and restricted intelligence material for mass distribution was inadequate. In the new JICPOA building we had two good offset presses so, for the first time, we had both personnel and equipment to do something about it. Within JICPOA we set up a Bulletin Section, which never consisted of more than eleven persons, to produce CinCPac-CinCPOA weekly intelligence bulletins. Volume 1, Number 1, was issued on 14 July 1944.

The first print order was for 2,000 copies. The project was a success from the beginning. Demand almost immediately jumped to 6,000 copies and many of the early issues had to be reprinted. By the end of the war, the weekly circulation was 14,000 copies. The bulletin published descriptions and pictures of enemy ships, aircraft, equipment, weapons, and installations; enemy accounts of past battles and battle tactics, action photographs, and any pertinent information on the enemy that could be disseminated under the "confidential" classification. Material was drawn from all sections of JICPOA, and liberal use was made of photographs. The photographic and lithographic departments of JICPOA took great pride in the bulletin. A "war photograph of the week" usually graced its cover. John Goodbody was bitter when the photograph of the flag-raising on Mount Suribachi escaped to the press before he could use it on the cover of the bulletin.

The bulletin confined itself to evaluated information on the enemy and emphasized accuracy, brevity, and simplicity. One of its virtues was the timeliness of the material it contained. This was achieved through vesting responsibility for its production in only a few persons. The bulletin staff did not have access to Ultra information. To avoid inconsistencies or any inadvertent disclosure of Ultra, I was held responsible for the classification of bulletin material. Behind this protective shield, the editors had wide choice of material and presentation. In my office, each Monday morning, we went over every word of the text and the layout. By noon everything was in the hands of the printers. By Wednesday the entire printing was ready for distribution. By Friday it was in Guam and Eniwetok being distributed to units of the fleet and of the amphibious forces. The promptness with which JICPOA material was delivered was a tribute to the efficiency of its Administration Section, at the heart of which were the Legendre brothers, Morris and Sidney.

When the Marianas fell, the Japanese frantically began to reinforce the Volcano Islands and the Ryukyus. To counter this move, carrier groups hit the Bonins and Iwo Jima, and the submarines continued their attacks on shipping. JICPOA had accumulated enough information of the East China mine barrier to map safe routes around its mine fields. On 20 June, three submarines, the *Tang*, *Tinosa*, and *Sealion*, entered the East China Sea behind the mine barrier to fall unexpectedly upon the convoys carrying troops to Okinawa. Before they withdrew, they sank sixteen marus. In Luzon Strait, wolf packs tore at the throat of Japanese sea communications with the Philippines and the East Indies.

Because of an increase in the number of American submarines and a decrease in the areas open to Japanese shipping, a subtle change occurred in submarine warfare. In the early years of the war, U.S. submarines waged a war of attrition, but by the middle of 1944 they were imposing a blockade on Japan. Although Japanese ships ran the blockade they paid a terrific toll. Decryption of the maru and five-digit codes continued to reveal important convoy and combat-ship movements. Ultra messages to submarines were of almost nightly occurrence, too many to enumerate, but a few instances stand out. On the night of 16 July, a wolf pack of three submarines, the *Piranha*, *Guardfish*, and *Thresher*, after being coached into contact by Ultra, sank six ships of a ten-ship convoy in Luzon Strait. The next week, the *I-29*, on the last leg of a long voyage on which it had carried quinine and rubber to Germany and was returning with prototypes of new scientific instruments and weapons, was routed through the South China Sea from Singapore. FRUPac decrypted its routing message in time for three submarines, the *Tilefish*, *Rock*, and *Sawfish*, to set up an ambush. The *Sawfish* sank the *I-29* with three torpedo hits.

While the Fifth Fleet and the Fifth Amphibious Force were engaged in the Marianas operation, the Third Amphibious Force was drawing up plans to take Palau. These plans were submitted to Nimitz on 7 July 1944. JICPOA had produced an information bulletin and air target folders, but our knowledge of Palau was meager, based only on photographs taken during carrier air strikes, a captured chart, and the observations of patrolling submarines. The *Seawolf* made a photographic reconnaissance of Palau, and the *Permit* did the same for Yap and Woleai, in the western Carolines, in July, but these photographs were not yet available.

From the Marianas there were three ways to advance against Japan, but I thought that the way through Okinawa was best. Okinawa, which is on the eastern side of the East China Sea, about twelve hundred miles from Saipan and about eight hundred miles from Tokyo, has good harbors and there was plenty of room for airfield development. From it, planes and surface ships could control the southern half of the East China Sea and cut off Japan from Formosa and the south. In their concentration on the defense of the Marianas, Palau, and New Guinea, the Japanese had neglected Okinawa and Iwo Jima.

I went up to the Geographic Section to confer with Lieutenant Commander Beverley Causey, who would have the job of preparing an information bulletin on Okinawa, to suggest that we get an early start so that we could exhaust all sources of information. Commander Denzel Carr, of the District Intelligence Office in Honolulu, had spent several months on Okinawa only a few years before the war, and he might be able to develop leads from the many Okinawans in Hawaii. I knew that Okinawa was the habitat of the habu, a snake as venomous as a rattlesnake and bigger. I suggested that we might get a good picture of a habu and information on the flora and fauna of Okinawa from Bishop Museum. With plenty of time, I expected Causey would turn out the best information bulletin ever. He did, but it was a long while before we needed it.

In early August the submarine *Burrfish* was sent out with an underwater demolition team to reconnoiter the beaches of Peleliu and Angaur, in the Palaus, and Yap, in the Carolines. I learned then that Admiral Halsey, with the Third Fleet and the Third Amphibious Force, was scheduled to take those islands and Ulithi, also in the Carolines, in September, in order to support MacArthur's advance to Mindanao. I thought it was a move in the wrong direction, away from Japan and not toward it. I wanted to be sure the War Plans Division knew what we had learned about Okinawa, so I went down to talk to Admiral Forrest P. Sherman, CinCPac's chief planner. The island was still inadequately defended although the Japanese were rapidly moving in reinforcements, despite heavy losses from our submarine operations.

"Could you take it with four divisions?" he asked.

I was over my head already. I thought we then could take it easily but, as happened at Guadalcanal, that would be only the beginning. Each side would throw in all available reinforcements until the last decisive battle of the war developed.

"Well, four divisions are all we can lift in the central Pacific," Sherman told me. "We have to keep the Japanese off balance after their defeat in the Marianas, but we are limited to a four-division objective."

Sherman's elementary logistic considerations easily shot down my suggestions. Although he may have been in sympathy with my ideas he must have considered me very naive. He had been involved in long controversy between the Navy's proposal to proceed directly to Formosa and MacArthur's plan to first retake the Philippines. In Nimitz's and MacArthur's conference with President Roosevelt at Waikiki on 26 July 1944, it was agreed that MacArthur would take Mindanao, Leyte, and Luzon with the assistance of the Pacific Fleet. The Joint Chiefs of Staff did not establish a timetable for these operations until 9 September 1944. I was not aware of all this high-level planning until much later.

Perhaps the premature JICPOA study of Okinawa had some influence, however. At the San Francisco conference between central and southwest Pacific planners on 29 September 1944, Spruance advocated Okinawa as the next objective after Luzon. He was the first high-ranking officer to do so. I cannot recall ever having discussed it with him, but Captain Charles H. Murphy, his intelligence officer, and Commander Slonim, his radio-intelligence and language officer, both spent much time at JICPOA and were familiar with all the work in progress there.

Task Force 38, led by Admiral Halsey, bombed the Palau Islands on 6 September and Mindanao on the ninth to destroy Japanese air forces that could interfere with the conquest of Peleliu, or with MacArthur's landing on Morotai, both scheduled to begin on 15 September 1944. The carriers met with no enemy opposition. Halsey then canceled further strikes on Mindanao and moved up to the central Philippines, where he destroyed 200 Japanese planes and many ships in harbors, but met little opposition. Encouraged by this apparent weakness of the Japanese, he sent a dispatch, on 13 September, to Nimitz and MacArthur recommending that CinCPac landings in the Palaus and Yap and MacArthur's landings on Morotai and Mindanao be canceled and the forces of the central Pacific and the southwest Pacific unite for the conquest of Leyte. This would advance the timetable for retaking the Philippines by at least two months.

Halsey's plan met with instant approval from MacArthur, except that he wanted to take Morotai to provide a staging base for planes en route to Leyte. Nimitz approved, except that he wanted to continue with the Peleliu-Angaur operation, also for staging into Leyte. The Joint Chiefs of Staff, then attending the conference in Quebec between President Roosevelt and Prime Minister Winston Churchill, quickly approved. MacArthur took Morotai with little difficulty but Peleliu proved to be very different. The forces intended for Yap were diverted to Leyte. Ulithi was occupied without opposition.

The Third Amphibious Force under Admiral Theodore S. Wilkinson, covered by the Third Fleet under Admiral Halsey, began landing operations on Peleliu on 15 September, as originally planned. JICPOA had prepared a new Palau Information Bulletin incorporating information gained from submarine and aerial reconnaissance during July and August, but no one could be found who had ever visited the Palaus, and nothing much had been written about them for a century or more. Information concerning the beaches was fairly good, but dense tropical foliage that aerial photography was unable to penetrate concealed jagged limestone ridges, honeycombed with caves, behind the beaches. Also at Peleliu, the Japanese changed their traditional tactic of "annihilation of the enemy at the beach" to a more-balanced, stubborn defense in depth. This, and inadequate knowledge of the terrain, was partly responsible for the heavy casualties. It might have been better if the landings in the Palaus had been called off, as Halsey recommended, because the cost in lives of the conquest of Peleliu and Angaur was too great a price to pay for their limited strategic value.

During the Marianas campaign Admiral Lockwood, in cooperation with the Fifth Fleet, directly controlled the submarines and results were excellent. During the Palaus operations the planners of Halsey's Third Fleet wanted to exercise direct control over participating submarines. Lockwood objected, but the question was resolved in favor of the Third Fleet. A group of ten submarines, under Halsey's direct control, was disposed in double reconnaissance lines, called the Bear Pit, and was to be on station by 13 September between the Palaus and the Philippines. The Japanese fleet made no attempt to interfere with the operations in the Palaus and maru traffic with those islands had long since ceased, so the Bear Pit submarines saw nothing during the campaign. Because of Halsey's wide-ranging carrier operations, the positions of the submarines had to be changed many times. On one occasion the staff of the Third Fleet ordered submarines to cross mine fields whose locations were known to ComSubPac and should have been known to the Third Fleet. Fortunately, these orders were changed after Lockwood protested, but the incident demonstrated the necessity for close cooperation between submarine operations and the intelligence organization—difficult to maintain with the staff of a flagship at sea.

Between 15 September and 20 October, the Third Fleet ranged the Philippine Sea from the Ryukyus to Mindanao, striking airfields and shipping in the Ryukyus, Formosa, Luzon, and the central Philippines. JICPOA and FRUPac were of little help to Halsey during this period of rampant action. Our knowledge of where Japanese airfields were in that area was incomplete. Through radio intelligence we knew that the Japanese fleet was divided, most of the surface ships being at Lingga Roads, near Singapore, while the carriers were training new pilots in Japan's Inland Sea, between Shikoku and Honshu. Although the exact locations of a few ships of the Combined Fleet might be in doubt, we had an accurate roster of all their names and characteristics. By collating radio intelligence, captured documents, and our own action reports, we also had excellent information on when and where each Japanese naval vessel, larger than an escort destroyer, had been lost.

Every morning CinCPac's Communications Division sent to the Estimate Section copies of incoming and outgoing dispatches that might be related to our work. One morning I was surprised to find a copy of a dispatch from Chungking, China, relaying a report by a Chinese observer that a powerful Japanese surface force had departed from Amoy, China, for Luzon. To meet it, Halsey would certainly have to change his plans for strikes on Luzon. I was at a loss to account for the existence of such a large force until I checked the names of the Japanese ships, which the informant had obligingly supplied. They were all ships that had been sunk but whose loss had been kept secret by the Japanese. Among the names, for instance, was *Mutsu*, the battleship that the Japanese did not know that we knew had been sunk by an accidental internal explosion in the Inland Sea.

I called Layton on the telephone and learned that he had already originated a dispatch to Halsey discrediting the message. Captain Marion C. "Mike" Cheek and Lieutenant Harris Cox, intelligence officers with Halsey in the *New Jersey*, also had good current information of Japanese naval order of battle and quickly spotted the hoax, as Cox later told me. The misinformation had probably been planted by a double agent for the purpose of distracting Halsey. China was then a multinational stew of secret agents and double agents.

The Third Fleet hit Okinawa, Formosa, and northern Luzon, between 10 August and 14 August, with repeated air strikes. The Japanese responded by counterattacking with every plane they could muster, including carrier planes with pilots in training, and their losses were heavy. Many of the planes of Air Squadron 901, specially trained and equipped for antisubmarine work, were lost, making life much easier for American submarines. Two Third Fleet cruisers, the *Canberra* and *Houston*, were hit by torpedoes but, by heroic efforts, were safely towed to Ulithi. None of the Third Fleet ships was sunk.

Japanese pilots enthusiastically reported that they had sunk eleven aircraft carriers and two battleships, damaged eight aircraft carriers and two battleships, and sunk or damaged many other ships. Radio Tokyo joyously reported that Admiral Halsey had been defeated, and the emperor decreed a mass celebration for the "Victory of Taiwan." Many thought that this was arrant propaganda but radio intelligence knew that the Japanese Imperial General Headquarters believed it. The Japanese Army made extensive changes in their plans for the defense of the Philippines. The Japanese apparently had no organization capable of assessing reports based on combat observations. The bombastic style of their action reports suggests that it would have taken great courage for any Japanese administrative organization to attempt such assessment, but without it, plans and decisions were apt to be based on dangerously fictitious values. One of the important functions of our Estimate Section was the realistic appraisal (and constant reappraisal, as evidence accumulated) of damage our forces had reportedly inflicted on the Japanese. I was thankful, however, that our task was only to ascertain the truth. Layton at CinCPac and Voge at ComSubPac had the unpopular job of convincing battle-hardened veterans that many of what they believed to be honest reports of damage to the enemy were overoptimistic.

U.S. Army forces, supported by naval gunfire and carrier-based aircraft, under the overall command of General MacArthur, landed on Leyte on 20 October 1944. The Seventh Fleet under Admiral Thomas C. Kinkaid provided naval support. The Japanese fleet responded by executing its "Sho-Go" plan for the defense of the Philippines.

A large Japanese surface force departed from Lingga Roads for Brunei, Borneo, on 18 October. Radio intelligence detected this movement and warned American forces. At Brunei the force divided into two parts. The Southern Force, with two battleships and one cruiser, left Brunei on 22 October and set course across the Sulu Sea with the intention of entering Leyte Gulf through Surigao Strait. According to the plan, the Center Force, with five battleships and twelve cruisers, was to proceed up Palawan Passage, go through the Sibuyan Sea and San Bernardino Strait, and rendezvous with the Southern Force in Leyte Gulf.

On 20 October the Northern Force, with four aircraft carriers (whose pilots were half-trained and which had less than half of their complement of planes), two carrier-battleships, and three light cruisers, sailed from the Inland Sea. This force was not sighted until the evening of 24 October, when it was off Cape Engaño, northeast of Luzon. Captured documents translated months before and distributed to Halsey and the task force commanders of the Third Fleet revealed a Japanese plan to use a diversionary attack force to draw the American fast carrier force away from a position covering landing operations. It should have been suspected that the Northern Force was that diversion.

U.S. submarines of the southwest Pacific forces sank two heavy cruisers, severely damaged two others, and shadowed the Center Force until it entered the Sibuyan Sea. On 24 October carrier planes from the Third Fleet sank the mighty battleship *Musashi* and severely damaged a heavy cruiser. That night Kinkaid's Seventh Fleet annihilated the Southern Force in Surigao Strait.

Overenthusiastic reports from his pilots led Halsey into believing that the Center Force had suffered disabling damage. Consequently, when his search planes reported the Northern Force off Cape Engaño, he assembled the Third Fleet and sped north, where he sank four Japanese aircraft carriers and other vessels, but left San Bernardino Strait unguarded.

Despite the damage it had sustained, the Center Force was stronger than the forces Kinkaid had in Leyte Gulf to meet it when it emerged from San Bernardino Strait into the Philippine Sea on the morning of 25 October. Between it and Leyte Gulf were only the thin-skinned and slow escort carriers and their destroyer screen. These put up such a furious resistance that, while losing one escort carrier and three destroyers, they sank three Japanese heavy cruisers and turned back the Center Force.

At Pearl Harbor CinCPac staff tensely followed the action, partly through intercepted dispatches from Halsey and Kinkaid. On the morning of the twenty-fifth I eagerly searched the Estimate Section's copies of these messages, reading victory in every dispatch, until I encountered the escort carriers' astounding report of being under gunfire from Japanese battleships. I assumed that when Halsey turned north to destroy the Northern Force, he left the battleships and cruisers of Task Force 34, under Admiral Willis A. Lee, to guard San Bernardino, but I could find no dispatch to that effect.

Layton, I thought, would have more and better information. I called him on the telephone and told him we did not have a dispatch directing Lee to form a battle line.

"Where is Task Force 34?" I asked him.

Layton was irate. In the absence of any message to the contrary, he concluded that Halsey had taken the battleships with him in pursuit of the Northern Force. I reasoned that Halsey might have given Lee orders by visual signals and, as we had only radio intercepts to go by, we would have no indication of them. Perhaps Task Force 34 was between the Japanese and San Bernardino, and closing in on the Center Force.

"I doubt it," Layton replied, and slammed down the phone.

But the seeds of doubt had been planted in the fertile soil of staff hope. That, I believe, was the genesis of Nimitz's dispatch to Halsey, "Where is Task Force 34?"

It is difficult to explain why Halsey swallowed the bait of the Japanese Diversionary Attack Force. Harris Cox told me afterward that he and Captain Cheek, on board the *New Jersey*, had all the necessary documents to support their conclusion that the Third Fleet was being enticed away from its covering position, but no one would listen to them. The Third Fleet staff seemed determined that night to reject any facts that might deter pursuit of the Japanese

Chester W. Nimitz
Courtesy: U.S. Naval History Division

carriers. Perhaps the criticisms of Spruance's decision at Saipan had something to do with their attitude.

The Japanese Army had planned to hold back their major forces for a decisive battle for the Philippines on Luzon. On 23 October Imperial General Headquarters changed these plans and elected to make a decisive stand on Leyte. Between then and 30 October, they landed forty thousand additional troops and ten thousand tons of supplies at Ormoc, on the west coast of Leyte, and staged in air replacements from Formosa and Kyushu. The U.S. Fifth Army Air Force, prevented by weather and terrain from completing airfields on Leyte, was slow in providing Army forces with air support. Attacks by kamikaze planes were horribly effective in damaging the ships of the Seventh and Third fleets. The schedule for the conquest of Leyte was delayed. On 15 December 1944 U.S. Army forces landed on Mindoro. On the twentieth, organized Japanese resistance on Leyte ended.

As the Japanese made desperate efforts to reinforce the Philippines, the Estimate Section continued to provide submarines with exact information on the routes and positions of many convoys. In October U.S. submarines sank seventy marus and air forces sank forty-seven, most of them in a lane from Formosa, through Luzon Strait, and along the west coast of the Philippines. In November fifty-seven marus were sunk by submarines but in December only twenty-one were sunk, and most of them small ships, because there were very few large ones left to sink. Japanese Army divisions, transported to the Philippines from Manchuria, suffered many casualties en route. The experience of the 23rd Infantry Division is an example.

This division embarked in a convoy of nine transports with four antisubmarine frigates as escorts, and the escort carrier *Shinyo* loaded with planes for the Philippines. A decrypted message enabled Voge to put two wolf packs on the track of the convoy in the northern end of the East China Sea. In a wild battle on the night of 17 November 1944, both wolf packs attacked the convoy, sinking four transports and the *Shinyo*. The remainder of the 23rd Division arrived at Manila in late November. Stocks of arms and ammunition were low and there were few effective antitank weapons. Poor transportation facilities and lack of provisions handicapped the Japanese defense.

———————

More than fifty tons of captured documents from the Marianas arrived at JICPOA, flooding the Translation Section and spilling over into the tents erected in the JICPOA compound. In November 1944 we learned a lesson in how important a single item in all the mass of paper could be. Voge had loaned the Estimate Section the services of a quartermaster to assist us in plotting mine fields and to maintain our growing file of charts. The young man could not read Japanese, but he developed a hobby of collecting a complete file of Japanese Notices to Mariners, which he selected from the piles of captured documents. The red-bordered ones, of course, were translated promptly but the ordinary ones were not considered to have much immediate intelligence value. In one of the ordinary ones, however, the quartermaster discovered a series of latitude and longitude coordinates in Arabic numerals. As a matter of curiosity, he plotted these on the chart. When he found that they outlined a square area in mineable waters off Inubo Saki, he called it to my attention.

A translator quickly confirmed that it was an area "closed to navigation," the phrase used to designate a mine field on the red-bordered charts. I telephoned the information to Voge. He sent out an urgent message to the submarine *Scamp* which, a few days before, had been ordered into that area as lifeguard for the first B-29 strike on Tokyo. We never heard from the *Scamp* again. We all believed she had struck a mine and that we could have saved her had we translated that scrap of paper a few days earlier. It shook up the Estimate and Translation sections badly. After the war I learned that in the area where the *Scamp* might have been there were three separate depth-charge attacks rated by the Japanese as certain "kills," and there were no mines in that particular area "closed to navigation."

Christmas dinner 1944 at 4009 Black Point Road was greater than ever. Izzy measured the oven and went shopping for the biggest turkey it could hold. The day before Christmas, she baked a big ham to go with the turkey. She improvised tables to turn the living room into a second dining room, and we invited thirty guests from JICPOA and FRUPac. They all came out from Makalapa in a bus. On Christmas Day 1944, victory seemed distant but assured. The road ahead might be rocky, but when a toast was offered to "The Golden Gate in forty-eight," the optimists replied "Back alive in forty-five."

CHAPTER 16

In January 1945 JICPOA had a complement of 500 officers and 800 enlisted men. FRUPac, separately organized and administered, probably had as many more. During 1944, JICPOA had been reorganized and expanded to meet new situations and conditions as the war moved westward. The Enemy Bases Section was merged with the Photographic Interpretation Section and reorganized into the Geographic Section and the Reference Section, reflecting increased reliance on photo-interpretation, as what little territory remained in Japanese hands came within range of photographic reconnaissance planes. Two air intelligence officers, trained in target-analysis, joined JICPOA to form the Target-Analysis Section and assist in designating and analyzing targets in the home islands of Japan.

In 1944 Commander, Air Force, Pacific Fleet, transferred to JICPOA responsibility for technical air intelligence in the Pacific Ocean Area. The Enemy Air Section was expanded, under Commander Lester Armour with Lieutenant Commander Kirke A. Neal as executive officer, to provide for this additional duty. On the recommendation of the Army Air Forces, the Flak Intelligence Section was organized under Colonel Earl W. Thompson for the purpose of coordinating all matters relative to flak intelligence in the Pacific Ocean Area. A Psychological Warfare Section was organized under Colonel Dana W. Johnston. An Escape and Evasion Section was formed at JICPOA when the Military Intelligence Service in Washington transferred a small group of specially trained people under Colonel Robley F. Winfrey to help any Allied personnel, whether free or imprisoned, in enemy territory. The Operational Intelligence Section was established to familiarize newly arrived operational intelligence officers with the Japanese naval order of battle, the geography of the western Pacific, current operations, and the organization of JICPOA. Operational intelligence officers scheduled for duty on the staffs of flag officers were trained in the

Estimate Section to handle Ultra material. Operational intelligence trainees liberally provided the Estimate Section with watch officers. Lieutenants Richard Huie and John English were transferred to the staff of the Fifth Fleet.

My administrative duties with JICPOA increased. I was promoted to captain and given additional duty on CinCPac's staff. Mac Showers took over most of the responsibility for the Estimate Section. He had been with it since the Battle of Midway. Dick Emory, who had worked in the Estimate Section nearly as long, was transferred to Washington, leaving naval air estimates to be made by Lieutenant Elden Chapman and army air estimates to be made by an Army officer, Captain Gordon Hamilton.

There were also changes made in FRUPac. The number of messages in the maru code declined rapidly with the decrease in Japanese shipping, but the five-digit code retained its great importance. Exchange and rotation of personnel between FRUPac and other communications intelligence units promoted cooperation between them. Jack Holtwick went to Chungking, China. Tom Birtley, who had been in charge of the unit at Pearl Harbor before the war, returned to FRUPac after a tour of sea duty and a long siege in the hospital. Redfield Mason and, later, Commander Rufus L. Taylor, another language officer and expert cryptanalyst, came out from Washington. Captain Goggins, who had been the able leader of FRUPac since Rochefort was detached, left to take command of the battleship *Alabama*. He was relieved by Captain John S. Harper, my friend and classmate.

Greater changes in JICPOA followed the establishment of CinCPac's advanced headquarters on Guam on 2 January 1945. On the twenty-eighth the first echelon of the Advanced Intelligence Center went out from JICPOA to Guam, to be followed by others until the center had sixty officers and fifty enlisted men. Commander Richard O. Green, who was also the fleet photographic officer, became the officer-in-charge of the Advanced Intelligence Center. This was a very happy choice. Photo-interpretation had become the primary source of operational intelligence, and Green had excellent qualifications for the job. He achieved close cooperation with the 21st Bomber Command and with CinCPac's Intelligence Division, to everyone's benefit.

When Admiral Nimitz moved to Guam, Captain Layton, the fleet intelligence officer, moved with him. Since the Estimate Section had always supported fleet intelligence by coordination of Ultra information with other sources, he asked to have Mac Showers go with him to set up a fleet combat intelligence center. This left a big gap in the Estimate Section, but Paul Yardley and Alex Johnson were well qualified to fill it. Admiral Lockwood moved the operational headquarters of his submarine command to the submarine tender *Holland* in Apra Harbor, Guam, on 24 January. Voge moved with him, ending his daily conference with the Estimate Section. To replace it, a special code was created and held only by the Estimate Section and the Submarine Force's Operations Division.

Guam rapidly developed into the center of operations for the war against Japan, and for a while it appeared that Pearl Harbor was destined to become a rear area of diminishing importance. However, both CinCPac and ComSubPac had to retain administrative headquarters at Pearl Harbor, and Admiral Spruance and the Fifth Fleet's planners remained there to map out that fleet's operations for 1945.

It was planned to move a large part of JICPOA forward, but this proved to be impossible because of the crowded conditions on Guam. Twitty had to spend much of his time there, but the administrative work of JICPOA continued to be done at Pearl Harbor. Most of the Translation and Interrogation sections were left behind, along with a large part of the photographic reproduction and lithography operations and the Bulletin Section. Other sections learned to operate with representatives forward, with most of the work being done at Pearl Harbor. The solution was found in greatly improving communications. The Army's intelligence communications were merged with FRUPac's and the joint code room was right across the hall from the Estimate Section in FRUPac's building. This made it more convenient for Captain Layton, in Guam, to communicate with CinCPac's administrative headquarters in Pearl Harbor through FRUPac than through CinCPac's regular channels, which sometimes resulted in giving me chores that had little connection with intelligence.

One morning a dispatch from CinCPac's advanced headquarters appeared on my desk directing me to send them twelve typewriters. There was a shortage of these potent weapons of modern warfare. We had stripped JICPOA of every extra typewriter to equip its own advanced center. It would take weeks to acquire new ones through regular channels, which was probably the real reason why the request was sent to me. I called in Morris Legendre, showed him the message, and told him to put twelve new typewriters on the morning plane to Guam. Both he and his brother Sidney were financially independent of any pittance the Navy paid them. I suspect they sometimes paid for items the Administrative Section needed out of their own pockets rather than bother with the red tape, but twelve typewriters were not then available at Pearl Harbor for money or love. The next morning Morris came into my office and blandly reported that twelve new typewriters had been shipped to CinCPac on the morning plane to Guam.

I was burning with curiosity to know how he did it, but I did not ask. When I was engineering officer of a small submarine in a big Navy Yard, I sometimes had to resort to moonlight requisitions and other quasi-legal methods to obtain equipment, so I knew it might be better for both of us if I did not know the details. Ten years later, when I had reverted to civilian status and was dean of engineering at the University of Hawaii, a harassed commander in the Supply Department at Pearl Harbor called me on the phone.

"Were you the senior naval officer at JICPOA during the war?" he asked.

When I admitted to the charge, he told me his inventory was missing twelve typewriters and the only explanation he had was a penciled notation that they had been delivered to JICPOA. I was confident that Morris had left no clear track behind him, so I asked:

"Commander, do you have my signature on a custody receipt for those typewriters?"

He confessed that he did not, and for a moment I was tempted to claim protection under the Fifth Amendment, but both Morris and Sidney Legendre were then dead and I felt adequately protected by the statute of limitations, so I told him the whole story. I hope that helped to clear his books.

General Arnold proposed to the joint planners in Washington, on 14 July 1944, that Iwo Jima be taken to provide for fighter protection and emergency-landing facilities for B-29 bombers when they began to strike Japan. At that time, Iwo Jima had a defense force of about 7,000 men, less than half the D-day strength of Peleliu, and its defenses were relatively undeveloped. The joint planners agreed, and the operation was scheduled for 20 January 1945, by which time it was expected that the Philippine campaign would be over. After the first B-29 strike on Japan, 24 November 1944, the Japanese staged, through Iwo Jima, several destructive raids on the B-29 bases in Saipan, making it practically imperative that Iwo Jima be taken.

In the event, the assault on Iwo Jima was postponed to 3 February 1945 and then to 19 February because the Luzon campaign required the Central Pacific Force to stay in the Philippines longer than planned. Each day's delay increased the final cost of Iwo Jima.

The Japanese, fully aware of the strategic value of the ugly little island, did everything in their power to strengthen its defenses. To avoid submarine attack, reinforcements and supplies were shipped from Japan to Chichi Jima and Haha Jima, in the Bonin Islands, whence they were forwarded to Iwo Jima by small craft. Both U.S. submarines and surface forces attacked this supply line with considerable success, but still could not prevent the Japanese from building up the strength of the defending force to more than 21,000 men by D-day.

This build-up did not escape attention. From 8 December 1944 to 15 February 1945, Iwo Jima was bombed by shore-based aircraft at least once nearly every day and subjected to five bombardments by cruisers and destroyers. Photo-interpreters detected evidence of the steady improvement of defense positions, despite clever camouflage that concealed the exact positions of many gun emplacements and strongpoints. From submerged positions a few hundred yards off the beach, the *Spearfish* took hundreds of periscope pictures revealing that Mount Suribachi was honeycombed with dug-in positions for coast-defense guns, mortars, machine-gun nests, and strongpoints, all interconnected by tunnels and caves like those on Peleliu.

During one of the cruiser bombardments, the *Archerfish* was on lifeguard station off Iwo Jima and, through her periscope, watched the rain of shells plow up the island until it seemed that nothing could be left alive. Yet, an hour after the sun had set and the cruisers had disappeared over the horizon, Iwo Jima came miraculously to life. More than a dozen planes from Japan landed in quick succession, were rapidly unloaded, and took off again. Throughout the night the island was a beehive of activity.

The Japanese constructed cave shelters more than thirty feet beneath the surface, interconnected with surface defense positions by deep tunnels. In these caves, they were safe from aerial bombing and naval gunfire, and as soon as a bombardment was over, they swarmed out to repair damages and man defense positions. They tried to make Iwo Jima impregnable, and very nearly succeeded.

Spruance, with the Fifth Fleet, made carrier strikes on Tokyo on 16 and 17 February to reduce Japanese air reaction to the assault on Iwo Jima, and battleships, cruisers, and destroyers bombarded the island for three days before the Marines landed on 19 February 1945. General "Howling Mad" Smith predicted to Admiral Spruance, during the planning, that Iwo Jima would be the toughest operation the Marines had undertaken. He was right; they had to fight for every yard of advance. Approximately 22,000 Japanese were killed on Iwo Jima, and about 1,000 eventually were taken prisoner. The Marines lost nearly 6,000 killed and more than 17,000 were wounded in action.

Admiral James Fife relieved Christie as Commander, Submarines, Southwest Pacific, on 30 December 1944. At Singapore there were several Japanese naval vessels, including the carrier-battleships *Ise* and *Hyuga*. The Japanese were so desperate for oil that the two big ships were ordered to take on deckloads of oil in drums and attempt to run the submarine blockade to Japan. Radio intelligence closely monitored Singapore's communications and intercepted these orders and the scheduled route of the two battleships.

Fife alerted all the submarines in the South China Sea. One of the British submarines under his command sighted the Japanese task force soon after it left Singapore on 11 February 1945 but could not get close enough for a torpedo attack. Four of the U.S. submarines that were patrolling along the track of the task force sighted the *Ise* and *Hyuga*, and two of them fired torpedoes, but missed. Both of the big ships got home to Japan unharmed. Despite this failure, however, the campaign Fife's submarines conducted against the Japanese oil supply was successful. Frequently aided by radio intelligence in finding convoys, the submarines sent more tankers to the bottom of the sea than got through to Japan. In March 1945, the Grand Surface Escort Force abandoned organized attempts to import oil from Southeast Asia and tankers became rare targets for submarines.

Lockwood's submarines also found targets to be scarce in the East China Sea and the Yellow Sea. Some Japanese convoys sailed close in along the coast of China, taking advantage of the shallow water and anchoring in harbors each night for protection. Radio intelligence could give the submarines very little help in finding such convoys. Commander, Naval Group, China, Admiral Milton E. Miles, had organized a system of coast-watchers along the China coast, and information supplied by them enabled the submarine *Barb* to attack a Japanese convoy in the harbor of Namkwan, China, on the night of 22 January 1945. Despite such aggressive tactics, however, targets for submarines were hard to find, unless the Estimate Section could provide helpful information.

By the end of January, the Japanese air force in the Philippines having been virtually destroyed, plane crews and pilots were trapped in northern Luzon. Four Japanese submarines were ordered to transport these aviators from Luzon to Formosa. FRUPac intercepted and decrypted the whole plan, and Voge sent a wolf pack to spoil it. Several U.S. submarines were involved but the *Batfish* was in the right position and had all the action. In three night attacks between 9 and 12 February 1945, she sank three of the Japanese submarines and broke up the evacuation operation.

Lockwood searched for new missions for his submarines. In the FM sonar he found a possibility. With this device, a submerged submarine could detect a mine as much as a quarter of a mile away. Submarines could, therefore, secretly search a strategic area for defensive mines before an operation. I confess it was a project that never appealed to me. Contemplation of conning a submarine a hundred feet beneath the surface, probing blindly for echoes from mines that could blow the submarine to kingdom come, gave me nightmares. I much preferred the safer method of translating red-bordered Notices to Mariners. Of course, the notices informed us only where certain mines were. They gave us little assurance that other mines had not been planted in areas through which major ships must pass.

Among the first submarines to have FM sonar installed were the *Tunny* and the *Tinosa*. After an intensive course of training, which Lockwood personally supervised, these two submarines were sent to the vicinity of Okinawa to search out Japanese mines. Every submarine had copies of JICPOA's charts of mine fields, including those of the great Japanese mine barrier along the eastern side of the East China Sea, to the west of Okinawa. We had no knowledge of mines between that barrier and the Ryukyu Islands, where our amphibious forces would soon be operating.

One night, the *Tunny*, pursuing her hazardous business of mine reconnaissance in this area, heard the bell-like tones that are characteristic of FM echoes from moored mines. Shortly afterward, she surfaced and her skipper, Commander George E. Pierce, sent a radio message to Lockwood at Guam, reporting what he had heard. Lockwood immediately forwarded the message to the Estimate Section at Pearl Harbor, asking for our evaluation of the report. I was home in bed, but fortunately Ed Blair, chief of JICPOA's Mine Warfare Section, was on watch in the Estimate Section. He called me on the telephone and in guarded language explained the situation. Of course, Blair knew more about mine fields than I did, so I told him to answer Lockwood immediately.

Early the next morning, I thumbed through the file of the previous night's dispatches. There was a copy of the *Tunny*'s message

Edward McC. Blair

reporting the position of Japanese mines she had located. That message was followed by Lockwood's message to the Estimate Section, and then by the Estimate Section's proper and correct reply:

"No known minefields in position reported."

Good!

The next message was Lockwood's reply to Pierce in the *Tunny*:

"Holmes says there are no mines there."

Not so good!

A couple of months later I encountered Pierce in the Submarine Base officers' mess. I asked him what had been his reaction to Lockwood's message. Pierce bluntly replied, "I told my exec, if Holmes knows so damned much about these mines, why isn't he out here in a submarine looking for them?"

———

Long before the Iwo Jima campaign was over, JICPOA was deeply involved in producing intelligence for Okinawa. Spruance's operation plans for Okinawa were issued on 3 January 1945, and Turner's followed on 9 February. The Fifth Fleet, the Fifth Amphibious Force, and the Service Force all had planning headquarters at Pearl Harbor. General Simon B. Buckner, Commander, Tenth Army, also established headquarters on Oahu. Later, the Tenth Army numbered 172,000 Army and Marine combat troops and

115,000 service troops on Okinawa. All these organizations, and others, were heavy consumers of intelligence.

The wind-down of the war in the Atlantic and the Mediterranean enabled the British to organize the British Pacific Fleet, with headquarters at Sydney, and to contribute a fast carrier task force, under the command of Admiral Sir Bruce Fraser, to the campaign for Okinawa. CinCPac directed that the British forces were to be serviced by JICPOA with intelligence material on exactly the same level as American task forces. Early in 1945 the Royal Navy sent a lieutenant commander to Pearl Harbor to arrange with JICPOA for this service.

To provide current intelligence to the British was no problem. It was necessary only to furnish ships' names and their organization to the chief of our Distribution Section. He would keep track of the movements of the ships and deliver the goods in standard quantity at the proper time. But providing old material was a different matter. JICPOA had already issued 200 or 300 bulletins, in addition to CinCPac-CinCPOA's weekly intelligence and maps, charts, and aerial photographs. We took the British intelligence officer into our stockroom to select what he wanted. He wanted nearly everything. When it was added up, and each item was multiplied by the number to be distributed to each unit, there were two plane-loads of intelligence material to be transported to Sydney.

Captain Lowe H. Bibby, U.S. Navy, on the staff of the Tenth Army, was a classmate with whom I had been closely associated ten years before, when we were both commanding submarines based at Pearl Harbor. He came down to JICPOA, and together we worked out a schedule to supply the Tenth Army with intelligence. Some of the three Marine and five Army divisions that made up the Tenth Army were already on our distribution lists, but others had to be supplied with copies of material that had been previously issued. Many of the bulletins were out of stock and had to be reprinted, swelling the total of material produced and distributed by JICPOA for the Okinawa operation to 127 tons.

Major Charles T. Kingston came through Pearl Harbor on his way to an intelligence assignment on the staff of General Curtis E. LeMay, Commander, XXI Bomber Command, which flew the B-29s in the Marianas. Lieutenant Colonel Fager, of the Estimate Section, arranged to have Kingston stop over for several days to become acquainted with the JICPOA setup. The XXI Bomber Command was independent of CinCPac-CinCPOA in the Pacific, and there was serious disagreement between Nimitz and LeMay over the use of B-29s in support of the Okinawa campaign, but that did not affect the cooperation between intelligence units. All of JICPOA's services were available to General LeMay's staff, and photographs taken by B-29s were of great assistance in planning carrier strikes on Japan. Duplicate negatives of such pictures were sometimes delivered by the bomber command to JICPOA's center on Guam within an hour after the bombers' return from their missions.

During his stopover at Pearl Harbor, Kingston had many discussions with Blair about mines. It is possible that the project of the XXI Bomber Command, to mine the Inland Sea of Japan, owed something to these conversations. Minelaying was as unpopular with aviators as it was with submariners, partly because they rarely could observe the results of their efforts. Later, Blair kept Kingston informed of evidence, accumulated by FRUPac and JICPOA, of the success of the Army Air Forces' mining operations, and this helped to make minelaying more palatable to the aviators.

The Fifth Amphibious Force and the Tenth Army had some intelligence problems to which JICPOA could find no adequate answers. One was the trafficability of the soil at potential beachheads on Okinawa. The loose volcanic sand on Iwo Jima had made everyone aware of the seriousness of the problem. The heavy, tracked vehicles of the Tenth Army could reduce anything but the most stable soil to a quagmire. At Tenth Army headquarters, botanists were studying low, oblique aerial photographs of the beaches in an effort to identify the foliage, which could furnish clues to the nature of the soil and its ability to withstand heavy traffic, but it was a far-out effort. What was needed were actual samples of the soil.

A beach reconnaissance party landed surreptitiously from a submarine at night might obtain soil samples, but Spruance, quite properly, vetoed any such expedition. The *Burrfish* had landed and successfully recovered a beach reconnaissance party at Peleliu, but when she attempted to repeat the feat at Yap, half the party failed to return, and no one ever learned what happened to them. The *Swordfish* had already been lost while making a photographic reconnaissance of Okinawa. Prisoners captured by the Japanese from a beach reconnaissance party or from a submarine sunk in shallow water, or even the detected presence of a submarine loitering off critical beaches, might provide the Japanese more valuable information than we could obtain from even a successful beach party.

Fortunately, our very early request to the Fourteenth Naval District's Intelligence Office to find someone with knowledge of the beaches at Okinawa paid off. Lieutenant Commander Neil C. Vanzant of that office found an eighty-year-old conchologist, Ditlev D. Thaanum, who had collected seashells on those beaches. Thaanum's notes, maps, and photographs were very valuable in the preparation of preliminary intelligence reports on Okinawa. Of even greater importance, they led directly to Daniel Boone Langford, a young man of sixty-three, another conchologist who had been a colleague of Thaanum's on his seashell expedition. Good detective work located Langford in Arizona, and Vanzant flew to the mainland to interview him. Langford proved to have such encyclopedic knowledge of Okinawa and its reefs and beaches that Admiral Turner, Commander, Fifth Amphibious Force, arranged to have him employed as a civilian expert. He went to sea in Turner's flagship, the *Eldorado*, and rendered very valuable service to the Fifth Amphibious Force and the Tenth Army throughout the Okinawan campaign.

When the final edition of the Okinawa Information Bulletin was ready to go to press, Lieutenant Commander Causey brought the proofs down for my approval. It was a beautiful piece of work, with many maps, photographs, illustrations, and tabulations, a minimum of text, and a standard JICPOA yellow cover. To reduce the number of fold-in maps, it was printed on oversize pages, a feature that was unpopular with intelligence officers who had to stow and transport it. I was then so deeply involved in administration that I did not have time for creative intelligence, so I told Causey there was nothing I could add to his masterpiece. However, I recalled our previous conversation about snakes on Okinawa, and I asked him if he had been able to find a good picture of a habu. Proudly he opened the bulletin and a habu in full color seemed to leap out of the page at me. It was a reproduction of a picture he found at the Bishop Museum. He had also tabulated Okinawa's snakebite statistics, which indicated that the habu would be about as much of a problem there as rattlesnakes would be to field maneuvers in Colorado.

The Tenth Army landed on Okinawa on 1 April 1945 against light opposition, and by ten o'clock that day had taken the two airfields scheduled as the objectives for the fourth day. The Japanese, profiting by their experience at Peleliu and Iwo Jima, where they abandoned their old tactics of trying to annihilate their enemy on the beach, had established their main lines of defense well back from close naval bombardment.

When I visited Guam a few weeks later, most of the war correspondents there had seen the Okinawa Information Bulletin. Apparently all were impressed with the picture of the habu, but few had read the statistics indicating that poisonous snakes on Okinawa would be a real but minor problem. During the first week after the landing no one reported seeing a habu. *Time* magazine printed a little item implying that naval intelligence had goofed in issuing warnings about venomous snakes. Medical officers of every unit had stocked up on anti-snakebite serum, causing a worldwide shortage. A good story making the rounds was that the Tenth Army had been able to make a "stand-up" landing on Okinawa because the Japanese had captured a copy of the Okinawa Information Bulletin and, after seeing that picture of the habu, their soldiers were reluctant to dig in at the beaches.

When the habu came out of hibernation, we did have some snakebite casualties, although, as far as I know, no deaths from habu bites. Several smart young officers in JICPOA intelligence teams sent me snake skins with tongue-in-cheek little notes:

"See, Captain, there really are habu on Okinawa, and here is the skin of one to prove it."

I had to learn the hard way that one good picture could overemphasize a subject as easily as a long, wordy text could conceal one.

On 6 April 1945 the last Japanese task force of surface ships departed from the Inland Sea through Bungo Suido. U.S. submarines shadowed it on its route around the southern end of Kyushu into the East China Sea. There, on the seventh, planes from Task Force 58 sank the super-battleship *Yamato*, the light cruiser *Yahagi*, and four destroyers. Only four destroyers survived.

The virtual destruction of the Japanese Navy and the drastic reduction in the number of marus brought about changes in radio intelligence. It also forced the Japanese to suicide weapons of many varieties. Most effective were kamikazes which, in April and May 1945, took off from Kyushu in mass flights to attack U.S. ships in the vicinity of Okinawa. Kamikazes were the most serious threat the Navy faced during the war.

In controlling and forming up planes over the airfield in preparation for these attacks, the Japanese made lavish use of voice radio. Their radio messages in abbreviated Japanese, amounting to codes intended to be intelligible only to Japanese pilots and controllers, were intercepted in Guam and the Marianas. Traffic analysts, language officers, and cryptanalysts soon learned that, by coordinating their work, they could milk these communications of vital intelligence. To assist them, I suggested that Dick Emory be brought back from Washington and put in charge of the work on kamikaze communications, but it was 7 June before he could arrive in Pearl Harbor and be flown out to Guam in Admiral Nimitz's private plane.

With intelligence gleaned from Japanese voice communications over Kyushu's airfields, radio intelligence was able to inform Admiral Spruance that kamikaze attacks were coming, in approximately what numbers and when, in time for him to alert all ships and planes and dispose them best to meet the attack. Large numbers of kamikazes were shot down but enough got through to sink or damage many ships. Without the timely warning radio intelligence provided, the casualties and the ship losses would have been much greater.

CHAPTER 17

THE LOSS OF OKINAWA banished Japanese shipping from the East China Sea. Across the Sea of Japan was the only way left for food and raw materials to reach Japan in significant quantities. Lockwood was determined to close that route also. There were three ways for submarines to enter the Sea of Japan; La Pérouse Strait on the north, Tsugaru Kaikyo between Hokkaido and Honshu, and Tsushima Kaikyo between Korea and Honshu.

Mines and adverse currents ruled out the narrow Tsugaru Kaikyo. Submarines entered the Sea of Japan through La Pérouse in 1943, but since the *Wahoo* went in that way in the fall of that year and failed to return, no submarines had attempted it. In the meantime, the Japanese had strengthened its antisubmarine defenses with deep-laid mines and controlled mines against submarines. The Russians still used La Pérouse en route to and from Vladivostok, but the Japanese patrolled it on the surface and from the air. Prevailing currents made La Pérouse more practical as an exit than as an entrance. That left Tsushima Kaikyo.

Early in the war the Japanese laid extensive mine fields both to the east and the west of Tsushima. JICPOA had translated the secret Notices to Mariners and the Mine Warfare Section had mapped the mine field that sealed the strait. Both U.S. submarines and the marus they hunted had sensibly stayed clear of these areas but Lockwood believed that, with the new FM sonar, submerged submarines could feel their way through them into the Sea of Japan. Nine submarines were organized to act as a group and carefully trained to run the mine fields. Lockwood requested Nimitz for permission personally to command this operation, which was scheduled to begin on the night of 3 June 1945. Nimitz refused the request.

The Mine Warfare Section of JICPOA considered the risk of this undertaking was too great for the potential gain. I envied no man his position in any of the nine submarines. We all did our utmost to ensure that they had all the information we could muster. Our charts of the areas closed to navigation were accurate, and we had some information about the location of the mine lines within those areas. We knew that, in the years since they were planted, many of the mines had broken loose, thinning the lines but, unknown to us, the Japanese had just recently reinforced them. We believed that mines had been laid to watch for submarines at the surface, at periscope depth, and at a depth of 100 feet, but that the Japanese had no magnetic bottom mines. This information probably was responsible for the happy decision to run through at a depth of 150 feet.

Marus often reported by radio the positions of floating mines, and we worked up charts based on our decryption of all these reports. The Mine Warfare Section also issued up-to-date charts of the Tsushima mine fields, an illustrated bulletin describing types of Japanese mines, and new bulletins of mine fields in the Yellow and East China seas. The Geographic Section contributed information bulletins on the Sea of Japan, the Yellow Sea, the Sea of Okhotsk, the Kuril Islands, and La Pérouse Strait. The Translation Section came up with a timely special translation, "Underwater Sound Wave Transmission Conditions in Japanese Waters." Several days before the submarines were due to depart from Guam, I sent to Voge a dispatch asking if there was any other information we could supply. Voge, a master of facetious dispatches, replied:

"We may have to take one torpedo off each submarine to provide space for intelligence material. Please do not repeat not send any more."

On the nights of 3 and 4 June we waited with fingers crossed, relieved when there was no flurry of radio activity from the Tsushima area. Then, on the night of the ninth, the date set for the submarines to begin attacking shipping in the Japan Sea, FRUPac intercepted an emergency transmission from a maru reporting a submarine attack in the Japan Sea, so we knew the operation was proceeding as planned. All nine submarines had successfully traversed the mine fields and entered the Japan Sea. The *Bonefish* was lost about 18 June in an attack by a Japanese patrol craft. The other eight submarines made their exit through La Pérouse, in a beautiful woolly fog. In seventeen days in the Sea of Japan, they sank 27 marus and one submarine.

When some of the submarines returned to Pearl Harbor, the Submarine Force held a critique to hear their skippers tell of their experiences. Ed Blair, chief of the Mine Warfare Section, and I were invited to attend. I have always regretted that we did not take Lieutenant Harriet Borland along with us. She assisted Blair in preparing intelligence material for the operation, and she deserved recognition strictly on the basis of merit. Besides, I would have enjoyed standing up to introduce to that group of hard-bitten submarine skippers a beautiful and talented woman who, as a mine-warfare intelligence officer, made significant contributions to their success.

Harriet was the first woman to boast one of the rectangular yellow pass cards, with a photograph, which each one of us had to wear hung conspicuously around our neck while we were in the FRUPac building. Admiral Nimitz had a strict rule—no women on his staff. Technically, Harriet was not in violation of that rule. She was attached to Mine Force headquarters, a short distance from JICPOA, down Makalapa Drive. She worked in the Estimate Section by tacit agreement between the Mine Force and me, but I was not so sure that Admiral Nimitz would have recognized the niceties of this logic if we had flaunted Harriet's position.

As did every other shore-bound admiral with a sea command, Admiral Nimitz had visions of some day uprooting his staff and putting out to sea in a flagship. If that had happened and women had worked their way into indispensable positions on his staff, he could have been seriously handicapped. After CinCPac and the Advanced Intelligence Center moved to Guam, however, there was little probability that any of us who were left behind would be needed at sea. CinCPac took with him, when he moved forward, nearly all the best male yeomen. Replacement with other male yeomen was impossible, and it was becoming difficult for JICPOA to get the work out. I wrote a letter to Admiral McMorris, Nimitz's chief of staff, explaining the situation and asking for permission to employ female yeomen at JICPOA. My letter came back with an appended note in Admiral Nimitz's copperplate handwriting:

"Tell Captain Holmes he can employ one female yeoman for every male yeoman he has sent to Guam."

That solved my problem. The women who joined JICPOA in the last few months of the war were proficient, hard-working, and dependable. I am convinced that JICPOA would have worked more smoothly if we had started out with a solid core of women in many of the stable jobs.

CinCPac-CinCPOA Weekly Intelligence Bulletin published in each issue a chart of the estimated locations of active Japanese submarines. Captain John Harper, officer-in-charge of FRUPac, tipped me off that some sharp-eyed security officer in Washington was suspicious of these charts because their consistent accuracy suggested that whoever prepared them had access to Ultra information. The security officer was right, of course, as I had to admit. I told Harper that I personally checked every item on every one of those charts. Any Ultra information we used was so carefully sanitized that even if the charts fell into enemy hands, there would be no way to connect them with decryption of Japanese messages. I intended to go on publishing them.

I should have paid more attention to John Harper's friendly warning. A few weeks later, in April 1945, a letter from Admiral King to Admiral Nimitz was passed to me for a statement. King directed Nimitz to cease publication of the submarine situation charts and to investigate the security breach. Then I prepared a full and careful explanation.

The submarine charts, I admitted, were prepared under my supervision and I accepted complete responsibility for them. I used my knowledge of Ultra to delete from the charts any erroneous information and to add some estimated positions of submarines derived from decryption of Japanese messages, being careful to attribute such information to direction-finder fixes, sightings by air searches, or reports from our submarines, as might be appropriate. I believed there was no danger that these charts could reveal the real source of my information. We had captured dozens of more elaborate Japanese charts of U.S. submarine activities, which JICPOA and the Submarine Force carefully analyzed. The only information we gained from them was the reassurance that the Japanese were crediting themselves with sinking eight times as many of our submarines as we actually lost, and we believed the Japanese could not derive even that much information from our charts.

On the other hand, I had to admit that the charts in the Bulletin were of minor importance. Under the best of conditions they could not reach interested operating forces in less than a week, and in that time most of the Japanese submarines would be long gone from the charted positions. Specific information acquired by decryption, upon which antisubmarine actions might be based, such as the *England*'s exploit of sinking six Japanese submarines in twelve days, was always handled by the fleet intelligence officer, and usually transmitted by dispatch. For security reasons, such information received extremely limited distribution. The virtue of the submarine situation charts was their wide distribution—to ships' officers, port directors, plotting officers, and others, who were thereby informed of changes in the level and areas of Japanese submarine operations. At the present stage of the war, the value of this information probably was low. Consequently, upon receipt of Admiral King's letter I had immediately ceased publication of the charts in the Weekly Intelligence Bulletins.

Shortly afterward, my statement was returned to me with an appended note from Admiral McMorris to Admiral Nimitz:

"Admiral King is wrong in this case but it is not of sufficient importance to argue the point. Holmes has already taken the only required action."

To this was added Admiral Nimitz's "O.K."

That was the last I ever heard of it.

The Japanese Submarine Force had suffered disastrous losses and, in early 1945, there was a marked decrease in its activity. Many surviving submarines were being modified to carry suicide weapons called *kaitens*. These were piloted torpedoes, carried on the deck and released from the submerged submarine when within range of an appropriate target. At first, they were used to attack anchored ships and to penetrate harbors, but later they were released to attack ships or convoys at sea. The Japanese deluded themselves with greatly exaggerated reports and estimates of their successes but, up to the middle of July 1945, only one ship had been sunk by a *kaiten*.

After January 1945, Japanese submarine operations were confined mainly to the vicinity of Iwo Jima and Okinawa. Little was known, by U.S. forces, about *kaitens*, although several encounters with midget submarines, which were actually *kaitens*, were reported. For several months preceding July 1945, there had been practically no Japanese submarine operations in the southern part of the Philippine Sea. There were occasional reports, from various sources, of periscopes or submarines sighted, but everyone knew from experience that most of them turned out to be false. Consequently, U.S. antisubmarine activity became lax.

In July, two *kaiten*-carrying submarines departed Japan, to operate in the southern part of the Philippine Sea. On the twenty-fourth, about 250 miles east of Cape Engaño, the *I-53* released two *kaitens* to attack a convoy, and sank the destroyer escort *Underhill*. Four days later the *I-58*, which was patrolling along the Guam-Leyte route, released two *kaitens* to attack a ship identified as a tanker and claimed to have sunk her. Actually, neither *kaiten* made a hit, and their attacks may have resulted only in a report by the cargo ship *Wild Hunter* that she had sighted a periscope. This information was broadcast to all ships. Shortly before midnight the next night, the *I-58* encountered the cruiser *Indianapolis*, proceeding unescorted at

16 knots, from Guam to Leyte. The *I-58* fired six conventional torpedoes, two of which hit. The *Indianapolis* went down in fifteen minutes, and her loss was not discovered for eighty-four hours. About 300 men went down with the ship, but sharks and three and a half days of exposure before the survivors were rescued brought the total loss to 883 men.

Several days before the *Indianapolis* sailed from Guam, FRUPac learned by radio intelligence that the *I-58* was on patrol in the middle of the Philippine Sea. This information was passed to CinCPac but, since it was Ultra-derived, its distribution had to be very limited. It probably never reached either the *Indianapolis* or the Naval Operating Base, Guam.

Shortly after the *I-58* torpedoed the *Indianapolis*, that submarine transmitted a report to Tokyo that it had sunk "a battleship of the *Idaho* class." This message was intercepted by FRUPac, decrypted, and passed to CinCPac about sixteen hours after the sinking. Apparently it was evaluated as just another of the many Japanese messages exaggerating their successes. It also was given very limited distribution, and probably no one had both essential bits of information—the position of the *Indianapolis* and the *I-58*'s report of sinking a battleship at that position.

If the port director at Guam had received positive information that the *I-58* was patrolling the Philippine Sea, he might have reassessed the need for an escort for the *Indianapolis*. If the right people had received information that the *I-58* had reported sinking a battleship at the estimated position of the *Indianapolis*, a search for her might have started earlier. To have broadened the distribution of Ultra, however, would have violated a policy that had been established by prewar agreement between the War Department and the Navy Department. The use of Ultra information was authorized only for action that might result in material advantage in major strategic situations. Instructions for its dissemination were:

> Those authorized to disseminate such information must employ only the most secure means, must take every precaution to avoid compromising the source, and must limit dissemination to the minimum number of secure responsible persons who need the information in order to discharge their duties. No action is to be taken on information herein reported, regardless of temporary advantage if such action might have the effect of revealing the existence of the source to the enemy. (*Hearings before the Joint Committee on the Investigation of the Pearl Harbor Attack. Congress of the United States. Seventy-ninth Congress. Part 29, page 2403, Proceedings of the Army Pearl Harbor Board.*)

These instructions were more liberally interpreted in the Pacific war than they were in the Atlantic, but despite several alarms the Japanese never learned the extent of the information we obtained by breaking their codes. The instructions were successful in preserving secrecy, but they left unsolved one of the major problems of the intelligence organization—identifying in advance those "who need the information in order to discharge their duties," and getting the information into their hands in time for them to act, without disclosure to many others. Secrecy is a double-edged weapon, and it sometimes inflicts deeper wounds on its wielder than upon his opponents.

After the Okinawa campaign JICPOA faced its largest problem —production of intelligence for Operation Olympic, the invasion of Kyushu. Planning for that operation was initiated in January 1945 and, by the end of the Okinawa campaign in April 1945, preliminary plans were virtually complete. Okinawa was being prepared as the advanced base. After VE-day, 8 May 1945, military and naval forces from all over the world began converging on the Philippines, the Marianas, and Hawaii as staging areas from which the great assault would be launched. Many of these forces had never before been in the Pacific, and their demands for intelligence were enormous.

JICPOA became a factory geared to the production of all types of intelligence material and staffed by 1,800 persons in Hawaii and hundreds of others on detached duty all over the Pacific. Its production averaged 2,000,000 sheets of printed intelligence and more than 150,000 photographic prints each week.

Based on the January estimates of Kyushu's defenses, the plan was to land on three beaches at that island about 1 November 1945. The defenses of Kyushu were being developed by the Japanese Army, and very little of this planning was reflected in the radio traffic intercepted by FRUPac. The U.S. Army's Signal Intelligence Service was our major source of information on the defense buildup. Colonel Fager's group in the Estimate Section was a part of the Signal Intelligence Service, and he was in constant touch with Washington and Manila.

By July 1945 it was apparent that Japanese strategists realized that the most probable landing places on Kyushu were those the American planners had picked. The Japanese Army in Manchuria was being moved to these areas at a rapid rate, and the strength of the defenders of Kyushu would soon exceed that of the planned assault forces. Since the ratio of assault forces to defenders in amphibious landings on defended beaches was usually about three to one, the prospects were ominous.

Then, on 6 August 1945, the first atomic bomb was dropped on Hiroshima, and on 14 August the war was over. President Harry S Truman estimated that his decision to use atomic bombs saved the United States a million and a half casualties. The estimate is conservative. If the first landings on Kyushu had been made as planned, and repulsed, the total of American casualties could well have been more than twice that number—and the Japanese casualties would have been several times greater.

Harris Cox and Molly Claridge invited Izzy and me to dinner at the Halekulani for the night of 14 August, when they announced their engagement. That was the day the war ended, and not all the fireworks and the dancing in the streets were for Molly and Harris. After dinner we went to Ed Blair's apartment in Waikiki.

We were preceded into Blair's small living room by a Navy band playing the Marine Corps song. Each time the tuba went "umpa-umpa" the walls of the apartment went in and out. It was like being in a boiler factory inside a boiler. Someone worked his way to my side and shouted in my ear that I was wanted on the telephone. I could just make out, over the din, that a message for me had been received at FRUPac, and the watch officer did not know what to do about it. I told him I would come out to Pearl Harbor, but it would take about an hour to get through the crowds.

Izzy said if I was going to drive to Pearl Harbor, through the riot in Honolulu, she was going with me. After we left Waikiki and gained the back streets, the traffic was not bad. The closer we came to Pearl Harbor, the quieter it became. Makalapa, where the senior officers were quartered, was dark and silent, but a light was on in the quarters of Captain Edwin R. Swinburne, commanding officer of the Submarine Base, so I stopped to leave Izzy with him. The Marine sentry at FRUPac would not have let her inside the compound, peace or no peace. Only a few weeks before, when I had forgotten my pass one morning, the sentry greeted me with a snappy salute and a "Good morning, Captain Holmes," but he would not let me in until the officer of the day came out and issued me a temporary pass.

The message was from CinCPac advanced headquarters on Guam. Captain Layton was about to accompany Admiral Nimitz to Tokyo and wanted twenty thousand Imperial Japanese yen to be sent to him on the morning plane to Guam—for what purpose I never knew.

Isabelle W. and W. J. Holmes at 4009 Black Point Road, Honolulu

There had been a suitcase full of Okinawa yen under my desk until a few days before, when I decided that its disposal was a problem for the fleet paymaster to deal with, and turned it over to him. That would not meet Layton's requirement, but perhaps the fleet paymaster had acquired Imperial Japanese yen the same way. I called his office on the telephone. No answer. I called the duty officer at CinCPac's Makalapa headquarters. The line was busy.

After several efforts to get through to the duty officer I picked up the dispatch and walked down to CinCPac headquarters. The duty officer, a major of Marines, was busy on two telephones. He motioned me to sit down and wait. He also had a problem. CinCPac's advanced headquarters had sent him a request for one hundred copies of the music for the Soviet national anthem, to go out on the morning plane.

As I listened to the major on the telephone, paging all possible sources of the music, a wave of nostalgia swept over me. All over the world, battleships would be scraping camouflage paint off brightwork, holystoning teakwood decks, mustering side boys, and boatswain's mates would be shining their pipes preparing for the spit, polish, and protocol of peace. When a Soviet man-of-war encountered the battleship *Missouri* in Tokyo Bay an ancient ceremony would be enacted, while junior officers shivered in their boots in fear that something would go wrong to disrupt the pageant. On the *Missouri*'s broad quarterdeck, a Marine guard in splendid dress uniforms would be mustered with the band. While saluting guns banged away, filling the air with black-powder smoke, the Soviet flag would be broken at the yardarm, and the band would play the Soviet national anthem.

"You have it?" the major said to the telephone. "Good! Hum the first few bars to me . . . That is *not* the Soviet national anthem. That's 'God Save the Czar'!" With a sigh the major hung up the phone and asked me what was my problem.

He did not know where to find the fleet paymaster, and anyway the time lock was set on the big safe and no one could get into it until morning. He volunteered to deliver my dispatch to the fleet paymaster first thing in the morning. I left my small problem in stronger hands than mine and went down to Ed Swinburne's quarters to pick up Izzy. Through the quiet back streets we drove home to 4009 Black Point Road, to spend the first night of peace in the same bed from which I had been aroused by the bombing of Pearl Harbor.

INDEX

Benson, Roy S., 137
Betio, Tarawa, 141, 143-45, 147, 150, 152
Biard, Forrest R., 36, 58, 121, 125
Bibby, Lowe H., 204
Birtley, Thomas B., 22, 197
Bishop Museum, 114, 131, 187, 206
Bismarck Sea, 133, 134
Black Chamber, 21, 44, 45, 49
Blair, Edward McC., 155, 156, 202, 205, 210, 211, 216
Bloch, Claude C., 9, 10, 25, 34, 37, 39, 59, 61, 62, 90, 91
Bonefish (submarine), 210
Bonin Islands, 185, 200
Borland, Harriet, 211
Borneo, 26, 80
Bougainville, Solomon Islands, 135, 146, 147, 165
Boulder, language school, 120, 121, 123, 152, 168
Bowers, Doctor, 108
British, 27, 47, 106, 139, 141, 144
    Eastern Fleet, 65
    Pacific Fleet, 204
Bromley, John R., 36, 128
Brunei, Borneo, 191
Bryan, Edwin H., 15
Bryan, J., 90
Buckner, Simon B., 203
Buin, Bougainville, 135
Buka, Solomon Islands, 171, 172
Bulletin Section, JICPOA: 184
    CinCPac-CinCPOA Weekly Intelligence Bulletin, 185, 198, 211, 212
Buna, New Guinea, 118, 119
Bungo Suido, Honshu, 74, 207
Burma, 41, 72
Burrfish (submarine), 187, 205
Butaritari, Makin, 150, 152

Cain, Chief Radioman, 67
Calhoun, Barney, 37
California (battleship), 37, 62
Canberra (cruiser), 190
Canton Island, Phoenix Islands, 143
Cape Engaño, Luzon, 191, 192, 213
Carlson's Raiders, 111, 150

Caroline Islands, 26, 57, 79, 110, 170, 171, 177
Carr, Denzel, 1, 121, 186
Castaway's Baedeker, 160
Catchpole, Operation. *See* Eniwetok
Causey, Beverley, 186, 187, 206
Cavalla (submarine), 182, 183
Central Pacific Force: 138, 146, 147, 199. *See also* Fifth Fleet, U.S.
Chapman, Elden S., 132, 157, 197
Cheek, Marion C., 190, 192
Chicago Tribune, 108
Chichi Jima, Bonin Islands, 200
Chikuma (cruiser), 25, 28
China, 23, 24, 52
Chokai (cruiser), 24
Christie, Ralph W., 138, 173, 181, 201
Chungking, China, 197
Churchill, Winston, 188
Chuyo (carrier), 161, 162
CinCPac. *See* Commander in Chief, Pacific Fleet
CinCPac Advanced Headquarters, Guam, 197, 198
CinCPOA. *See* Commander in Chief, Pacific Ocean Area
CIU. *See* Combat Intelligence Unit
Claridge, Molly, 216
Coast Guard, U.S., 15, 128
Cole, Allyn, 36
Combat Intelligence Unit (CIU), 5, 9, 167
    as cover name for FRUPac, 14, 16, 18, 30-35, 40, 46, 53, 56, 57, 60, 61, 69, 86, 88, 93, 104, 106
    as section of ICPOA, 113, 114, 125, 126, 130, 132, 135-38, 140, 144.
    See also Estimate Section, JICPOA
Combined Fleet, Japanese, 24, 26, 51, 79-85, 96-98, 165, 178, 189
CominCh. *See* Commander in Chief, U.S. Fleet
Commandant, Fourteenth Naval District (ComFourteen), 9, 31, 90, 109, 112, 123. *See also* Bloch, Claude C.

Huckins, Thomas A., 18, 22, 55, 69, 86, 125, 167
Hudson, Alec (pen name of W. J. Holmes), 9, 60, 61, 75, 83
Hudson, Robert E., 121, 122, 123
Huggins, David, 152
Huggins, Frank B., 152
Huie, Richard, 197
Hull, Cordell, 45, 50, 51
Hydrographic Office, Navy Department, 111, 120, 164, 177
Hydrographic Section, JICPOA, 132
Hyuga (battleship), 24, 201

I-class fleet submarines, Japanese:
I-1, 124, 125
I-7, 40
I-16, 31, 172
I-22, 31
I-23, 60
I-28, 74
I-29, 186
I-32, 171
I-53, 213
I-58, 213, 214
I-70, 40
I-168, 98
I-175, 170
I-176, 171
ICPOA. *See* Intelligence Center, Pacific Ocean Area
Idaho (battleship), 214
Imperial General Headquarters, 83, 88, 190, 193
Navy Order Number 18, 83, 88
Indianapolis (cruiser), 181, 213, 214
Inland Sea, between Shikoku and Honshu, 26, 137, 189-91, 205, 207
Intelligence Center, Pacific Ocean Area (ICPOA), 112-16, 120, 121, 122, 130, 131, 138, 140, 144, 160, 167. *See also* Joint Intelligence Center, Pacific Ocean Area (JICPOA)
Interprons. *See* Photographic Interpretation Section, JICPOA
Interrogation Section, JICPOA, 152, 198

Ise (battleship), 24, 201
Isuzu (cruiser), 25
Iwo Jima, Volcano Islands, 185, 199-201, 203, 205, 206, 213

Jaluit, Marshall Islands, 57, 59, 144, 145, 147
Japan Sea, between Japan and Korea, 115, 153, 154, 209, 210
Japanese fleet organization, 24, 25
Japanese war plans:
first phase, 78-81
second phase, 81
Java Sea, Battle of, 65
Jenkins, Logan H., 184
JICPOA. *See* Joint Intelligence Center, Pacific Ocean Area
Jintsu (cruiser), 25
Johnson, B. Alexander (Alex), 171, 172, 198
Johnston, Dana W., 196
Johnston Island, 31, 32, 72, 82
Joint Chiefs of Staff, 140, 142, 170, 187, 188
Joint Expeditionary Force, Marianas operation, 181, 182
Joint Intelligence Center, Pacific Ocean Area (JICPOA): 140, 167
in Gilbert Islands operations, 143, 145, 150, 151
JICPOA bulletins, 152, 158-60, 164, 169, 178
in submarine operations, 153, 154, 156, 162, 194, 209
in Marshall Islands operations, 157, 158, 159, 161, 164
in Eniwetok and Marianas operations, 165, 167-69, 176-78, 181, 184, 185
in Palau operations, 186, 188, 189
in Okinawa operations, 187, 188, 203-7
reorganized, 177, 196-99, 215.
See also Intelligence Center, Pacific Ocean Area (ICPOA)

Kaga (carrier), 25, 28, 64, 97
Kahoolawe, Hawaiian Islands, 158, 163

Myoko (cruiser), 24, 71

Nachi (cruiser), 25, 132, 154
Nagara (cruiser), 25
Nagato (battleship), 24
Nagumo, Chuichi, 28, 82, 83, 97
Naka (cruiser), 25
NA line, 171, 172
Nansei Shoto, 64
Narwhal (submarine), 64, 153
Nashville (cruiser), 67
Natori (cruiser), 25
Nauru Island, 139-43
Nautilus (submarine), 104, 105, 111, 143
Naval General Staff, Japanese, 78-82, 96
Naval Intelligence, Office of (ONI), 47, 49, 106, 131
Naval Special Landing Forces, Japanese, 81, 113, 144
Naval War College, 89
Neal, Kirke A., 196
Neches (oiler), 57, 59
Nevada (battleship), 4
New, William A., 95
New Britain, 72
New Guinea, 14, 64-66, 69, 70, 72, 118, 133, 138, 170-73
New Jersey (battleship), 167, 190, 192
Nimitz, Chester W., 42, 62, 192
  relieves Kimmel, 40, 41
  in Battle of Midway, 75-77, 81, 86, 88, 90, 91, 93, 107, 182
  in correlation to Rochefort, 89, 94, 95, 110, 116, 117
  in operations on offensive, 136-38, 142, 146, 167, 170, 172, 186-88
  moves to Guam, 205, 209, 211-13.
  See also Commander in Chief, Pacific Fleet; Commander in Chief, Pacific Ocean Area
Northern Force, Japanese, 25, 97, 133, 137
North Pacific Force (NorPac), 88, 137, 139
Notices to Mariners. *See* Mine Warfare Section, JICPOA

Nouméa, New Caledonia, 120, 144, 184

Objective Data Section, ICPOA, 113, 130, 131. *See also* Enemy Bases Section, ICPOA/JIC-POA
Ogalala (minelayer), 4
Ohmae, Toshikazu, 39
Ohnishi, Takejiro, 79
Oi, Atsushi, 154
Oi (cruiser), 24
Okhotsk Sea, 153, 210
Okinawa:
  early plans for, 185-87, 190
  campaign, 169, 202-5, 209, 213, 215
  Information Bulletin, 206, 207
Oklahoma (battleship), 3, 4
Olympic, Operation, plan for (Kyushu invasion), 215
ONI. *See* Naval Intelligence, Office of
Op-20-G (Communication Intelligence Center, Washington), 45-48, 51, 53, 63, 70, 88, 89, 114, 115
Operational Intelligence Section, JICPOA, 196
Oro Bay, New Guinea, 134
Owen Stanley Mountains, New Guinea, 65, 118, 119
Ozawa, Jisaburo, 181, 182

Palau Islands (PP), 19, 26, 28, 59, 88, 120, 166, 170, 171, 178, 180
  invasion operations, 186, 188, 189
Palawan Passage, Philippines, 191
Papua, New Guinea, 65, 119, 133, 134
Paramushiro, Kuril Islands, 133
Parry Island, Eniwetok, 167, 168
PC-1135 (submarine chaser), 171
Pearce, Edward S., 77, 84
Pearl Harbor:
  attack on, 1-8, 28, 32, 44, 54, 79-81, 103, 121, 122, 166
  combat intelligence before the attack, 9, 11, 14, 31, 38, 39, 48

227

Pearl Harbor (*cont.*)
post-attack conditions, 34, 35, 37, 40, 43
second bombing of, 59, 60, 83, 85
during Battle of the Coral Sea, 72, 73, 76, 77
during Battle of Midway, 89, 94, 96, 99, 111
as base of operations, 146, 152, 198
the day the war ended, 216, 217
Peleliu, Palau, 187–89, 199, 205, 206
Permit (submarine), 186
Philippine Islands:
prewar situation, 14, 26, 27, 52, 57, 78, 79, 103
recapture of, 41, 170, 178–80, 187–90, 194, 199
Philippine Sea:
Battle of, 180–82
Japanese submarines in, 213–14
Photographic Interpretation Section, JICPOA, 196
Interprons, 177
Photographic Reconnaissance and Interpretation Section Intelligence Center (PRISIC), 113, 130, 139–45, 152, 160, 164, 177
Pickerel (submarine), 153, 156
Pierce, George E., 202, 203
Pike (submarine), 95
Piranha (submarine), 186
Pis Island, Truk, 167
Plunger (submarine), 153
Pollack (submarine), 144
Pompano (submarine), 154–56
Port Moresby, New Guinea (MO), 65, 69, 70–74, 82–86, 118, 119, 134
Pownall, Charles A., 157
PP. *See* Palau Islands
Pratt, Fletcher, 21
President Coolidge (transport), 131
Princeton (carrier), 147
PRISIC. *See* Photographic Reconnaissance and Interpretation Section Intelligence Center
Psychological Warfare Section, JICPOA, 184, 196
PT. *See* Truk

Purple code, 45, 46, 47
Pye, William S., 42

Rabaul, New Britain:
identified as RR, 59, 88
as Japanese base, 57, 64, 69, 70, 72, 73, 110, 157, 166
air strike on, 134, 135, 147
Raby (destroyer escort), 172
Radio Intelligence. *See* Fleet Radio Unit, Pacific
Rainbow Five war plan, 11, 26
Reeves, Joseph M., 42
Reference Section, JICPOA, 196
Richmond (cruiser), 133
Rio de Janeiro Maru (submarine tender), 171
RO–104 (submarine), 171
Roberts Commission, 42–44
Roberts, Owen J., 42–43, 49
Rochefort, Joseph J.:
officer-in-charge, CIU, 3, 4, 11, 14–16, 18, 20, 21, 25, 26, 28, 167
after Pearl Harbor attack, 31, 32, 37, 38, 55, 56, 121
interviewed by Roberts Commission, 42, 43, 53
and second bombing of Pearl Harbor, 59, 61, 79
makes special estimates, 66, 69, 79
in intelligence for Battle of Coral Sea, 64, 65, 68, 71–75
in intelligence for Battle of Midway, 83, 85, 86, 89, 90, 94, 101
starts ICPOA, 108–14, 123
ordered to Washington, 115, 116, 117, 197
Roenigk, John G., 36, 128
Roi Island, Kwajalein, 17, 162
Roosevelt, Franklin D., 40, 50, 187, 188
Rorie, Durwood G., 3, 36, 56
Rota, Mariana Islands, 170
RR. *See* Rabaul
Rundle, Chief Radioman, 67, 68
Runner (submarine), 153, 156
Russia, 47, 153, 173, 209
Ryujo (carrier), 25, 28
Ryukaku (carrier), 70, 71, 73, 101.
See also *Shoho*

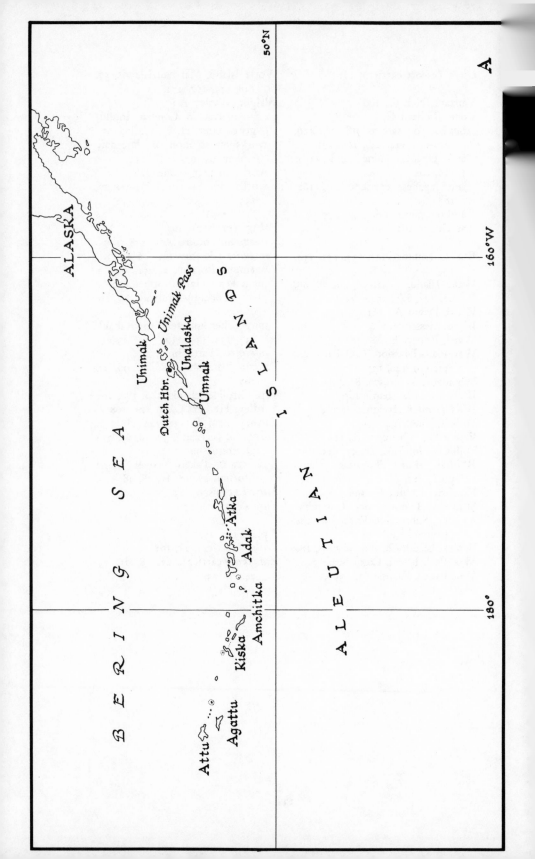

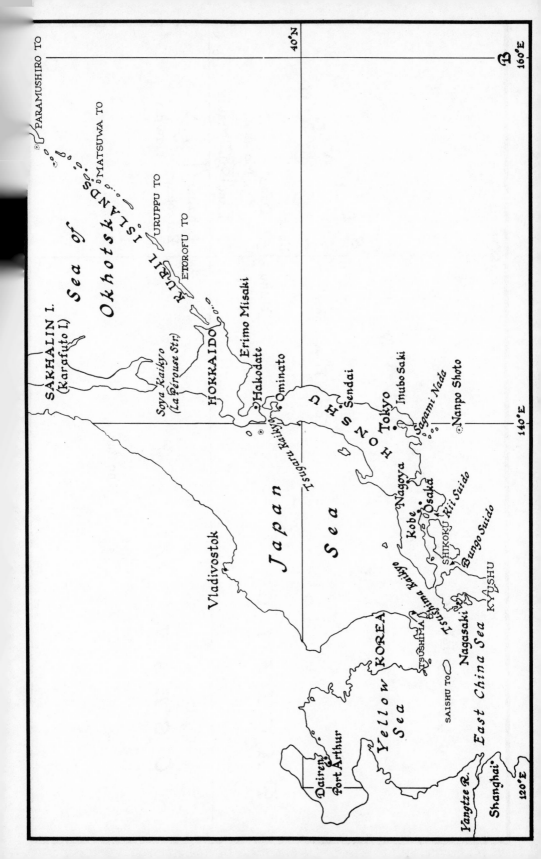

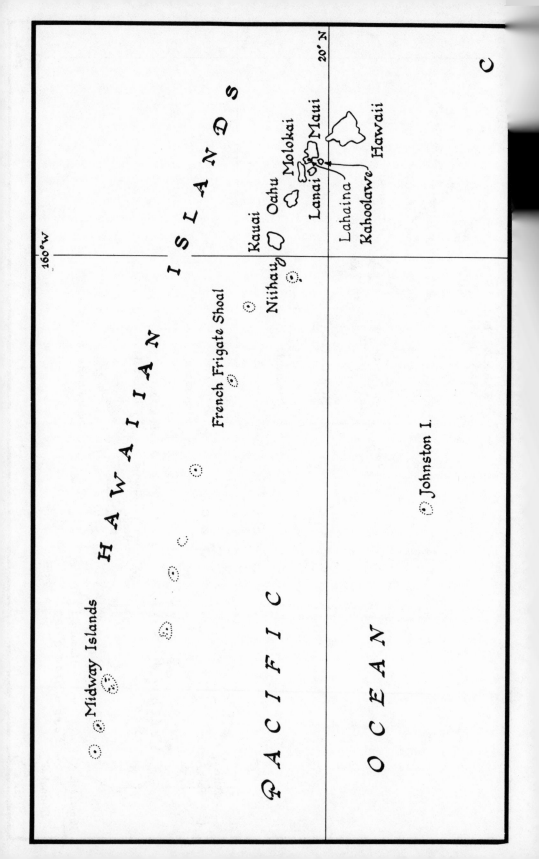

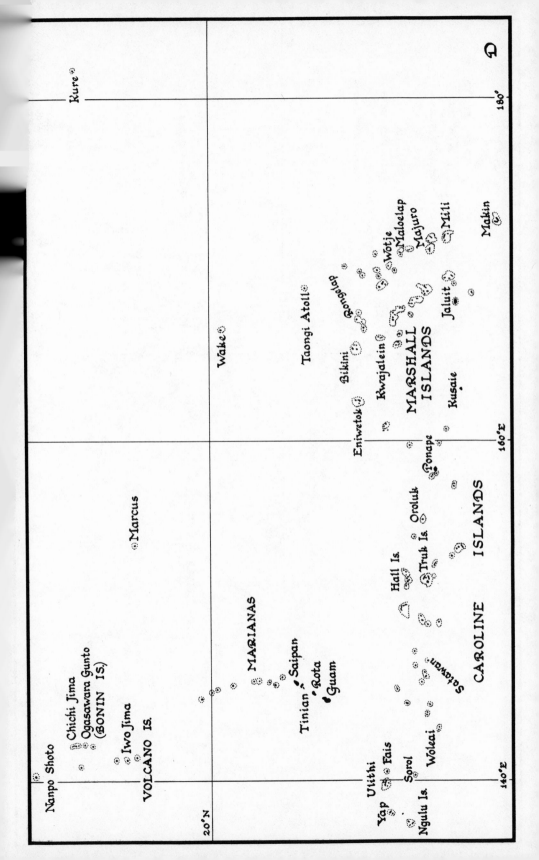

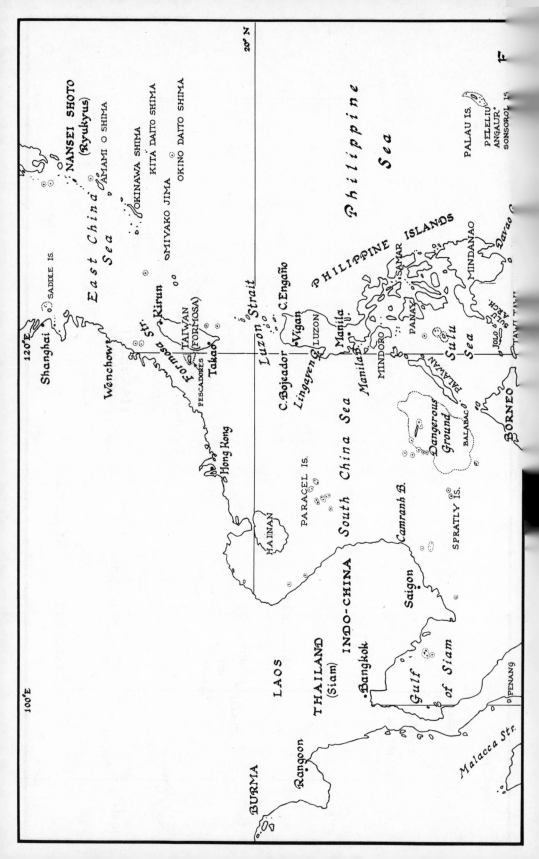

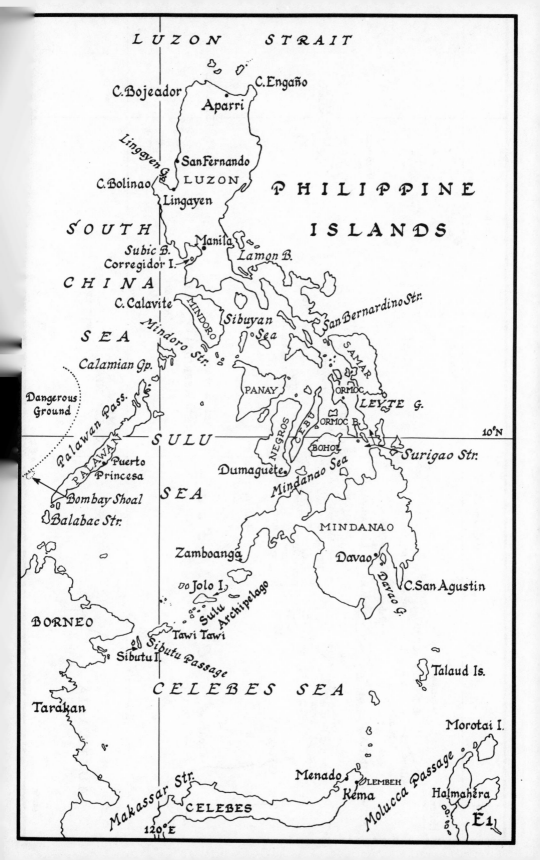

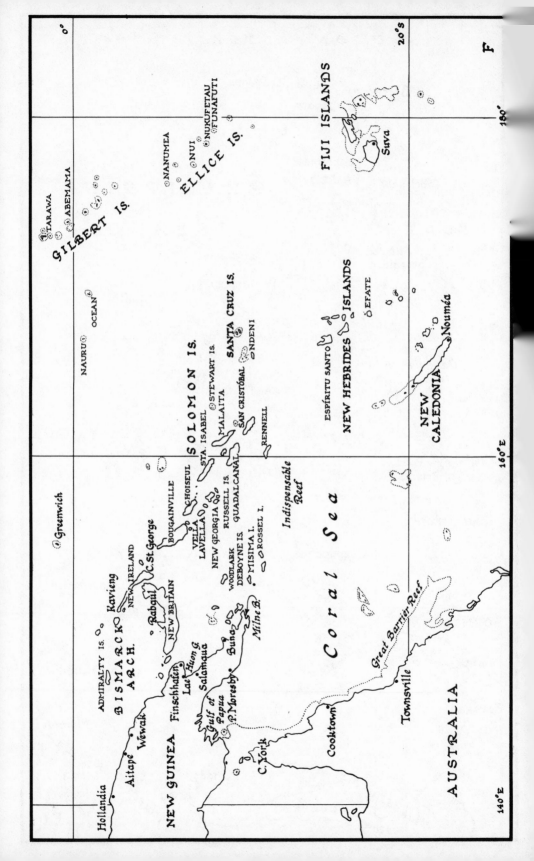

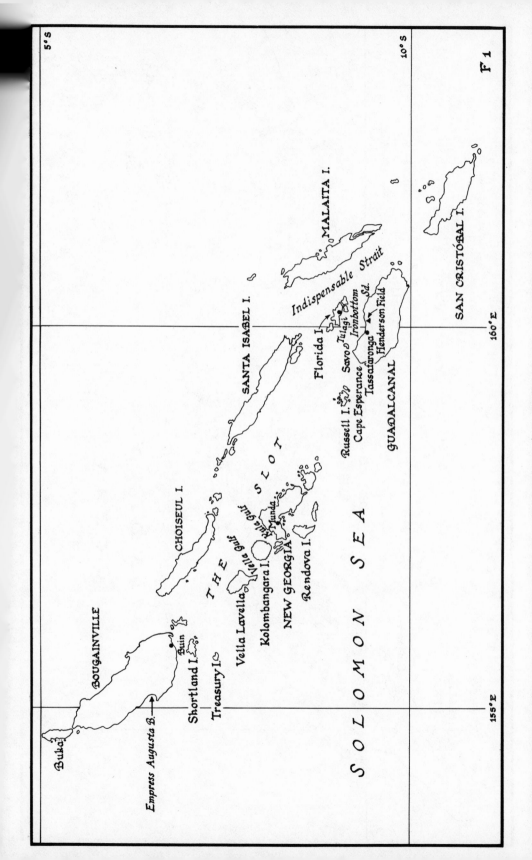

5° S

10° S

F 1

BOUGAINVILLE

Buka

Empress Augusta B.

Buin

Shortland I.

Treasury I.

Vella Lavella

CHOISEUL I.

Vella Gulf

Kula Gulf

Kolombangara I.

Munda

NEW GEORGIA

Rendova I.

THE SLOT

SANTA ISABEL I.

SOLOMON SEA

MALAITA I.

Indispensable Strait

Florida I.

Russell I.

Savo

Tulagi

Ironbottom Sd.

Cape Esperance

Tassafaronga

Henderson Field

GUADALCANAL

SAN CRISTÓBAL I.

155° E

160° E

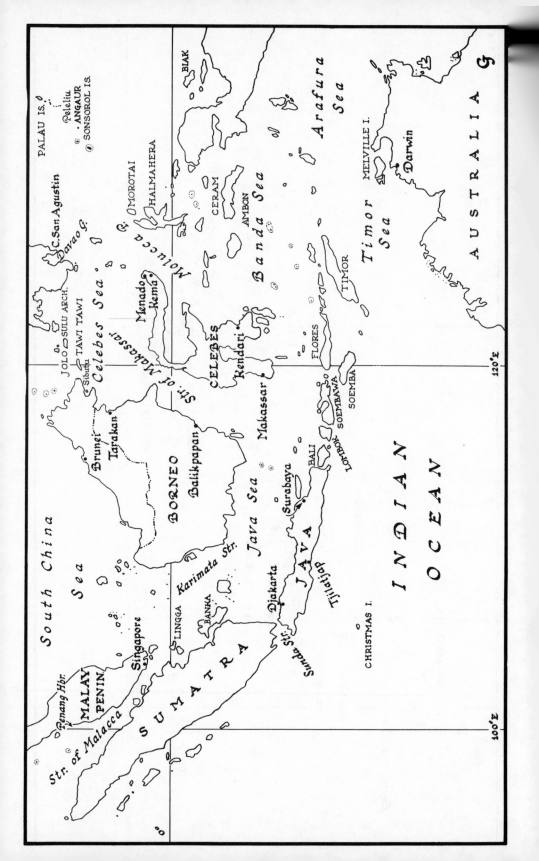

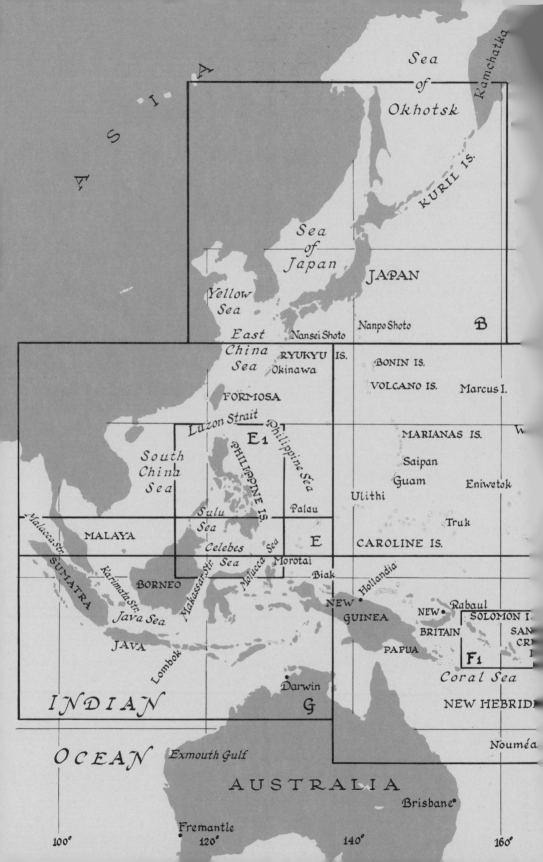